Journey from Genesis to Genocide
Hate, Empathy, and the Plight of Humanity

by

Peter J. DiDomenica and Thomas G. Robbins

DORRANCE PUBLISHING CO., INC.
PITTSBURGH, PENNSYLVANIA 15222

The contents of this work including, but not limited to, the accuracy of events, people, and places depicted; opinions expressed; permission to use previously published materials included; and any advice given or actions advocated are solely the responsibility of the author, who assumes all liability for said work and indemnifies the publisher against any claims stemming from publication of the work.

Dorrance Publishing Co., Inc.
701 Smithfield Street
Pittsburgh, PA 15222
Visit our website at *www.dorrancebookstore.com*

ISBN: 978-1-4349-3001-9
eISBN: 978-1-4349-2353-0

Contents

Chapter One
American Airlines Flight 63

All that is necessary for the triumph of evil is that good men do nothing.

- Edmund Burke

A small black dot appeared out of the northwest and pierced the veil of a pale blue afternoon sky. The late December chill enveloped Logan International Airport in Boston as the plane settled into its final approach over runway 4 Left. A small army of officials, some in uniform, some in casual weekend clothes, stood looking skyward clutching their coats against the ever-present runway wind.

The Boeing 767 looked much wider than usual as it approached low over the Boston skyline, as if it were stretched from wing to wing. In a split second, the plane appeared to shudder and spread apart at the wing tips. Suddenly, with an earsplitting roar, two F-15 Eagle fighters from the 102nd Fighter Wing punched the afterburners and rocketed skyward. The fighter jets were scrambled from Otis Air base on Cape Cod to escort American Airlines flight 63 and its Al-Qaeda-trained terrorist to touchdown at Logan Airport. The 102nd Fighter Wing has a proud history of defending America, from Cold War escorts of Soviet surveillance planes just off the Atlantic coast, to arriving first on the scene in the skies over New York City after the deadly terrorist attacks on the World Trade Center. The fighter jets, having finished another historic detail, were now out of sight, leaving behind a gray swirl of contrails across the pale sky as the dull gray American Airlines plane touched down on the runway and turned on to an abandoned taxiway far from the passenger terminals. As the plane lurched to a stop in the cold December air, several police cars and rescue trucks pulled alongside and alternately showered the skin of the plane with blue, red, and yellow lights as black clad members of the security teams quietly moved into place.

As a team of officers, weapons drawn, surrounded the plane carrying 183 passengers and 14 crew members, a large white vehicle was driven slowly towards the front cabin of the plane. The vehicle was strange looking, kind of like an oversized pickup truck with a set of stairs rising from the bed and extending over the roof and above the front hood. The vehicle was used for those occasions, like now, when a plane had to safely unload passengers away from the terminals. The incident commander was standing ramrod straight on the tarmac behind the communications van, quietly choreographing the entire scene. As the senior law enforcement official, it was his job to bring this incident to a successful conclusion. His outward actions did not reveal his innermost thoughts as to how this scenario might end. He was in constant communication with the control tower, the pilot, and the team of SWAT officers that had taken up positions around the plane.

As the events slowly unfolded on the tarmac at Logan Airport, the Boston office of the FBI had begun to assemble its anti-terrorist group for what could possibly be another hoax threat. The special agent in-charge of the Boston office was on his way into the city. His agents assigned to the intelligence group had provided a briefing of what they knew at this moment in time, which wasn't much. All the FBI and other police officials knew at this moment was that a plane bound to Miami from Paris had been diverted here to Boston. The FBI chief couldn't help but to afford himself a quiet chuckle as he recited in his head the infamous Bogart line, "Of all the gin joints...in all the world, she walks into mine." He had been briefed that the original diversion plan crafted by the FAA was designed to land the plane in Bangor, Maine, but as the pilots and crew provided updated information to the FAA while jetting over the Atlantic, it was decided that this bomb threat had some disturbing aspects to it and would be better handled at Boston's Logan Airport, the FBI chief's "gin joint."

Two days earlier and 14 miles east of Paris, France, a tall, thick, scruffy-looking man waited in line at Terminal One at Charles de Gaulle International Airport to board the transatlantic flight to Miami. The Paris-Roissy airport, as it is known locally, is the second largest airport in Europe, handling over 200,000 passengers a day. On this day, the tall, scruffy man attracted the attention of the security supervisor. At 6 feet 4 inches tall, the man was half a foot taller than the others waiting in the security line. The man had a big head, with big hair that ran thick and matted around his ears and down the back of his neck. He stood uneasy, shifting back and forth but never diverting his eyes from the front of the line, as if in a trance. He was focused hard on his goal, like a solider on a mission as he approaches the front lines to face the enemy. All he needed to do at this moment was to reach the other side of the security checkpoint, board the plane, and accomplish his mission: to kill as many infidels as he can in the name of Allah.

Richard Colvin Reid was the name listed on the passport. The picture identically matched the man now standing before the principal inspector for the airport police authority. With no checked baggage, no carry on luggage, and a one-way ticket for a flight from Paris to Miami, security had ample reason to pull Richard Reid aside and ask him a few questions and they did just that. He was detained by the local police at Paris-Roissy, interrogated and searched from the top of his head down to the soles of his shoes. In the end, the police came up with nothing to hold Richard Reid from his flight into martyrdom. As fate would have it on this day, the delay due to his detention caused him to miss the last flight out. Having missed his flight, he took advantage of American Airlines hospitality by availing himself of the offer of free accommodations for the night at a local hotel. That night as he gently slipped his shoes far under his bed, he thought he might sleep a little easier, comforted in the knowledge that he had taken the best that security had to offer. He was still free and nestled comfortably in bed just inches above a pair of shoes that will forever change how the world looks at terror. *Tomorrow, I will please Allah*, he thought as he drifted slowly to sleep

December 22 was a soggy, rainy day in Paris, the kind of cold, wet, and dreary day that seeps to the bone. The day had begun early for Richard Reid as he tugged on his shirt and pants then slowly and methodically slipped into his shoes, first pointing his toes and placing them far forward into the shoe and then pulling up the back of the shoe gently over his heel. The last step was to tuck a thick cord under the tongue of the shoe to secrete it from prying eyes. Richard Reid stepped quickly from the hotel lobby through the soaking rain and delicately ascended the shuttle bus stairs, stepping gingerly on the balls of his feet. He arrived once again at Terminal One, the international terminal, and took his place in the security checkpoint line for American Airlines flight number 63 bound from Paris to Miami. He felt an uneasy confidence knowing that, although he did not make it through the crucible the day before, he was not under arrest and he still had with him the device that would forever emblazon his name into history. He stood stoically, unflinching and staring straight ahead. Once again, he attracted the attention of security officials who noticed this large man, the way he carried himself, the arrogance in his stare, and the utter contempt for all those around him that seemed to ooze from his being. Security officials pulled Richard Reid out of line and once again, they put him through the crucible of inspection and interrogation. In the end, with no evidence of any wrongdoing and nothing to legally detain him further, Richard Reid stepped lightly onto flight 63 with his 182 fellow passengers and slipped comfortably into his plush window seat to await his date with destiny.

Flight 63 turned off the runway and slowly came to a stop on a midfield taxiway, the circle of armed police officers tightened around the plane. The communications from the captain to the tower indicated that there was one passenger aboard, bound and drugged, who had attempted to light his shoes on fire during the flight. The shoes were taken from the person and placed near the rear of the plane away from the wings, cockpit, and most of the passengers. A bomb was suspected, but the pilot and crew had no experience with the type of explosive device that was aboard; had they known, they probably wouldn't have been so calm and methodical in their words and actions.

The incident commander stood behind the mobile command vehicle listening to the chatter on the police and emergency response radios. He was hastily putting together a plan to secure the plane, remove the passengers, and to get the son-of-a-bitch who started this circus in motion off the plane and into FBI custody. What most disturbed him was the fact that the flight crew was *certain* that there was a bomb on board, thereby jeopardizing the passengers, crew, and the men assembled in a tight circle around the aircraft. He had no idea what type of bomb was aboard the plane or its killing potential. His concern focused on getting the passengers and crew off the plane and safely away from any potential detonation.

The decision was made to bring a set of truck stairs forward to the aircraft and quickly remove all the passengers and crew. The stairs were hastily brought around to the side of the plane and driven straight forward towards the cockpit in front of the wing. As the stairs bumped against the skin of the airplane cabin, the driver of the truck immediately shut off the ignition, jumped from the cabin of the truck, and retreated to a position of safety away from the now silent aircraft. In a flash, two uniformed troopers bounded up the stairs with submachine guns strapped across their chests. A third, unarmed trooper followed on their heels and, as if on cue, the door to the cabin was pulled inward. Within seconds, the troopers were out of sight, swallowed up by the gray steel. Simultaneously, two large shuttle buses rumbled to a stop near the front of the plane. The bus doors pulled open wide with an audible hiss that seemed to mock the wind that continued its steady assault on those who stood guard outside the plane. The officers remained steadfast, exposed to the elements, but hidden from view of the passengers who were now rising to exit.

Once the passengers were safely off the plane the incident commander bounded up the steps and ducked into the cabin. He looked directly at the only passenger still aboard and seated, Richard Reid, who was restrained crudely in his seat by several seat belt straps rising from the seat up over his shoulders and back down to bind his large hands. Reid appeared a bit groggy to the troopers who had begun to carefully unwrap the belts that bound him to the seat. He was stoic and seemed unaware, or more accurately, unconcerned about the events that were quickly unfolding. The groggy haze was induced in part by the antihistamine and sedatives, Valium and Narcan, injected into him during flight to aid the crew and passengers in their attempt to subdue this crazed madman. His stupor was also due in large part to his failure to complete his mission: blow up flight 63 in midair. The hatred, rage, and visceral reaction to those brave crew members and passengers who had wrestled with him in midflight were gone, replaced now by a palpable disdain for everything and everyone around him. The seatbelt shackles had now been removed and replaced by stainless steel handcuffs ratcheted tight on his thick wrists. He was assisted to a standing position and pulled toward the cabin doorway, a trooper on each side. His head brushed against the ceiling of the plane as the trooper escorting him to the front cabin maintained a tight grip on his upper arm. By now, all the passengers and crew had been safely removed, loaded onto the shuttle buses, and were on their way to the safety of the passenger terminal where they were sequestered to await FBI investigators.

Shuffling slowly out of the cabin and onto the stairs, Richard Reid had apparently expected much more than he got. Still staring straight ahead, he asked, to no one in particular, where the television crews and cameras were. The trooper standing to his left, holding firmly to Reid's arm, asked with an inquisitive tone, "Why, what are you up to?"

Reid replied dejectedly and almost inaudibly, "You will soon find out."

Reid was then hustled down the stairs to an awaiting police cruiser and driven off the runway. As the cruiser slowly made its way across the active runway, a large, blue box type truck proceeded towards the plane from its remote location at the water's edge.

The vehicle was big and bulky with the letters EOD clearly emblazoned on each side. Members of the Explosive Ordinance Disposal Unit are a breed apart. They are experts at detecting explosives and rendering them harmless. This day would test their mettle and provide those close to the scene a glimpse into the world of bomb technicians. As the vehicle slowed to a stop at a precise distance mid-plane, several team members quickly alighted from the vehicle, moved to the back, and opened wide the doors at the rear. Like a well-choreographed play, the team donned protective suits, extracted the necessary equipment they needed to analyze any suspicious item found aboard the plane, and to render it safe. Walking from behind the large doors of the bomb truck, the trooper looked like one of those deep water divers in an oversized helmet. A SWAT team member, noticing the bulbous figure slowly approaching the plane, thought he was headed in the wrong direction; with the dive suit on, he should be heading towards the calming waters of the ocean behind them. The SWAT team member did not know the bomb technician was thinking the same thing.

The EOD members carefully entered the now abandoned plane and cautiously approached the rear of the aircraft, as they had been directed by the captain and the crew. When they arrived at the back of the plane, they observed a pair of heavy, thick soled shoes that looked abandoned and out of place in the aft cabin. They carefully surveyed the shoes and noticed a wire protruding from one of them in the area around the tongue. They both scanned the immediate area for other dangers before they executed their prearranged plan. Minutes before they entered the aircraft, they issued the standard orders to halt all radio communications. They then shut their own radios and cell phones off, completely cutting themselves off from the outside world. Alone and squeezed in the aisle of this deserted plane, the two men approached the shoes carefully, with the full knowledge that any mistake in this dance of death would spell catastrophe.

Even before the EOD truck rumbled from its secure berth to the flight line, a full plan that was very detailed and clearly understood by all members was developed. It described the path and speed of approach to the plane, where it would come to a stop alongside, and most importantly, who would suit up and head inside the cabin. The chosen ones were now at the critical moment of discovery. They trained and rehearsed these scenarios for years trying to perfect their craft in an ever-changing terror landscape. They synchronized every movement as they pulled equipment from bulky packs strapped to their backs and began to position devices around and behind the shoes. Satisfied to their exacting standards, they "shot the picture." They examined the x-ray and validated their worst fears: Centered in the frame was a wire that began at the tongue of the shoe and ended abruptly in the sole. A detonation device was clearly visible at the tip of the wire, but what would be puzzling to the uninitiated was there appeared to be no explosive. Instead of breathing a sigh of relief, they motioned each other with well-practiced signals that each understood clearly. They both knew that far from the danger being over, things just got a hell of a lot worse.

They both knew at this precise moment that they were dealing with a bomb. It was a well-crafted, ingenious device that was as deadly here on this quiet plane as it was at 33,000 feet over the Atlantic Ocean. Undoubtedly crafted meticulously by expert hands, this was most likely a very volatile mixture of explosive chemicals extremely sensitive to heat—any heat. There was extreme danger with this special explosive mixture. It was unlike anything that most of us think of when we think of a bomb, certainly not a black bowling ball-looking object with a fuse stuck into the top, nor was it a briefcase with wires protruding out from the hinges. This sinister cocktail can be placed in almost any vessel—backpacks, phones, bottles, and even shoes.

Many would-be terrorists have met their fate while attempting to create this deadly mixture. So fragile is this deadly cocktail that oftentimes, the heat from a human hand can trigger a deadly blast. Right now, as they approached the shoes with sweat dripping inside their protective suits, both men were keenly aware that their own body heat could cause an explosion and, as if on cue, they instinctively looked at their gloved hands, turning them over and pulling them to their faces as if in search of their lifelines. Both men trusted the material specifications of the gloves—designed to keep body heat in—yet wondered, in this confined space, if the gloves would work.

With all their instruments secure back into their packs, one man faced the front cabin as the other carefully placed both hands on one shoe and lifted it gently to his midsection. His desire was to keep his arms outstretched, but in this confined space, he bent both arms toward his midsection as a running back, pulling a football in tight. With the shoe securely in his grasp, he carefully turned toward his partner, now at the front of the cabin. While his partner signaled to the outside security team, he headed to the front stairs. He gracefully walked the length of the cabin and exited down the truck stairs. Upon reaching the bottom stair, he walked toward the EOD truck and placed the shoe on a grassy area at the midline of the vehicle. He then headed back into the plane and gathered the second shoe, mimicking his previous actions with exacting precision.

Inside the terminal, the passengers of flight 63, isolated from the public, were huddled inside a makeshift assembly area. Several FBI agents and state police investigators were also huddled inside police headquarters, finalizing the plans to process the passengers and crew. Every crew member and passenger of flight 63 was positively identified and thoroughly interviewed. Richard Reid was now in federal custody and on his way to a holding cell to await his arraignment in the Federal District Court of Massachusetts. Thirteen months later at his sentencing hearing in that same court, Reid would affirm his allegiance to Osama bin Laden and tell the court that he was at war with the United States. In response, Judge William Young would admonish Reid that he was "not a soldier in any war" and was simply "a terrorist." Young would scold Reid, telling him, "We do not negotiate with terrorists.... We hunt them down one by one and bring them to justice."

The bomb squad was in the process of rendering safe the device found in Reid's shoes. Once completed, the explosive device would be photographed, analyzed, and held for evidence in the trial of Richard Reid.

The Federal Aviation Operations Commander in Washington actively monitored the situation at Boston's Logan airport to gather information and pass it along to his federal counterparts. His involvement began with the first radio call from the flight crew that something was happening inside the cabin of the plane while in midflight over the Atlantic Ocean. Now with the plane safely on the ground at Logan, he was anxiously awaiting a call back to find out exactly what caused the diversion of American Airlines flight 63. He carried a professional demeanor but was anxious inside as he thought about his role today and that fact that it was only three months ago that he was at the helm when the first ever national "ground stop" was initiated, which meant every plane in flight over American airspace and of American origin or destination was ordered to land at the nearest airport that could accommodate them. No one in the country, especially those living in the flight paths near large airports, will forget the eerie, unsettling silence in the skies. With that remembrance vividly etched in his mind, he stood staring at the bank of phones, each with an airport name boldly spelled out above the receiver. He wondered if he would once again call the White House and ask for permission to ground the entire fleet of aircraft.

The Richard Reid story is several years in the past but it is still emblazoned in our consciousness as a reminder to America and the world that terrorism will never stop in its attempt to further its political goals by inflicting mass casualties on innocent populations. A stark reminder of this is the number of international terrorist attacks and attempts, as well as the attempted terrorist attacks in America since Richard Reid's failed attempt. Internationally, there have been hundreds of terrorist atrocities since 2001 that have resulted in thousands of innocent deaths.

Eight years later, and nearly to the day, in an eerily similar attack to Richard Reid's shoe bomb incident, a terrorist attempted to blow up an airplane in midflight over the skies of Detroit, Michigan, on Christmas day 2009. This terrorist attempt took place on Northwest Airlines international Flight 253, traveling from Amsterdam to Detroit. Witnesses to the attempt reported that as the plane began its approach into Detroit's Metro Airport, the bombing suspect went into the bathroom for a period of about twenty minutes. When the bomber returned to his seat, he complained of stomach pains and pulled a blanket up over himself. As the plane was nearing Detroit's Metro airport, the bomber ignited an explosive device containing white powder, similar to the explosive substance used by Richard Reid. A small explosion and fire erupted as the device failed to properly detonate. The bomber, severely burned by the ignition, was subdued and handcuffed by the passengers and crew. Although eight years had passed without an aviation incident, this terrorist plot serves as a stark reminder to the world that the global terror threat remains undaunted.

Chapter Two
Bridging the Gap

*Can there be a more important subject than human nature? If the subject can be
truly fathomed, then our species will be more precisely defined,
and our actions perhaps more wisely guided.*

- Edward O. Wilson[1]

I n the kingdom of animals, only two families on the planet engage in
interspecies warfare involving attacks by massive armies: The family
formicidae, also known as ants, and Homo sapiens, also known as humans, the
last remaining species of the family *hominidae.* Renowned Harvard biologist
Edward O. Wilson observes that "Ants are the most warlike of all of the
creatures on Earth."[2] We are a close second. Having members known as
"suicide bombers," as exemplified by Richard Colvin Reid, is another feature
of human and ant societies that is uniquely shared.

> They blow themselves up by contracting their body muscles violently when
> near enemies. They're the suicide bombers and the extreme altruists, as far as
> their colonies are concerned. They rupture, and the body sprays poisonous
> liquid. That's [aimed] chiefly against other ants—the greatest enemy of ants
> is other ants. Does that sound familiar?[3]

A New Way of Thinking

The incident on December 22, 2001 on American Airlines flight 63 leaves
us asking several questions: What motivated Richard Colvin Reid to try and
end his life and murder nearly two hundred passengers and crew? Was Reid's
behavior the product of a diseased mind or the product of social forces on a
normal but vulnerable and exploited mind? What motivated the politico-

ideological movement that inspired Reid to use murder of innocents as a tool of achieving its ambitions? Are groups such as al-Qaeda, presumably behind the attempted destruction of flight 63, a collection of psychologically aberrant individuals or a group populated by mostly psychologically normal individuals guided by social and environmental forces and perhaps a small number of charismatic and narcissistic leaders? And, most importantly, can we identify principles of cause and effect that allow for the creation of monsters such as Reid and allow violent groups such as al-Qaeda to coalesce? For, if we can identify the principles of such cause and effect, we then can use that knowledge to prevent needless death and destruction such as that attempted by Reid on flight 63.

The authors are not scientists but are public safety officials who were thrust into homeland security roles in commercial aviation immediately after the 9/11 attacks. In that role, we were required to develop security systems and procedures designed to keep the next Richard Reid off commercial aircraft. We developed a behavior assessment system for screening passengers that sought to do something unprecedented in American law enforcement: deny access to aircraft and other critical infrastructure based on the belief that a person is involved in planning or about to carry out an act terrorism without the legal standard of proof required to detain or arrest.[4] This was a paradigm shift for the law enforcement profession that has traditionally sought to identify and prosecute people who have already committed a crime. Our jobs at places like airports were expanded to include conducting threat assessments of human beings and denying access to those deemed to be "high risk." This screening system became the basis for the U.S. Transportation Security Administration behavior screening program known as Screening of Passengers by Observation Techniques (SPOT), used at every major airport in the nation, and the British Transport Police behavior assessment program being used as a response to the July 7, 2005 bombings of the London Underground. Thus began our ten-year journey to seek answers to fundamental questions about human nature and the root causes of human conflict and aggression.

The drawback to our lack of formal scientific training will be perhaps a less than desirable level of scientific rigor and accuracy expected in scientific publications and a tendency to reach conclusions based on a less than desirable quantity of scientific proof also expected in such publications. The benefit, if you will, of this lack of formal scientific training is our holistic approach, which is not biased towards any particular scientific discipline and which is directed towards achieving practical results. The exigencies of 9/11 and the subsequent years of combating terrorism and insurgency have made many in the fields of intelligence, national security, defense, and law enforcement sudden students of human nature who needed to act quickly without the benefit of years of education and research. In the United States, we seem to have done a pretty good job so far. We hope this book invigorates an interest by the scientific community, government, and citizens into probing our fundamental human nature so we can change course in time to avert potential global catastrophes that threaten our very survival. This chapter explores the broad outlines of the material to be presented in the rest of the book.

The authors believe that various disciplines of natural and social sciences separately contain enough objective truths on human nature that can be woven together to provide answers to the questions raised by the incidents such as that which occurred on December 22, 2001 on flight 63 and much more devastating occurrences involving social aggression such as the Holocaust and the 1994 Rwandan genocide. This understanding of human aggression is necessary not only to prevent mass murder and genocide, but is essential to tackle issues that threaten the whole of humanity such as the proliferation of nuclear weapons and other weapons of mass destruction, global warming, pandemic disease, overpopulation, poverty, food shortages, and droughts. To solve these problems, involving the very existence of the human race, will require the collective effort of all nations and peoples. No such collective effort is possible in a world plagued by uncontrolled human aggression, self-interest, mistrust, and exploitation of natural resources, economic resources and human life.

We are all well aware of threats to humanity posed by nuclear weapons and global warming, but even food shortages may pose a threat to global civilization. Lester R. Brown, in an article in *Scientific American,* believes that food shortages may lead to failed states and, ultimately, to the end of global civilization itself.[5] Brown sees increased food shortages due to rapid population growth, loss of topsoil, water shortages, and rising temperatures. Food scarcity and the resulting higher food prices will put "severe stress on the governments of countries already teetering on the edge of chaos," leading to increasing numbers of failed states that become "a source of terrorists, drugs, weapons, and refugees, threatening political stability everywhere." The Fund for Peace and the Carnegie Endowment for International Peace, in *The Failed States Index 2008,* list countries that are close to collapse based on twelve social, economic, political, and military factors. Twenty countries are listed, including Somalia (ranked number one), Sudan (ranked number two), Iraq (ranked number five), Afghanistan (ranked number seven), Pakistan (ranked number nine), and North Korea (ranked number fifteen). Each of these countries already is either in the midst of a humanitarian crisis, violent insurgency, or threatens world stability. Brown ends his article stating:

> It is hard to overstate the urgency of our predicament. Every day counts.... We desperately need a new way of thinking, a new mindset. The thinking that got us into this bind will not get us out.[6]

In this book, we hope to offer "a new way of thinking, a new mindset" that will remove the barriers preventing the type of international cooperation needed to prevent world instability and, perhaps, the end of global civilization.

Scientific Reductionism and Emergence

In understanding and preventing human aggression, we must first began by understanding and bridging the gap between natural sciences such as biology, cognitive neuroscience and evolutionary psychology, and the social sciences and humanities, such as anthropology, sociology, and political science. Harvard biologist Edward O. Wilson, in his book, *Consilience: The Unity of Knowledge,* believes that "all tangible phenomena, from the birth of stars to the working of social institutions, are based on material processes that are ultimately reducible…to the laws of physics."[7] This extreme belief in scientific reductionism is no doubt rejected by many philosophers, the deeply religious, and even some natural scientists, but the ability of science to build from the bottom up a coherent understanding of the world has been growing steadily since the Enlightenment and has accelerated rapidly in the last century. Physicist Stephen Hawking seems to agree with the reductionism of Wilson: "Since the structure of molecules and their reactions with each other underlie all of chemistry and biology, quantum mechanics allows us in principle to predict nearly everything we see around us, within the limits set by the uncertainty principle."[8] Quantum mechanics is the most fundamental branch of physics dealing with phenomena on smallest scales imaginable, such as the interior of protons and neutrons.

For people living in developed nations, almost all aspects of life, including virtually all improvements in the quality of life, owe their origin to the scientific developments made since the Enlightenment. Things such as clean water, food production, transportation, energy production, hygiene, medicine, communication and information technology, education, and exploration have all developed from the adoption of the scientific method and contributed to the betterment of mankind.

Much of the natural sciences that can be used to inform the social sciences and humanities use principles derived from Darwinian evolution and natural selection, presenting another obstacle to acceptance of scientific knowledge as a means to prevent human conflict and aggression. For some, the idea of Darwinian evolution and natural selection as a physical process, similar to the rate of acceleration of an object under gravity, becomes an insurmountable obstacle to acceptance based on deeply held religious beliefs. The authors take an agnostic point of view on this issue and simply look at evolution and natural selection as reliable means for constructing models of human behavior. Interestingly, while Darwin is associated by most as the epitome of anti-creationism, his views on the subject of the creation of the very first life forms was equivocal and probably best described as agnostic. The last sentence in *The Origin of Species* was changed in the second edition (1860) and subsequent editions to include reference to "the Creator" breathing life into the original forms of life.

There is grandeur in this view of life, with its several powers, having been originally breathed *by the Creator* [italics added] into a few forms or into one; and that, whilst this planet has gone cycling on according to the fixed law of gravity, from so simple a beginning endless forms most beautiful and most wonderful have been, and are being, evolved.[9]

In the first edition published in November 1859, the words *by the Creator* were not present. Darwin was troubled by the addition of this phrase in the later editions and, in a letter written in about three and a half years after *The Origin of Species* was published, stated, "I have long regretted that I truckled to public opinion, and used the Pentateuchal* term of creation, by which I really meant 'appeared' by some wholly unknown process."[10]

We believe the utility of evolution and natural selection as a means for constructing models of behavior is possible without the need for rendering a verdict as to whether it is the ultimate truth as to the origins of humanity. We hope those who are turned away by evolution and natural selection can accept, as we have done, the utilitarian role of such concepts to further understanding of human nature.

The debate about the role of science and religion in society goes beyond being a possible obstacle to advancement in the fields of cosmology, physics, biology, and social science, but has itself been a source of conflict and aggression that threatens global stability and peace. We believe both disciplines can and should peacefully coexist, provided they understand and abide by their limits and do not attempt to disrupt or disparage each other.

Science, following the traditions of Aristotle, Francis Bacon, Descartes, and John Stuart Mill, consists of the formulation and modification of hypotheses through systematic experiment, observation, and the gathering of empirical data. Science attempts to answer "why" phenomena occur using principles of cause and effect but not the big "Why" in the sense of an ultimate reason for the existence or nonexistence of certain phenomena such as life. Religion seeks to provide guidance for living based on answers to the ultimate meaning of life, the big "Why" questions, adduced through faith. This faith is not based on the scientific method but a belief that the truth of our existence and purpose is self-apparent based on the very design of the Creator or creative forces.

As long as the scientific establishment stays out of business of imposing its views on the big "Why" questions and organized religions do not seek to forcibly impose faith-based reasoning on the little "why" questions, there can be a respectful and peaceful coexistence that does not fuel the already highly divisive nature of societies and nations. If you needed to cross a bridge over a high canyon, would you chose the bridge built by engineers trained at the Massachusetts Institute of Technology using modern scientific principles tested by the scientific method, or would you chose the bridge built by clerics based

---

* Pentateuchal is reference to the Five Books of Moses that comprise the Old Testament.

13

on faith that the Creator or creative force willed that the bridge hold for your trip? What may give you pause is not the ability of the Creator, but your belief in the cleric to accurately interpret divine will in a matter of practical significance to your safety. The world is filled with religious leaders who purport to interpret the will of the Creator; we have seen many mislead us due to, at the least, honest mistake, and, at the most, deliberate exploitation. We have also witnessed recently the emergence of an extremist form of atheism that seeks to mock and disparage religious beliefs. Let the scientists build the bridges we cross and let the clerics answer the question "Why" we need to cross those bridges.

From Quarks to Humans

The broad outlines of consilience already exist despite large gaps such as the natural/social science gap. Reductionism has brought us to the point of being able to explain nearly everything we see in the universe from objects as small as atoms and from a time when the universe was only a fraction of a second old.

Beginning with the world of the subatomic particles, a theory of physics called *quantum chromodynamics* unites fundamental particles, such as quarks and gluons, into baryons such as protons and neutrons. How these protons and neutrons form an atomic nucleus and how the atomic nucleus combines with electrons to form atoms is explained through another theory of physics called *quantum electrodynamics*. Using the underlying knowledge of physics, another branch of science, chemistry, explains the formation of molecules that form the building blocks of life, the nucleotides and amino acids. Molecular biology, using the underlying knowledge of chemistry, provides the theories that explain the formation of the building blocks of life, DNA and RNA, from the five nucleotides (adenine, guanine, thymine, cytosine, and uracil) and the formation of proteins from amino acids. This branch of science then explains the formation of the genetic code, the blueprint for life forms, from strands of DNA and RNA. Cellular biology takes these molecular components and explains how they interact to form the living cell and how such cells combine to produce complex life forms such as human beings. Evolutionary biology shows the evolution of life forms to their present state based on the Darwinian principle of natural selection in which differential rates of survival and reproduction based on genetic mutations lead to creation of new species. Neuroscience, drawing upon the foundations of chemistry and biology, can explain the executive or brain functions of complex life forms through the storage and transmission of electrochemical impulses of nerve cells. An emerging field of neuropsychology is using understanding of neurotransmitters, chemicals such as serotonin, dopamine, and noradrenaline involved in the linking of neurons, to treat mood disorders, such as depression. Evolutionary biology or sociobiology has begun to show, in humans and to a limited extent in primates, a basis for understanding behavior based on the coevolution of genes and culture in which genes prescribe "epigenetic rules" that guide the acquisition of culture that in turn help to determine which genes survive and alter the epigenetic rules of the population.[11] In Humans, cultural evolution takes place at a much faster rate, over years and decades, than genetic evolution, which can take thousands of years.

Now comes the gap where a greater understanding in the social sciences and humanities can be gained from the underlying natural sciences. Social psychology, anthropology, sociology, and political science stand to grow in their ability to understand and explain complex human behavior through incorporation of the more fundamental theories of biology, neuroscience, and sociobiology, just as chemistry is informed by physics. According to Wilson, "Most of the issues that vex humanity daily—ethnic conflict, arms escalation, overpopulation, abortion, environment, endemic poverty, to cite several most persistently before us—cannot be solved without integrating knowledge from the natural sciences with that of the social sciences and humanities."[12]

The Emergence of Emergence

A small but growing group of scientists believe that scientific reductionism—the ability to describe all complex phenomena as the sum of simpler rules governing constituent parts—has run its course and that further fundamental understanding of complex phenomena will require acceptance of physical laws as arising from the collective behavior of complex entities. Or, in other words, the physical laws are said to be *emergent*. Robert B. Laughlin, professor of physics at Stanford University and winner of the Noble Prize in Physics, believes that "science has now moved from an Age of Reductionism to an Age of Emergence, a time when the search for ultimate causes of things shifts from the behavior of parts to the behavior of the collective."[13]

> In other words, we are able to *prove* in these simple cases that the organization can acquire meaning and life of its own and begin to transcend the parts from which it is made. What physical science thus has to tell us is that the whole being more than the sum of its parts is not merely a concept but a physical phenomenon. Nature is regulated not only by a microscopic rule base but by powerful and general principles of organization. Some of the principles are known, but the vast majority are not.[15]

Ironically, Newton's laws of motion and gravitation that for centuries were the epitome of reductionism turn out to be emergent laws describing collective behavior.[15] For more than three centuries, these simple laws—governing the motion of planets and billiard balls with deterministic precision in a "clockwork universe"—were thought to be fundamental rules of nature. With the advent in the early twentieth century of quantum mechanics—the physics of the microscopic world of atoms and subatomic particles—nature became fuzzy and probabilistic. Under Heisenberg's *uncertainty principle*, it is impossible to know exactly the position and momentum of a particle, wherein the more precise one measurement is, the less precise the measurement of the other. What is even more striking about this fundamental principle of nature is that the amount of uncertainty can be determined with mathematical precision using Heisenberg's uncertainty equation! Under the wave-particle duality of matter, atoms and subatomic particles are not like miniature billiard balls but spread out through space like a wave spreading across a pond. A subatomic particle such as an electron has a nonzero probability of being anywhere in the universe! What is even more striking as with the uncertainty equation is that the probability of the location of the electron can be determined with mathematical precision using equations describing the wave function of matter. Once you accept these quantum mechanical concepts as fundamental to nature, as science in general has for more than eight decades, then strange experimental results of microscopic behavior seem to "make sense." For example, an individual electron, not being measured at the moment it has a choice of either going through one slit or another slit in a screen, will go through both slits at the same time, producing wave that interferes with itself just like two waves interfering on a pond.˙

The phases of matter as vapor, liquid, or solid and the properties of transition between phases are a familiar phenomena that can be predicted and explained, not through reductionist laws of individual atoms and molecules, but through the emergent rules of collective behavior. According to Laughlin, the "granddaddy" of emergent phenomena "is the functioning of large organisms, such as people."[16] The idea that consciousness and self-awareness as being an emergent property of the collection of atoms that make up an individual is very appealing as the essence of your being is truly (we would hope) something more than the sum of the parts that you are made of.

Yes, we have strayed a bit into the philosophical and metaphysical here. We will continue to make occasional forays into various disciplines that may appear to be tangential at best to the subject of this book, yet it is this process of exploring these tangent disciplines that has given us a better understanding of human nature—of conflict and aggression and ways of preventing and reducing it. So, we ask the reader to indulge us in this respect because we firmly believe that when you finish the journey with us, you will have a greater and more meaningful understanding of yourself and human nature.

In the social sciences, an emergent view of the development of human societies is brilliantly propounded by Jared Diamond in his Pulitzer Prize-winning book, *Guns, Germs, and Steel: The Fates of Human Societies*. Going back 13,000 years ago, all people on the planet were still living the primitive lifestyle

---

˙ However, if the electron is being observed, it will make a choice of one slit to pass through and not interfere with itself. The wave nature of atoms and subatomic particles exists only when not being measured; as soon as measurement is made, the wave form collapses and the particle behaves like a "classical" particle having a specific location. One of the great mysteries of 21st century physics is the apparent ability of an observer to affect the nature of matter and to cause instantaneous changes in matter that defy the universal speed limit on the transmission of information based on the speed of light.

of hunter-gatherers as were the first humans more than five million years ago. With the rise of food production through domestication of wild plants and animals beginning 11,000 years ago in an area of Southwest Asia known as the Fertile Crescent, large sedentary societies that allowed for complex societies with a political elite and specialized roles for members, including soldiers and scientists, arose. In explaining why we see complex industrialized societies with wealth and power today, principally in Eurasia and derivative societies in North America, while in many parts of the world there exist poor non-literate farming societies and even more primitive hunter-gatherer societies, the answers do not lie in the biology of the individual societies or through racist explanations. In a summary of his book, Diamond states, "History followed different courses for different peoples because of differences among peoples' environments, not because of biological differences among peoples themselves."[17]

"Guns, germs, and steel" are Diamond's symbolic representations of the outcomes of food production that led to the dominance of some societies over others. The large and stratified societies that developed due to food production were able to develop the technology (guns and steel), political organization, writing, and even epidemic diseases (germs) used to overcome less advanced cultures. Members of these dense food-producing societies eventually developed resistance to epidemic diseases that spread to humans through close contact with domesticated animals. When members of these advanced food-producing societies migrated to areas inhabited by hunter-gatherers, the germs literally wiped out whole cultures that were defenseless against the germs. The most severe example of the catastrophic role of germs in history is seen in the European conquest of the Americas that resulted in the decimation of up to 95 percent of the native population due to infectious disease brought by the Europeans.

Food production, the original source of the growth of powerful societies, "followed straightforwardly from the differing suites of wild plant and animal species available for domestication, not from limitations of the peoples themselves."[18] In essence, the broad outlines on the development of civilizations—history—was largely determined not on the basis of the nature of individuals, but on the emergent principals of humanity based on climate, environment, and the availability of wild plants and animals suitable for domestication.

In the spirit of Edward O. Wilson's belief in the unification of the natural and social sciences, Diamond would like to see the subject of human history treated as a science: "The challenge now is to develop human history as a science, on par with acknowledged historical sciences such as astronomy, geology, and evolutionary biology.... One cannot deny that it is more difficult to extract general principles from studying history than from studying planetary orbits.... But recall 'science' means 'knowledge'...to be obtained by whatever methods are most appropriate to the particular field."[19]

In Harvard, history professor Niall Ferguson's book, *The War of the World: Twentieth-Century Conflict and the Descent of the West*, the explanation offered for the extreme violence of the twentieth century does not include individual people despite such notorious leaders such as Stalin, Hitler, and Mao Zedong. In the "bloodiest century in modern history, far more violent in relative* as well as absolute terms than any previous era," a century in which more than 160 million perished through organized violence, Ferguson cites environmental and situational factors to explain the violence.[20]

"Three things," states Ferguson, "seem to me necessary to explain the extreme violence of the twentieth century, and in particular why so much of it happened at certain times, notably the early 1940s, and in certain places, specifically Central and Eastern Europe, Manchuria, and Korea. These may be summarized as ethnic conflict, economic volatility, and empires in decline."[21]

Ferguson's explanation implies that looking to individual personalities to understand the causes of massive organized aggression will not result in understanding the causes, that situations determine the fates of large collections of people. This is clearly an emergent view of society.

We need not decide at this point whether the ultimate description of the universe will be a reductionist or emergent set of laws or a combination thereof. Just as in pure sciences such as physics, where both reductionism and emergence help us to understand the physical properties of the universe, we will use reductionist and emergent principles of the social sciences to explain the Shoe Bomber and the Holocaust. Dispositional psychology is a kind of reductionist psychology that looks to understand human behavior through understanding the disposition of an individual. When we look later at organizational aggression such as that perpetrated by the German Nazi Party before and during World War II, the dispositions of key individuals clearly play an important role in explaining the aggression. However, we will see there were mind-boggling acts of aggression committed by the most normal people, acts that cannot be fully explained by individual disposition but can only fully be explained as *emergent* collective behavior. A striking example of this will be seen in the story of Reserve Police Battalion 101, a group of ordinary men too old for military service pressed into service as police units for the Nazi-occupied territories of Eastern Europe during World War II. This battalion of slightly less than 500 ordinary men was responsible for the executions of 38,000 civilians in a four-month period as part of Hitler's "final solution." Emergence as a concept for the social sciences is not referred to as such but is known as "situational" psychology.

---

* Steven Pinker in his book *The Better Angels of Our Nature* makes compelling arguments based on several sources of data that although the 20th Century was the deadliest due to planned aggression in actual numbers, it is not the deadliest in relative terms as measured in terms of the percent of world population who died as a result of planned aggression. For example Pinker shows that an average of 15 percent of people in hunter-gatherer and hunter-horticultural societies from 14,000 BCE to 1770 CE died violent deaths while the estimated 180 million deaths due to warfare and genocide during the 20th Century amounts to only 3 percent of the world population. Pinker notes that "Modern Western countries, even in their most war-torn centuries, suffered no more than around a quarter of the average death rate of nonstate societies, and less than a tenth of that for the most violent one."

Situational psychology has developed over the last five decades, beginning with two famous experiments in social psychology: Yale University psychology professor Stanley Milgram's Obedience Experiment conducted in 1961 and, a decade later, Stanford University psychology professor Philip Zimbardo's Stanford Prison Experiment. In the Milgram Obedience Experiment, ordinary people, serving as "teachers," followed the instructions of an "experimenter" and were led to believe they were involved in an experiment on memory and learning through the use of punishment. The experiment involved the "teacher" administering progressively stronger electric shocks to a "learner" when the "learner" failed a memory test involving memorization of word pairs. In reality, the "teacher" was the actual subject of the experiment; there were no actual electric shocks being administered to the "learner," who was in reality a confederate in the experiment. The "learner" was seated in an adjacent room with whom the "teacher" could communicate over a speaker system. The "teacher" operated a shock generator starting at 15 volts that progressed by 15 volt increments to a maximum of 450 volts at the 30th increment or level. The 25th level at 375 volts was labeled on the generator "Danger, Severe Shock" and the 29th and 30th levels (435 and 450 volts) were simply marked "XXX," implying a possible lethal dose of electricity. The real experiment would end with either the "teacher" refusing to go on further or after the administering of three shocks at the maximum "XXX" 450 volts. The experiment was scripted with recorded responses from the "learner" in which the "learner" progressively complains of increasing pain, screams that he does not want to continue, complains of having a heart condition, and finally, above the 300-volt level, there is dead silence. Despite any protestations by the "teacher" that the experiment should stop or the well being of the "learner" should be established, the "experimenter" is scripted to tell the "teacher" that "the experiment requires that you continue," that the "shocks may be painful but they're not dangerous," and that the "experimenter" is responsible for the health of the "learner."

In the original experiment, 65 percent of "teachers" administered the final "XXX" voltage three times despite the "learner's" pleas and the dead silence at the end. In subsequent experiments in which a condition was altered, the compliance rates would go as high as 90 percent or could be reduced to less than 10 percent, lending further support to the notion that situations rule. A group of forty psychiatrists was polled by Milgram and asked to estimate the percentage of "teachers' in the original experiment format who would go through to the very end and administer the "XXX" voltage. They predicted that less than 1 percent would go all the way to the end! The Milgram Obedience Experiment has been replicated by other researchers numerous times in numerous countries with similar results. The results of the obedience experiments prompted Milgram to boldly state, "If a system of death camps were set up in the United States of the sort we had seen in Nazi Germany, one would be able to find sufficient personnel for those camps in any medium-sized American town."[22]

In the Stanford Prison Experiment, Philip Zimbardo set up a mock prison in the basement of the Psychology Department building at Stanford University in Palo Alto, California. Twenty-four male college students from the U.S. and Canada were selected after diagnostic interviews and personality tests used to screen out persons with psychiatric or medical problems or a history of crime or drug abuse. This group of "ordinary, normal, healthy young men"[23] was randomly assigned to roles as guards or prisoners. The purpose of the experiment was to see what effect the roles of guard and prisoner within a prison system would have on ordinary and normal young men; "to differentiate between what people bring into a prison situation from what the situation brings out in the people who are there."[24] There was no specific training for the guards except for instructions to "maintain law and order" without using violence and to prevent escapes.[25] Guards were provided uniforms, mirrored sunglasses, batons, and whistles. The Palo Alto police were recruited to pick up the prisoners and place them under arrest and bring them to the "Stanford County Prison." Upon arrival, the prisoners were blindfolded and led into the jail. Guards ordered the prisoners to strip and sprayed the prisoners with powder to simulate delousing. Prisoners were given a numbered uniform that consisted of simply a smock and a nylon stocking was placed on their heads as a substitute for head shaving.

The experiment was designed to last fourteen days, but was stopped on the sixth day due to the abusive and sadistic behavior of the guards and the extreme stress levels of the prisoners, five of whom had already been released due to severe emotional and cognitive disorders. Already on the first day, prisoners were being made to perform humiliating acts such as singing and to perform physical punishments such as push-ups and jumping jacks. Zimbardo notes that on day one, guards were already "beginning to take pleasure in giving commands and forcing the prisoners to execute them" and that punishments were becoming "cleverly inventive...the first signs of creative evil." By day five, the prisoners were simulating acts of sodomy.

> It is hard to imagine that such sexual humiliation could happen in only five days, when the young men all know that this is a simulated prison experiment. Moreover, initially, they all recognized that the "others" were also college students like themselves. Given that they were all randomly assigned to play these contrasting roles, there were no inherent differences between the two categories. They all began the experience as seemingly good people.... Yet, some guards have transformed into perpetrators of evil, and other guards have become passive contributors to the evil through their inaction.[26]

Zimbardo himself become so immersed in his role as prison superintendent that he lost his objectivity and scientific detachment, allowing the experiment to continue when it should have been stopped after the first day. With similar boldness of Milgram's statement about staffing of death camps, Zimbardo states that the Stanford Prison Experiment "reveals a message we do not want to accept: that most of us can undergo significant character transformations when we are caught up in the crucible of social forces. Any deed that any human being has ever committed, however horrible, is possible for any of us—under the right or wrong situational circumstances."[27]

Just as we are confident in walking across a frozen pond based on our understanding of the collective behavior of water molecules, when looking at groups of people, societies, and nations, and the interactions between them, understanding the dynamics of behavior and the ability to predict behavior will occur principally through emergent rules dependent on situational and environmental factors.

The Other Gap: Hate and Empathy

Later in this book, we will begin to explain human behavior using the "triune brain" model developed by Paul MacLean, the former director of the Laboratory of the Brain and Behavior at the United States National Institute of Mental Health. In this model, the brain is functionally and structurally divided into three parts that were established successively in response to evolutionary need so that the brain is in effect three brains in one.[28]

The Three Human Brains

The most primitive brain is referred to as the *reptilian complex,* consisting of the brain stem and cerebellum which are located at the base of the brain and top of the spinal column. The structure and functions of this brain are the same for the entire brain of reptiles, and these functions have been in place for over 300 million years. The reptilian complex is concerned with basic survival through automatic processes that are highly resistant to change such as "fight or flight" response, breathing, circulation, reproduction, social dominance, and establishing home territory.[29] The *limbic system* is the second brain to evolve. It is located in the center of the brain.[30] It, too, is designed for ensuring survival and reproduction, but does so through initiating and controlling emotional responses and pain and pleasure. It is also referred to as the *mammalian brain,* because the reptilian complex and limbic system structure and functions are what comprise almost the entire brain of a mammal. These functions have been in place for 200 million years. The third and most highly evolved brain is the *neocortex,* also called the *cerebral cortex,* which constitutes most of the mass of the human brain. The neocortex, the seat of conscious thought, is responsible for the higher level functions such as language, speech, planning, voluntary movement, and processing sensory information.[31] These three brains are all interconnected and are involved in all human behavior, although one brain tends to dominate in any particular behavior.

The Primitive Emotion of Hate

Rush W. Dozier, Jr., author of *Why We Hate: Understanding, Curbing, and Eliminating Hate in Ourselves and Our World*, refers to the two older brains as the "reptomammalian" brain constituting the "primitive neural system" while the neocortex constitutes the "advanced neural system."[32] Dozier believes hate is a primitive emotion that arises in the primitive neural system "that combines intense dislike, anger, stereotyping, and us-versus-them distinctions…that marks for attack or avoidance those things that we perceive as a threat to our survival or reproduction."[33] He describes hate as "a kind of anger phobia" and "relic of the distant past…formed in the world that existed millions of years ago."[34] The greatest danger occurs when a belief system, such as ideology, religion, or nationalism, is rationalized and merges with hate directed at a particular person, group, or nation.

> History makes it painfully apparent that when hate pervades a meaning system, there is virtually no limit to the atrocities an individual, group, or society can perpetrate. The structure of the human mind provides no assurance that people will behave rationally. This is why hate is such an urgent problem in the post-cold war era, when weapons of mass destruction are spreading. If a group or nation with a hate-filled meaning system that exalts martyrdom obtains such weapons, it may well be willing to use them and face—even welcome—the ghastly consequences…. As our tools have evolved over the past hundred thousand years from stone axes and spears to firearms, hydrogen bombs, and intercontinental missiles, the consequences of the darkest part of our nature become infinitely more ominous.[35]

We propose (and will discuss in greater detail in the following chapters) that hate (which we also believe includes revenge) is more than an emotion as described by Dozier, but a hybrid *emotional-cognitive state* involving the fusion of primitive survival instincts of the limbic brain with the planning and purposeful neocortical "thinking" brain. In particular, where *human causation* is identified as a threat to survival or reproductive interests, the primitive limbic brain and highly functioning neocortical brain unite to eliminate the threat at almost any cost, including, in extreme cases, paradoxically, one's self. True hate does not arise when calamity affects us where there is no nexus to human causation. People who have lost loved ones to natural disasters such as hurricanes, tornadoes, and earthquakes experience sadness, distress, depression, anxiety, and anger but are not consumed with true hate. They may loosely say "I hate tornadoes" but they are not experiencing that special emotional-cognitive state called hate. In some cases, out of a need to find something to hate in order to feel some form of control, people may personify natural disaster through ascribing blame to a supernatural deity. How often have we heard the victim of some calamitous natural disaster lament, "I hate God"? There are no social groups committed to a hatred of tornadoes like the numerous hate groups that exist committed to the destruction of another group of people such as Nazis or al-Qaeda. In true hate, a feedback loop between the limbic and cortical areas of the brain exists in which primitive fears provoke identification of a human cause and the identification of a human cause provokes primitive fears. Once this loop is created, it is extremely difficult to interrupt it because the most primitive survival mechanisms of the brain are in sync with the most highly evolved cognitive parts of the brain. Thus, intergenerational warfare and rivalry, such as the present conflict between Israel and its Arab neighbors, can exist and thrive for decades and even centuries.

Fortunately, empathy serves as an antidote to hate. Hate and empathy are polar opposites that can lead to the most vicious and destructive acts or the most sacrificial and compassionate acts toward our fellow humans. Empathy involves experiencing for one's self the emotional state of another. Empathy is a neurological process that allows us to actually feel what another person is feeling. Empathy inspires altruism—compassion and the desire to act in other's interests—because it creates the sensation that the other person is the same as you or your immediate kin. It blurs the distinction between you and another so that you are more inclined to act in the other's best interest. This type of altruism, known as "reciprocal" altruism, is based on the expectation of the act of kindness being returned. "If I treat you as though you are me, you are likely to treat me as though I am you." The Golden Rule is the embodiment of empathy. While we are genetically predisposed to support close relatives ("kin altruism"), our behavior towards people outside of immediate family is fluid and dynamic, depending on our culture and experience. Unfortunately, who we hate and who we are empathic towards is subject to easy manipulation by others.

Hate and empathy evolved as social controls during our primitive hunter-gatherer past, consisting of small bands of related people numbering no more than about 150 who were known to each other. This way of life constitutes more than 99 percent of our history as humans. We are naturally empathetic towards any person identified as part of our "band" or "tribe," cautious around anyone outside the "band" or "tribe," and easily provoked to hate anyone who presents a threat to the survival of ourselves and our kin or our reproductive interests. In our past as hunter-gatherers, hate and empathy were in balance; empathy was the normal condition and hate limited to truly human-caused existential threats. Modern industrial society now threatens our very existence because it tends to promote the development of hate and limit the exercise of empathy. In dense urban environments, our anonymity decreases our sense of responsibility to others and increases our suspicion of others. Globalization has thrust distant and unfamiliar cultures into direct contact promoting fear. Large populations of different "tribes" in close proximity with decreasing resources easily provoke suspicion, fear, and, eventually, hate. This was the demographics of the Jewish Pale of Settlement in Central and Eastern Europe in the early twentieth century, which contributed to the severity of the Holocaust. Because of our *negativity bias*—the tendency of our limbic brain to

23

fixate on bad events—the global news media constantly feeds us with all the bad news and minimally reports good news, thus reinforcing our fears and fueling our hate. Finally, hate is the most highly evolved emotion involving the co-opting of the thinking brain to set in motion destructive behavior, whereas empathy relies almost exclusively on feeling to motivate helpful behavior. The delicate balance of hate and empathy that allowed humans to succeed as a species has been disrupted with far too much hate and far too little empathy.

There are perhaps three human beings on the planet who could unleash the destructive forces of hydrogen bombs to wipe out humanity and most species, while there are perhaps a dozen who could detonate nuclear bombs that would kill hundreds of thousands, destabilize the world, and create an environmental catastrophe. Control of these nuclear bombs is so far under the control of nations but soon could be in the hands of terrorist organizations. The people in control of these devastating weapons have reptomammalian brains that can be easily provoked into irrational hate. Leaders of terrorist organizations are already consumed by such hate and will no doubt deploy these weapons without mercy. Part of being human means "a primitive animal lives in your mind and brain" that "knows it must feed, have sex, and fight or flee if threatened."[36] The fate of the world is truly in the hands of a few individuals who we hope will not make any decisions regarding aggression without the full influence of the advanced neural systems of their neocortex.

North Korea, a totalitarian state with nuclear weapons, was, until recently, under the control of an emotionally unstable leader. The question is not whether Iran is seeking to construct nuclear bombs and delivery systems, the question is, once Iran has such weapons and systems, will it choose to use them? India and Pakistan have fought three wars over territory over the last five decades, are presently in a state of cold war over the Kashmir region, and both have nuclear weapons. Are the leaders of North Korea, Iran, India, and Pakistan analyzing the world using their rational neocortex or are they under the spell of reptomammalian-induced hate?

Leaders have the ability to cause needless death and destruction, not only through control of weapons of mass destruction, but also through their influence over the minds of their followers. Various situational factors involving conflict with an *out-group* such as disputed territory, present state of war, or previous history of war or violence, and limited resources can easily be woven by leaders into a compelling story to alarm the primal fears of their followers related to survival and reproductive fitness. The occurrence of a present crisis and the identification of a responsible *out-group* are all that is needed to evoke these primal reptomammalian fears and convince the thinking neocortical mind that the annihilation of the out-group is necessary or, at least, create an indifference to and lack of empathy towards the *out-group*. In Nazi Germany, Adolph Hitler was able to inspire a small but critical mass of ideological followers to carry out the Holocaust but, more importantly, was able to create indifference and lack of empathy towards Jews and other *out-groups* in the a majority of the population.

The Banality of Evil

Adolf Eichmann, considered the architect of the Holocaust for his role in the mass deportations of Jews in Eastern Europe during World War II to extermination camps, was tried before an Israeli court in Jerusalem in 1961 for crimes against humanity and crimes against the Jewish people. Attending his trial as a reporter for the *New Yorker* was the political theorist and philosopher Hannah Arendt.[37] Expecting to find Eichmann a monstrous incarnation of evil, she instead found a man whom she referred to as the embodiment of the "banality of evil," a man who was "terribly and terrifyingly normal." Arendt portrayed Eichmann as a dutiful bureaucrat of shallow intellect who abdicated his conscience in furtherance of improving his career. Eichmann himself declared at his trial he abdicated his conscience in obedience to the leader principle (*Fuhrerprinzip*). Eichmann was examined by six psychologists who found no evidence of abnormal personality. This included one psychologist who found his attitude towards his family and friends as "highly desirable." Arendt observed, "The longer one listened to him, the more obvious it became that his inability to speak was closely connected with an inability to think, namely, to think from the standpoint of somebody else."

The transformation of Eichmann, who was a traveling salesman for the Vacuum Oil Company before joining the SS, into an architect of genocide shows the power of situational forces on shaping the behavior of "terrifyingly normal" people. As we shall later see in greater detail, lack of empathy for the *out group*, cultural norms for obedience, personal need for success and acceptance, psychological distance from the actual acts of murder, and relief from personal responsibility through sanctioning by authority figures created fertile soil for the growth of monsters like Eichmann.

Time is quickly running out to bridge the *hate-empathy gap* created by our limited capacity for empathy and our ability to be easily provoked into hatred that incorporates the brain's most powerful cognitive functions. The dire consequences of this gap are compounded by the extreme destructiveness of our instruments of hate—firearms, explosives, and atomic bombs—and the limited power of our empathetic response to effect major change. Is there a benevolent equivalent to the destructiveness of an atomic bomb that can create an instantaneous profound improvement in the lives of millions? Would that there could be an "empathy bomb" capable of reversing the misfortunes of millions in an instant! "To successfully cope with enormous dangers of the globalizing world of the twenty-first century, we need to use recent breakthroughs in the understanding of the brain and behavior to address the problems of hatred and violence."[38] We need to immediately apply the advances being made in bridging the gap from the natural sciences to the social sciences and humanities to bridging the gap between hate and empathy. The ability of our primitive reptomammalian brain to co-opt our rationale thinking brain to justify and plan for the annihilation of whole populations, our ability to use weapons of mass destruction, and the ability of the few, through our political-social systems, to inspire the many to seek the annihilation of whole populations threatens our very survival. There are few warriors in American history who could compare to General Douglas MacArthur who served as brigadier general in World War I, as a general and commander-in-chief of U.S. Army Forces Pacific during World War II (where he accepted the Japanese surrender ending the war), and as commander-in-chief of the United Nations Command during the Korean War (until his dismissal by President Harry Truman on April 10, 1951). Yet, in retirement, MacArthur, disturbed by the destructive power of the hydrogen bomb, called for the abolition of war. In a speech to the Los Angeles County Council of the American Legion on January 26, 1955, MacArthur had these words:

> You will say at once that although the abolition of war has been the dream of man for centuries, every proposition to that end has been promptly discarded as impossible and fantastic. Every cynic, every pessimist, every adventurer, every swashbuckler in the world has always disclaimed its feasibility. But that was before the science of the past decade made mass destruction a reality…. Now, the tremendous and present evolution of nuclear and other potentials of destruction has suddenly taken the problem away from its primary consideration as a moral and spiritual question and brought it abreast of scientific realism. It is no longer an ethical question to be pondered solely by learned philosophers and ecclesiastics but a hardcore one for the decision of the masses whose survival is the issue…. Sooner or later, the world, if it is to survive, must reach this decision. The only question is, when? Must we fight again before we learn? When will some great figure in power have sufficient imagination and moral courage to translate this universal wish—which is rapidly becoming a universal necessity—into actuality? We are in a new era. The old methods and solutions no longer suffice. We must have new thoughts, new ideas, new concepts, just as did our venerated forefathers when they faced a new world. We must break out of the straightjacket of the past. There must always be one to lead, and we should be that one. We should now proclaim our readiness to abolish war in concert with the great powers of the world. The result would be magical.

As Richard Reid stood in line at Charles de Gaulle International Airport like a soldier facing the enemy lines, was the homicidal/suicidal mission he embarked on the product of a deranged mind or had the leaders in his world tapped into his primitive neural system to create an existential crisis to which the only way out was destruction of the enemy and himself? We believe the latter explanation to be accurate not only for Reid but for the vast majority of other similar homicidal/suicidal attacks linked to terrorist organizations that seem to occur on a daily basis.

Human conflict and aggression, and likewise cooperation and empathy, are principally the result of situational and environmental factors with the dispositional nature of individuals one variable among many leading to the probable outcome of human interactions. We have reached a stage where multidisciplinary application of scientific knowledge is sufficient to predict the potential for conflict or cooperation and can be used to minimize the former and maximize the later.

In the next two chapters, we will explore our *Genesis* from the creation of the universe to the arrival of complex life on earth using the generally accepted scientific theories and principles. This is a rather ambitious journey for two small chapters but one we believe is worthwhile to place a different perspective on our place in nature and to appreciate even more how science can provide answers to the critical issues facing humanity.

Chapter Three
Genesis

In the beginning God created the Heavens and the Earth.

- Genesis 1:1

*In the context of inflationary cosmology, it is fair to say
that the universe is the ultimate free lunch.*

- Alan H. Guth[39]
Professor of Physics, MIT

In the beginning, there was Absolute Nothingness: no matter, energy, space, or time. About 14 billion years ago, a *quantum fluctuation* in the Emptiness allowed an ounce of positive energy to appear, offset by the negative energy of its gravitational field, so that the total energy of the universe remained a zero. This ounce of energy was confined to an area a billion times smaller than a proton, 10^{-26} centimeters*, with incredible density 10^{80} (1 followed by 80 zeros) times that of water. After the smallest amount of time allowed by physics, 10^{-43} seconds known as *Planck time*, the temperature of the universe was a trillion trillion times hotter than the interior of the sun (10^{32} Kelvin†). The three other forces of nature in addition to gravity—electromagnetic, weak nuclear and strong nuclear forces‡ —were unified as a

---

* This extremely small number using exponential notation is a decimal point followed by 25 zeros and the number 1. The conversely extremely large number 10^{26} is 1 followed by 26 zeros.

† Kelvin (K) is a temperature scale referenced to absolute zero which is the absence of all thermal energy. 0 K equals absolute zero or -273.15 °C or -459.67 °F.

‡ The electromagnetic force is the attractive and repulsive forces associated with particles that have electric charge and produces electromagnetic radiation which, depending on frequency,

single force and matter was a dense super-hot plasma of its basic constituent particles: quarks, electrons, neutrinos, and their antiparticles. This seed for the universe began expanding and cooling. Thus began the Big Bang˙.

While the laws of nature do not allow for the creation of matter or energy out of nothing (the law of the conservation of mass-energy), the gravitational field created by the presence of matter or energy represented negative energy balancing out the presence of the mass and energy. Imagine holding a marble in your right hand attached to a rubber band anchored in your left hand. As you separate your hands, the energy of the marble moving away in your right hand is cancelled out by the tension in the runner band. In this example, the marble represents mass and the rubber represents the gravitational field, each equal in force and each canceling each other out, leaving zero net energy. Mass represents positive energy because mass and energy are interchangeable under Albert Einstein's famous equation $E = mc^2$ from his special theory of relativity. The energy (E) of an object is equal to its mass (m) times the speed of light squared (c^2). Since c^2 is such a large number, a small amount of mass converts into a huge amount of energy. Converting just 1 kilogram (2.2 lbs.) of mass to energy would produce an explosion equivalent to 22 million tons of TNT! Thermonuclear bombs, or H-bombs, using the mass to energy conversion process that powers the sun, have been built with the explosive power of 50 million tons of TNT, more than a thousand times as powerful as the atomic bomb detonated over Hiroshima during World War II that killed about 90,000 people.

Later in this book, we will talk about the H-Bomb of the mind, a bomb fueled not by hydrogen but fueled by hate. This "Hate Bomb" of the mind produces the motivational energy for a human destructive force that is on par with the energy produced by the hydrogen bomb. The hate bomb is fueled not by the fusion of hydrogen into helium but by the fusion of a perceived existential threat with primitive "us versus them" thinking. The greatest threat to humanity today is the potential for the confluence of the hate bomb with the hydrogen bomb or other weapons of mass destruction.

How does energy, even when balanced by equal negative energy, appear out of nothing? Even in the vacuum of zero energy space, the *uncertainty principle* of quantum mechanics does not permit the universe to exist with an

---

takes the form of waves such as radio waves, microwaves, light waves, x-rays, and gamma rays. The weak nuclear force has an effective range smaller than an atomic nucleus and is responsible for radioactive decay of neutrons into protons. The strong nuclear force is limited to the area of an atomic nucleus and holds protons and neutrons together inside the nucleus of the atom and binds quarks together to form protons and neutrons.

˙   Cosmologists and physicists generally agree on the evolution of the universe after the first fraction of a second however the reason for the existence of the initial singularity and the initial state of the singularity lead to numerous speculative views. The view of creation of the universe *ex nihilo* (out of nothing) is one of such speculative views although consistent with Judeo-Christian-Islamic beliefs on creation. The Catholic Church pronounced the Big Bang theory as being in accordance with the Bible in 1951.

energy field of exactly zero with a rate of change of exactly zero. "There must be a certain minimum amount of uncertainty, or *quantum fluctuations*, in the value of the field."[40] The uncertainty principle was formulated by the German physicist, Werner Heisenberg, in 1927. In mathematical terms, the uncertainty principle expresses the limits with which we can precisely measure the position and velocity of particles or the force and rate of change of energy fields. Greater precision in measuring the velocity of an electron results in greater the imprecision in measuring its position and vice versa. We cannot precisely measure both. The effects of uncertainty while applying to all objects are negligible for everyday objects. The effects only become noticeable at the atomic scale. The uncertainty principle also means that the energy level of a particle can fluctuate and the amount of the fluctuation increases with shortness of time. The effect of this energy uncertainty is a process known as *quantum tunneling* in which a particle such as a photon of light can occasionally reappear outside of its container due to a sudden increase in energy. In extremely small submicroscopic areas of space for extremely brief times, quantum fluctuations due to uncertainty result in the creation of subatomic virtual particle/antiparticle pairs that instantly meet and annihilate each other, as gravitational fields violently fluctuate. Nature will not permit observers to confine it to precisely known values and within those extremely small areas for extremely brief instants of time out of view to us, nature is wild, chaotic, and unpredictable.

Returning to our creation story, from 10^{-36} to 10^{-34} seconds after the Big Bang (ATB), there was a brief period time of exponential expansion of the universe in which it doubled in size 100 times over, increasing its size by 10^{30} (1 followed by 30 zeros) times its original size in a minuscule fraction of a second. Starting from a size much smaller than a proton, our universe was now the size of a grapefruit[41]! The temperature of the universe cooled enough (10^{28} K) for one of the forces of nature, the strong nuclear force, to separate from its unified state with the electromagnetic and weak nuclear forces. This separation is called a *phase transition*, much like when liquid water freezes and forms ice crystals. In the case of the universe, as can happen with water, the cooling was so fast the universe became *supercooled* so that the phase transition of the strong nuclear force was delayed, resulting in the creation of an unstable *false vacuum* state of the universe. The negative pressure of the false vacuum, similar to the collapsing of a plastic soda bottle when you suck the air out, created a gravitational repulsive force that fueled the exponential expansion of the universe. Unlike a true vacuum that has zero energy density, the false vacuum had an enormous energy density, equivalent to 10^{80} grams per cubic centimeter. Also, the energy density of a false vacuum cannot decrease, so that the energy density remained constant as the universe expanded. Each time the universe doubled in size, the positive energy doubled so as to maintain a constant energy density. However, since the gravitational energy also doubled, which is negative energy, the net total energy of the universe remained at zero. After 100 doublings in size and 100 doublings in energy density, the universe now contained something like 10^{80} particles, enough matter to fill today's observable universe containing 100 billion galaxies! This filling of the universe with all we can see from an ounce of mass-energy is, according to the MIT physicist Alan Guth, "the ultimate free lunch."

With the inflationary epoch over, the universe, still superhot and super dense plasma of matter and force particles, resumed its regular expansion rate. At 10^{-12} seconds ATB, the temperature dropped to 10^{15} K (still about 100 million times hotter than the center of the sun), and the final phase transition of the energy forces occurred with the electromagnetic force separating from the weak nuclear force. Quarks, the constituent particles of protons and neutrons, and antiquarks, the constituent particles of antiprotons and antineutrons, began to annihilate. Because there were 300,000,000 quarks for every 299,999,999 antiquarks, these annihilations left a small excess of quarks, which accounts for all the nuclear matter in the universe today and the rarity of antimatter.[42] Had the quarks and antiquarks existed in equal numbers, there would be no atoms in the universe to form stars, planets, and us! At 10^{-6} seconds ATB, the temperature dropped to ten trillion (10^{13}) K (about a million times hotter than the center of the sun), and the remaining quarks combined in groups of three to form protons and neutrons. At one second ATB, the temperature was now 10 billion K (about a thousand times hotter than the center of the sun) and the universe consisted of a hot plasma of photons, electrons, antielectrons (positrons), neutrinos, antineutrinos, protons, and neutrons. As occurred with the quarks, the electrons and antielectrons annihilated each other, leaving a residual of electrons. Neutrons began decaying into protons, electrons, and neutrinos, leaving about one neutron for every five protons. For the next three minutes, the universe cooled down to a billion K and protons combined with the remaining free neutrons to form hydrogen (a single proton) and helium (two protons and two neutrons) with traces of deuterium (known also as heavy hydrogen, with a single proton and neutron) and the heavier elements of lithium and beryllium. The forging of protons and neutrons into heavier elements occurs today in the sun and stars (and through the occasional detonation of H-Bombs here on earth) through a process known as *nucleosynthesis*. The process that forged these heavier elements in the few moments after the Big Bang (ATB) is called the period of *primordial nucleosynthesis*. The theory of the Big Bang predicts that this period of nucleosynthesis should have produced a universe that is composed of about 75 percent hydrogen and 23 percent helium, which has been confirmed through measurement by astronomers.

Let there be light[43]

Photons are the minuscule packets of energy that transmit the electromagnetic force that includes visible light, microwaves, and radio waves. Visible light and radio waves make up part of the electromagnetic spectrum, which, at the lowest energies, is in the form of radio waves and, as the energies increase, pass through microwaves, light waves, x-rays, and, finally, at the highest energies, gamma rays.[·] Up until about 380,000 years ATB, the temperature of the universe was too hot for the positively charged hydrogen and helium atomic nuclei to capture the negatively charged electrons to form electrically neutral atoms. The photons interact with charged particles so were continuously being deflected and absorbed. After about 380,000 years, the universe cooled to a few thousand degrees, which allowed the electrically neutral atoms to form and allowed photons to stream out through space across the entire universe. The universe was now transparent and light could travel freely. These photons have been traveling through space ever since and form what is known as the *cosmic background radiation* and can be "seen" today as a faint afterglow of the Big Bang. In the fourteen or so billion years since the Big Bang, these photons, as predicted in the Big Bang theory, have cooled down to a mere 2.7 degrees (2.7 K) above absolute zero, which puts them in the form of microwaves. These microwaves are below visible light in the electromagnetic spectrum and therefore cannot been seen with the human eye. A satellite placed in orbit by NASA called COBE (Cosmic Background Explorer) in the 1990s has measured in every direction a background microwave radiation with a temperature of about 2.7 K as predicted by the Big Bang Theory. "In concrete terms, in *every* cubic meter of the universe—including the one you now occupy—there are, on average, about 400 million photons that collectively compose the vast cosmic sea of microwave radiation, an echo of creation."[44]

After several hundred million years, areas of the universe that were slightly denser began to collapse due to gravitational attraction, forming galaxies. Within these galaxies, clouds of hydrogen and helium began to collapse due to their own gravity. When these collapsing clouds of gas got hot enough, nuclear fusion began and the first generations of stars were born. The stars stopped contracting when nuclear fusion, converting hydrogen into helium (nucleosynthesis), released energy in the form of heat and light, which provided enough pressure to counter the gravitational attraction. When a star's hydrogen supply diminishes, it will contract and get hotter, causing helium to be converted into heavier elements such as carbon, oxygen, and, for massive stars, heavier elements such as iron. The star will keep collapsing as the gravitational attraction becomes stronger than pressure from the output of heat and light. Stars having a mass about equivalent to the sun or less, which is the majority of stars in the galaxy, will stop nucleosynthesis and die as *white dwarfs*, a dense ball of carbon and oxygen about the size of the earth with each cubic centimeter weighing about as much as an elephant. Stars about 1.4 times as massive as the sun but less than about twenty times the mass of the sun will further collapse into a *neutron star*, a sphere with a diameter of 10 kilometers

---

[·]   Although electromagnetic radiation is composed of discrete particles, it travels through space in the form of waves like the ripples on a pond after you drop a stone into the water.

made of neutrons in which a teaspoon weighs as much as a mountain! The most massive stars will collapse into a *black hole,* whose gravitational field is so strong not even light can escape. The collapse of massive stars can result in cataclysmic stellar explosion called a supernova, in which most of the mass of the star is violently expelled as a cloud of gas and dust. The core that remains will form a neutron star or black hole. Supernovae can shine with the brightness of 10 billion suns and release the same amount of energy as the sun will in its entire 10 billion year life. The elements heavier than helium produced towards the end of the star's life, such as carbon, oxygen, and iron, and even heavier elements such as uranium produced during the supernova are blasted into interstellar space, forming a stellar nursery from which a new generation of stars is born. The sun and the planets, including the earth, began forming about 4.6 billion years ago from a rotating cloud of dust and gas containing the remnants of an ancient supernova. About 4.5 billion years ago, the planet earth formed from the accretion of heavier elements in the solar nebula. Virtually all the elements heavier than helium that you and the earth are made of, is made of star dust from the explosion of an ancient dead star.

The earth was without form, and void[45] ...Let the waters under the heaven be gathered together unto one place, and let the dry land appear.[46]

Let us take a look at the young earth 4 billion years ago as described by Paul Davies, a professor at Arizona State University and acclaimed physicist and astrobiologist:

> The whole world is almost completely submerged beneath a deep layer of hot water. No continents divide the scalding sea.... The atmosphere is crushingly dense and completely unbreathable. The sky, when free of cloud, is lit by a sun as deadly as a nuclear reactor, drenching the planet in ultraviolet rays. At night, bright meteors flash across the heavens. Occasionally, a large meteorite penetrates the atmosphere and plunges into the ocean, raising gigantic tsunamis, kilometers high, which crash around the globe. The seabed at the base of the global ocean is unlike the familiar rock of today. A Hadean furnace lies just beneath, still aglow with primeval heat.[47]

The solar system today is a relatively peaceful family of planets compared to the time of the earth's birth and childhood. Shortly after the birth of the earth, it is believed that a protoplanet a little smaller than the planet Mars collided with the earth, ejecting material from the mantel and crust of the earth and impacting protoplanet into orbit around the earth. This material, due to the influence of its own gravity, became the spherical body known as the Moon. Ending at about 3.8 billion years ago, the earth was subjected to an intense bombardment by comets, asteroids, and meteorites that resulted in cataclysmic changes such as the obliteration of the atmosphere and oceans. Impacts from these objects were also responsible for providing the earth with the water that became the oceans and the gases that formed its early atmosphere of carbon dioxide, methane, ammonia, and nitrogen. This water and these organic (carbon and hydrogen-based) compounds provided the ingredients necessary for more complex molecules that self-organized into life forms. The ingredients in the recipe for life turn out to be quite common in the universe. The key chemical elements of carbon, oxygen, hydrogen, nitrogen, and phosphorus have been found in outer space and in impact objects that have struck earth. Water and organic molecules including complex ones such as amino acids have been found in interstellar gas clouds and meteorites. In a famous experiment carried out by Harold Urey and Stanley Miller in 1953, a flask was sealed with water, methane, hydrogen, and ammonia (elements believed present in the early Earth atmosphere) and electricity was passed through the mixture to simulate lightning. After a week, the flask was found to contain several types of amino acids, thus recreating what was believed to be the "primordial soup" out of which life was assembled. While this experiment is now not believed to represent the model for conditions for the creation of life, it does prove how easy it is for the building blocks of life, amino acids, to assemble from basic chemical elements.

The Earth of 4 billion years ago could not support the type of life we are familiar with on the surface and oceans of the earth. The atmosphere contained no oxygen and, without ozone in the atmosphere, the surface of the earth was bombarded by a deadly stream of ultraviolet radiation. Every several million years, a large impacting comet, protoplanet, or asteroid would sterilize the surface of earth by creating a fireball that displaced the atmosphere, boiled the oceans dry, and melted rock to a depth of almost a kilometer.[48] Yet, somewhere on the earth, primordial forms of life were able to self-organize from water and organic molecules and survive. It turns out that today there is a thriving ecosystem of microbes living in undersea hydrothermal vents in the seafloor where temperature of the water approaches the boiling point. The metabolism of these microbes does not use sunlight (as plants do in photosynthesis) or oxygen (as animals do) to produce energy but uses hydrogen. It is in such an environment that life, about 4 billion years ago, most likely arose.

Life in Lost City

Through genetics, it is possible to determine which present living microbes have evolved the least and therefore are most like early life. The least evolved organisms are a microbe called hyperthermophiles, which can be found living today near hydrothermal vents and volcanic vents under the ocean called black smokers. Hyperthermophiles have been found living in water temperature as high as 110 C, which is above the boiling point of water.˙ These deep ocean hydrothermal and volcanic vents, in addition to protection from the harsh conditions of the early Earth surface, provided a ready source of chemicals needed for life and the seafloor provided channels for organic material to

˙ The water does not actually boil due to the immense pressure deep under the ocean.

concentrate. Hyperthermophiles do not get energy for metabolism from photosynthesis or by consuming other organisms; neither sunlight nor oxygen is used to produce energy. They obtain energy from combining sulphur, a common element of early Earth, with hydrogen to produce hydrogen sulfide.

In 2000, researchers discovered a new kind of hydrothermal vent system called Lost City[49] about 15 kilometers west of the tectonic plate boundary of the Mid-Atlantic Ridge. Discovered were several pillars of limestone, some rising as tall as a 20-story building, that were emitting heated seawater up to temperatures of 90 C. Water is heated by circulating through warm rocks below the pillars. The vents at Lost City have been shown to support conditions necessary to create organic compounds and have high concentrations of hydrogen that support the metabolism of microbes such as hyperthermophiles.

Life: Self-Replicating Units of Negative Entropy

To understand how and where life may have first arisen, we must understand what distinguishes life from the inanimate world around us. The key to life is a concept known as *entropy,* which is the amount of disorder or chaos in any closed system. Under the *second law of thermodynamics,* the amount of entropy (or disorder) in any closed system always increases with time until a state of *thermal equilibrium* is reached. Thermal equilibrium means that the temperature of a system is equalized and no further transfer of energy is possible. As an example, imagine a container of water separated by a barrier into to two compartments, one containing cold water and one containing hot water. When the barrier is first removed the amount of entropy (or disorder) would be low since there is a distinct region of cold water and a distinct region of hot water. As time goes on the heat from the hot water will transfer to the cold water increasing the entropy of the system until a uniform temperature is reached (thermal equilibrium) at which time no further heat transfer will occur. Our sense of time moving either forward or backward is based on our intuitive sense of entropy. If you were to watch a movie in which scrambled eggs were reconstituted into whole eggs or shards of glass assemble into a drinking glass, you would know that this movie was being run in reverse. We intuitively understand that as time moves forward, the world on its own seems to become more disorganized and disordered unless we intervene to create a pocket organization and order. For those of us "control freaks" obsessed with keeping everything in its place and organized, the second law of thermal dynamics has some depressing news: by cleaning and organizing your house and workspace, you have increased the net disorder (entropy) in the universe due to the breakdown of highly organized molecules in your body needed for the energy to clean and organize! One of the characteristics of living entities is their ability to create self-organization against the general trend of systems to greater disorder and hence, to create *negative entropy.*

The creation and storage of information also requires a reversal of entropy or *negative entropy*. If you took all the letters in a Shakespeare sonnet and scrambled them, the odds of randomly reassembling the sonnet from these letters are astronomical. Likewise, the odds of molecules self-assembling and being able to store and replicate information, such as done by the DNA and RNA molecules in all living entities, are astronomical. So, while the creation of the first living collection of molecules was a chance occurrence of extremely unlikely odds, the subsequent copies from this "accidental" replicating collection of molecules represent a process we call life. The actual remoteness of possibility for self-replicating complex molecules is subject to debate, leading some scientists to believe life on earth is unique and others to believe life is commonplace in the universe.* Paul Davies summarizes the qualities that distinguish life as broadly involving "two crucial factors: metabolism and reproduction."[50] Both metabolism and reproduction involve countering, within the body of the life form, the universe's inexorable progression to disorder and thermal equilibrium: metabolism through the creation and storage of complex molecules used for energy and reproduction through the ability of complex chains of molecules (DNA and RNA) to transfer useful information necessary for the replication of the life form. Oxford University professor and author Richard Dawkins refers to these first large molecules that were capable of self-replication as *replicators*. Once the replicator molecule existed, the process of natural selection could drive the development into more complex life forms through errors in copying of the molecule that proved to be advantageous to survival. These original replicators that existed nearly four billion years ago are no longer with us but their descendants, the DNA and RNA molecules, live on.

Life, like a computer, is a cooperative arrangement between software and hardware.[51] The software contains the instructions for the creation and metabolism of life forms and is contained in DNA and RNA molecules. The hardware is contained in protein molecules that provide the structure of cells and catalyze the processes used for energy and reproduction. The instructions contained in DNA and RNA are encoded in an alphabet of four different molecules called nucleobases. The four nucleobases in DNA are designated by the letters A, G, C, and T, standing for the molecules adenine, guanine, cytosine, and thymine†, with A pairing with T and G pairing with C. These pairs of nucleobases (*base pairs*) in the thousands or millions form the rungs of a ladder twisted together in a spiral known as the "double helix" polymer (chain of molecules). The backbone for the double helix polymer is sugar and phosphate molecules that form part of each nucleotide rung. We know already that the building blocks of proteins—amino acids—existed naturally and could

---

* Probably the strongest argument for the creation of life through supernatural force lies in the fact of the astronomical odds against the random collection of complex molecules forming that are capable of accurate self-replication without any external assistance other than the laws of chemistry and physics.

† In RNA, the letter T is replaced with U for uracil.

easily be assembled in the conditions of the early Earth. The building blocks for the other key molecule of life—nucleotides that constitute DNA and RNA—can also assemble spontaneously from simple chemicals present on the early Earth. Nucleobases can assemble from water, cyanide, and acetylene and sugars from warming a solution of formaldehyde. A mineral common in certain meteors releases phosphorus in water. Experiments in 2009 at the University of Manchester in the U.K. using simple chemicals present in the early Earth succeeded in producing two nucleotide bases (C and U).

> DNA is nothing less than a blueprint, or more accurately, an algorithm or instruction manual for building a living, breathing, thinking human being. We share this magic molecule with almost all other life forms on Earth. From fungi to flies, from bacteria to bears, organisms are sculpted according to their respective DNA instructions.[52]

An organism's complete set of DNA is called its *genome*. The smallest known genome contains about 600,000 base pairs for bacteria, while the human genome contains a little more than three billion base pairs. Human DNA is arranged in 23 paired chromosomes, each containing a range of about 50 million to 250 million base pairs, which are separate polymers (molecular chains) contained in the nucleus of every cell. Because of the chromosomes contained in the nucleus, each cell in the body contains the instructions for the creation of a complete human being.* Each chromosome contains numerous *genes*, which are discrete strings of nucleotide bases (averaging about 3,000 base pairs in humans) that each encode the production of a specific protein and are considered the basic physical and functional units of heredity. Variants of a gene occupying the same position on a paired set of chromosomes are called *alleles*. It is the variation of the alleles that make each one of us different (except for identical twins). For example, there are three known gene pairs that determine a person's eye color. Genes make up only about 2 percent of the DNA contained in the entire human genome; the remaining DNA is non-coding whose functions are largely unknown and have even been referred to as "junk DNA." Human beings have an estimated 20,000 to 25,000 genes that provide the code for all human traits—a surprisingly low number considering the complexity of the human mind and human behaviors. The proteins that the genes provide instruction for assembling are the stuff of life that perform most life functions and constitute a majority of cellular structures. Proteins are polymers assembled in sequences of typically a few hundred amino acid molecules from a group of 20 amino acids common to all life.

There is a "chicken and egg" paradox with DNA being the first living molecule because proteins serve as the enzymes involved in extracting the information contained in genes and in transcribing the information into

---

* The exception is mature red blood cells, which lack a nucleus and therefore lack chromosomal DNA.

proteins. So, to make DNA, you need proteins and to make proteins you need DNA. Most biochemists believe that the first replicator molecule was probably similar to RNA, which, in today's cells, transcribes and relays the instructions from DNA. RNA stores genetic information using a four-letter alphabet that includes three of the same letters as DNA (A, G, and C) and replaces T with U. RNA also can serve as a weak catalyst so, like enzymes, RNA may also serve as a catalyst for its own replication. Potentially, RNA could contain the instructions for its own replication along with the capability to catalyze its replication.

Evolution of More Complex Organisms

Once a successful replicator existed, life, through the forces of natural selection, mutated, leading a proliferation of more complex life forms adapted to various environments that used varied forms of metabolism and reproduction. About 3 billion years ago, microbes evolved that stored energy in complex organic molecules assembled using sunlight, carbon dioxide, and water. This energy-producing process—photosynthesis—released oxygen into the atmosphere, transforming the atmosphere into its present state. Some of this oxygen was transformed by ultraviolet radiation from the sun into ozone, which collected in a layer in the upper atmosphere, providing protection from deadly ultraviolet radiation. This layer of ozone allowed microbes to colonize the surface of the ocean and land more than 2 billion years ago. It is only in the last billion years that multicellular organisms evolved with fish, the first vertebrates, evolving about 530 million years ago and mammals evolving about 310 million years ago.

The Selfish Gene

While it is universally accepted by evolutionary biologists that natural selection drove the evolutionary changes to life forms once a replicator existed, there is less agreement on what it is that is actually "selected." In the groundbreaking book *The Selfish Gene* published in 1976, Richard Dawkins proposed that it is the gene that is actually selected, this being the entity "that survives, or does not survive, as a consequence of natural selection."[53] Today, this view of the gene is generally accepted by most evolutionary biologists. The personification of genes as being "selfish" is clearly not meant to imply that genes have a will of their own but is used as a device to convey the nature of competition that takes place at the level of genes where there are those genes that continue replicating and those that do not. The notion of selfishness is useful for understanding evolution because, from the perspective of the gene, their behavior is best understood as though they were seeking immortality through successive replications. In terms of understanding human nature, the nature of the entity that is selected for by natural selection plays an important role in such understanding. As Dawkins states:

> My purpose is to examine the biology of selfishness and altruism. Apart from its academic interest, the human importance of this subject is obvious. It

touches every aspect of our social lives, our loving and hating, fighting and cooperating, giving and stealing, our greed and generosity.[54]

According to Dawkins, because genes dictate the way survival machines and their nervous systems are built, genes control behavior in an indirect but powerful way.[55] Individual acts of altruism can be analyzed as selfish genes assisting replicas of itself sitting in other bodies.[56] For example, *kin altruism*, the tendency of mammals to expose themselves to risk for the sake of close relatives, especially by parents to offspring, is viewed as a consequence of natural selection favoring genes that selfishly protect replicas in other bodies. Altruism between individuals who are not related can also be viewed as the consequence of selfish genes when members of a species can remember each other and a good deed leads to the expectation of repayment. This "you scratch my back and I'll scratch your back" behavior is known as *reciprocal altruism*. Does pure altruism, in which the behavior is strictly for the benefit of a stranger without any expectation of a return benefit even exist in human nature? Do people who consciously strive to be pure altruists not feel pleasure and emotional reward for the selfless acts?

Of equal interest to the notion of the gene as the unit of natural selection is Dawkins' characterization of the larger living entities that genes occupy such as cells and organisms, including human beings, as "survival machines." Dawkins believes that when these original replicators became numerous, resources for survival started to become scarce, leading to competition. The replicators did not actually know they were engaged in a struggle "or worry about it; the struggle was conducted without any hard feelings—indeed, without feelings of any kind. But they were struggling, in the sense that any miscopying that resulted in a new higher level of stability, or a new way of reducing stability of rivals, was automatically preserved and multiplied."[57] Dawkins believes that some of these early replicators built a wall of protein around themselves for protection, which may have been the origin of the self-contained living cell. These first living cells were bacteria (known as prokaryotic cells that lack a nucleus and organelles) that were the only living organisms for at least 2 billion years and continue to be the most abundant organism on the planet. Continuing this logical progression, we can imagine that the bacteria began to combine in mutually beneficial relationships to form the eukaryotic cell: complex DNA molecules inside a walled-in cellular nucleus and cellular organelles such as the energy-producing mitochondria and (in plants) chloroplasts. The mitochondria and chloroplasts were once free-roaming bacteria that entered into a symbiotic relationship with a host bacteria, ending up taking up a permanent residence, although retaining some of their own DNA and replicating on their own. About 1.5 billion years ago, eukaryotic cells began attaching to each other and undertaking specialized functions, forming the first multicellular life organisms that came to include fungi, plants, and animals.

The Tree of Life and the Age of Bacteria

Biology's most basic classification (taxonomy) of life is the three domains of bacteria, archaea, and eukarya. Bacteria and archaea are the oldest and simplest single cell microbes that are classified as prokaryotes. Eukarya, consisting of eukaryotic cells, include complex single-celled organisms and all multicellular organisms. In the tree of life in which branches represent the various kingdoms of life and their length is representative of evolutionary distance in time since divergence from a common ancestor, "Animals, plants, and fungi constitute just three small branches."[58] Prokaryotic life (in loose terms, bacteria) has been around the longest and contains most of the diversity of life forms. Harvard paleontologist and biologist Stephen Jay Gould considered the entire span of life on Earth as the "age of bacteria" because of bacteria's great success, longevity, diversity, adaptability to a wide range of environments, and indestructibleness. He noted that the number of bacteria in one human gut outnumber the total number of humans that has ever lived.[59]

Hope for Humanity: From Genes to Memes

Our 14 billion-year journey took us from an unimaginably dense and hot point that marked the beginning of space and time to the universe of today containing 100 billion galaxies. In one of these galaxies around one star among 100 billion stars, we found a planet that formed 4.5 billion years ago from a cloud gas containing heavy elements from the supernova explosion of a dead star. Over the course of hundreds of millions of years, a collection of molecules, most likely deep in the crust under the ocean, copied itself using ambient energy sources to store information against the tide of entropy. The process of natural selection allowed some errors in copying to lead to more complex and more successful organisms. Despite the complexity of life we see around us, the most numerous and longest lasting life forms are simple bacteria and the driving force of evolution is the selfish nature of individual genes that use the body of cells and complex life forms as a temporary vehicle for transmission through the ages. The journey has been awe inspiring and humbling.

The question remains: Are we destined, because of our selfish genes, to continued levels of selfishness and altruism, war and peace, and hate and love as we experience today? If the answer is yes, then the extinction of humanity and possibly many other plant and animal species is inevitable. Our legacy will truly be to have restored the "Age of Bacteria." Our highly evolved neocortical "thinking" brain has given us the knowledge and tools to create massive urban societies and weapons that capture the awesome energy of the sun and stars. Our much less evolved and primitive limbic brain, responsible for the emotions that guide us, is still living in the world of small hunter-gatherer societies whose most dangerous arsenal contained stone axes and spears. The pace of genetic evolution is much too slow for our genes to adapt to the dangers of modern society. However, there is another type of evolution that adapts at a much quicker pace and that is *cultural evolution*. Culture involves the ability to learn about the world and use that knowledge to change behavior. Culture can be transferred through generations as genetic information does and can adapt to changes in the environment much more quickly. Dawkins calls units cultural transmission "memes": individual ideas that are passed on and evolve as genes do.

Edward O. Wilson attributes the capacity for cultural evolution not to specific rules of our genes but as a product of genetic evolution through *epigenetic* rules. According to Wilson, epigenetic rules "are innate operations in the sensory system and brain."

> They are rules of thumb that allow organisms to find rapid solutions to problems encountered in the environment. They predispose individuals to view the world in a particular innate way and automatically to make certain choices as opposed to others. With epigenetic rules, we see a rainbow in four basic colors and not in a continuum of light frequencies. We avoid mating with a sibling, speak in grammatically coherent sentences, smile at friends, and when alone fear strangers in first encounters. Typically emotion-driven, epigenetic rules in all categories of behavior direct the individual toward those relatively quick and accurate responses most likely to ensure survival and reproduction. But they leave open the potential generation of an immense array of cultural variations and combinations. Sometimes, especially in complex societies, they no longer contribute to health and well-being. The behavior they direct can go awry and militate against the best interests of the individual and society.[60]

These epigenetic rules are an intermediate step in the acquisition of culture and are an integral part of *gene-culture coevolution* whereby genes direct the acquisition of culture. Culture in turn helps determine which genes survive in succeeding generations, which, in turn, alter the epigenetic rules of populations.[61]

According to Dawkins and Wilson, there is hope for humanity in our culture:

> The point I am making now is that, even if we look on the dark side and assume that individual man is fundamentally selfish, our conscious foresight— our capacity to simulate the future in imagination—could save us from the worst selfish excesses of the blind replicators.... We have the power to defy the selfish genes of our birth and, if necessary, the selfish memes of our indoctrination. We can even discuss ways of deliberately cultivating and nurturing pure, disinterested altruism—something that has no place in nature, something that has never existed before in the whole history of the world. We are built as gene machines and cultured as meme machines, but we have the power to turn against our creators. We alone on earth can rebel against the tyranny of the selfish replicators.[62]

Human nature is, moreover, a hodgepodge of special genetic adaptations to an environment largely vanished, the world of the Ice Age hunter-gatherer.

Modern life, as rich and rapidly changing as it appears to those caught in it, is nevertheless only a mosaic of cultural hypertrophies of the archaic behavioral adaptations. And at the center of the second dilemma [the conscious choices that must be made among our innate mental propensities] is found a circularity: We are forced to choose among the elements of human nature by reference to value systems created in an evolutionary age now long vanished. Fortunately, this circularity of the human predicament is not so tight that it cannot be broken through an exercise of will…. In the process, it will fashion a biology of ethics, which will make possible the selection of a more deeply understood and enduring code of moral values.[63]

Wilson refers to an age long vanished, when the family of human species existed as hunter-gatherer societies, as forming the template for available human behavior. Let us now look more closely at our ancestral past and at our closest living relatives, the chimpanzees, for insight into what is driving the societies we build today. In this chapter, we ended our journey with the arrival of mammals a little more than 300 million years ago. We will now jump ahead to about 6 million years ago, the time at which our lineage, the family of hominidae, diverged from our closet living relatives, the chimpanzees.

Chapter Four
The Bipedal Apes

I suspect that if hamadryas baboons had nuclear weapons,
they would destroy the world in a week.

- Edward O. Wilson[64]

If we could understand our past, understand what shaped us,
then we might gain a glimpse of our future.

- Richard Leakey[65]

Our Closest Relatives

Gorillas, chimpanzees, and bonobos, our closest animal relatives, live in small nomadic bands of close relatives, just as humans have for about 6 million years. It has only been since a relatively recent time in our history, about 40,000 years ago, that humans have lived in societies larger than bands that generally consist of a few dozen individuals. Nomadic hunter-gatherer bands of people still exist in remote parts of New Guinea and the Amazon.[66] After the 6 million years or so since human and chimpanzee lineages split from a common ancestor, we still share 99 percent of the same DNA with chimpanzees. "Of the three billion letters that make up the human genome, only 15 million of them—less than 1 percent—have changed" from the common ancestor.[67] Of these 15 million letters that have changed, the sequences that have undergone the most mutation—a hallmark of positive evolutionary selection—were found to control distinctive human traits: development of the brain's cerebral cortex; brain size (which has tripled over the last two million years); facial movements needed for human speech;

digestion of starch; digestion of milk sugar in adults; and, fetal development of the wrist and thumb.[68]

Frans de Waal, the C.H. Chandler Professor of Psychology at Emory University, is one of the world's leading primate researchers. He believes that understanding our closest relatives will lead to greater understanding of ourselves. In his words, "primates live in highly structured cooperative groups in which rules and inhibitions apply and mutual aid is a daily occurrence."

> If we look at our species without letting ourselves be blinded by the technological advances of the last few millennia, we see a creature of flesh and blood with a brain that, albeit three times larger that that of a chimpanzee, does not contain any new parts. Our intellect may be superior, but we have no basic wants or needs that cannot also be observed in our close relatives. I interact daily with chimpanzees and bonobos, which are known as anthropoids precisely because of their human-like characteristics. Like us, they strive for power, enjoy sex, want security and affection, kill over territory, and value trust and cooperation. Yes, we use cell phones and fly airplanes, but our psychological makeup remains that of a social primate.[69]

De Waal has found that primates exhibit empathy and reciprocity, including chimpanzees consoling others who have been attacked and sharing food with others who have supported them in power struggles. Chimpanzees also engage in reconciliation by such activity as kissing and embracing after a fight. In one experiment de Waal carried out with pairs of capuchin monkeys, sophisticated human emotions of resentment and envy were observed for an unfair distribution of a food reward, a distinctly human reaction that economists have labeled "inequity aversion." Each monkey took turns trading a pebble with the researcher for a cucumber slice. The monkeys did this 25 times without any problem. When one of the monkeys began receiving a grape, a favorite food, instead of a cucumber, the monkey still receiving the cucumber slice "would get agitated [and] hurl the pebbles out of the test chamber, sometimes even those measly cucumber slices. A food normally devoured with gusto had become distasteful."[70] Anyone who has ever worked for a living as a waiter or waitress has probably rejected a measly tip either saying or thinking to themselves, "Keep your lousy money you cheapskate!"

Jane Goodall, considered the world's foremost expert on chimpanzees, spent thirty years studying chimpanzees in their natural habitat at Gombe National Park in Tanzania. In 1960, she observed chimpanzees making tools, thought to be an exclusive attribute of humans, by trimming blades of grass for use in extracting termites from the narrow passage of termite mounds. This discovery prompted famed archeologist Louis Leakey to send Goodall a telegram: "Now, we must redefine tool, redefine man, or accept chimpanzees as humans."[71] Goodall found that chimpanzee populations each have their own tool-using culture passed on from one generation to the next.

Chimpanzee bands are highly structured societies called "communities" with a clear hierarchy led by the alpha male. Goodall documented the rise to the top-ranking position through the life of a chimpanzee named "Figan" who, as an adolescent, showed exceptional intelligence and strong motivation to climb the social ladder. Male chimpanzees assert their dominance through a "charging display."

> This display serves to make chimpanzees look bigger and more dangerous than he may actually be—his hair stands on end; he leaps up to shake the vegetation; he drags huge branches noisily along the ground, then hurls them ahead of him; he picks up and throws rocks with such vigor that they fly unpredictably ahead, behind or to the side; he stamps and slaps loudly upon the ground or some tree trunk; his lips are tightly compressed, pulling his face into a ferocious scowl. And the wilder and more impressive his display, and the more carefully it is planned and executed, the better his chance of intimidating his rivals without recourse to actual physical combat—during which he himself, as well as his opponent, might be injured.[72]

Figan practiced his charging display as an adolescent which, along with a strategic alliance with his brother Faben, would assure his rise to the top. Over the course of one and a half years, Figan, with the support of Faben, would eliminate from competition his main contender for power, Evered (his childhood playmate) and, finally the alpha Humphrey. Goodall notes "the tremendous importance of coalitions" in the struggle for power, and that Figan might not have made it to the top without the help of his brother, Faben. In about a one month period from the end of April to the end May 1973, Goodall observed a series of three "major conflicts" involving Figan and Faben taking on their rivals. At the end of April, Figan and Faben attacked Evered, "who took refuge up a tree, whimpering and screaming. The brothers continued to charge about below for over half an hour until, during a lull, their victim finally managed to escape." Four days later, under the watch of his brother Faben, Figan attacked Humphrey twice, causing Humphrey to flee. More than half the *Kasekela* community (the name of the chimpanzee band) had observed the decisive victory and Figan's assent to the alpha position was assured. For good measure, Evered was attacked once more by Figan and Faben to eliminate any possible threat from him. "Figan had made it to the top."[73]

What was the payoff for all this effort to get on top and stay there? According to Goodall, it was "the respect of all the other members of his social group and the right of prior access to any feeding place or sexually attractive female he fancied. Power."[74] To reward his brother Faben for his support, Figan shared access to females and food. Faben continued to support Figan by keeping an eye on "the current lady friend when Figan was momentarily busy elsewhere." Despite the efforts of Figan and Faben, when their attention was diverted, the chosen female occasionally engaged in "clandestine intercourse with one or other of the frustrated lower-ranking males." When caught in the act by Figan "he would race towards the pair and, very often, bash the female for her faithlessness."[75]

Adult female chimpanzees enter a period of estrus (also referred to as being "in heat") for about 10 days every 36 days during which they are sexually receptive. During estrus, the skin around the sex organs and rear end swells and becomes pink, attracting the attention of the males. It is during the last few days of estrus that ovulation occurs and the female is most likely to conceive; it is also during this time that the female becomes the most sexually attractive and sought after by the males. Females in estrus may stay in the community and mate with multiple partners—Goodall reported that a female may copulate with six or more males in ten minutes—or may leave with a single male and enter into a temporary exclusive relationship called "consortship" for a period coinciding with estrus. "The goal of a consorting male is to keep his female away from rival males during the time when she is most likely to conceive— the last few days of her sexual swelling."[76] Goodall suggests that these consorts indicate "that chimpanzees have a latent capacity for the development of more permanent heterosexual pair bonding: a relationship more similar to the pattern of monogamy—or at least serial monogamy—that has become the cultural tradition in much of the western world."

Perhaps monogamy is more than a cultural tradition and has some foundation in our genetic heritage. The chimpanzee consorts generally lasted as long as the period of estrus, which was clearly visible due to the female swellings and pink coloration. Sometime after the split from the common ancestor of humans and chimpanzees, a mutation arose in our hominid ancestors in whom a group of females stopped displaying signals advertising ovulation and, therefore, the likely time for conception became indeterminate. In order for the "consortship" to become effective in assuring conception by a particular male, the male would have to constantly stay in close contact with the female to prevent copulation with other males. The males and females who maintained these long-term relationships tended to produce more offspring due to the investment of the male in child rearing, resulting in a genetic predisposition for maintaining permanent bonding which we refer to as marriage. The transformation was not complete, however, as the size difference in human males and females—called sexual dimorphism—indicates there is still some competition by males to have multiple partners. *Polygyny* describes the basic mating system of mammals in which one male bonds with multiple females to form harems.[77] The level of polygyny corresponds to the amount of sexual size dimorphism: the larger the difference in size between male and female primates, the more females each male tends to mate with.[78] "Male gorillas average three to six mates and weigh nearly twice as much as females. Male gibbons, which are monogamous, don't outweigh their consorts."[79] Where human males are moderately larger than females—about 20 to 30 percent heavier, it follows that humans are "moderately polygynous, with males initiating most of the changes in sexual partnership. About three-fourths of all human societies permit the taking of multiple wives, and most of them encourage the practice by law and custom."[80] "The anthropological record suggests that polygyny is natural in the sense that men given the opportunity to have more than one wife are strongly inclined to seize it."[81]

Primates have been shown in experiments to plan for future events. Goodall reported chimpanzees preparing tools for use on termite mounds several hundred yards away and out of sight.[82] This planning behavior was also confirmed by the behavior of a chimp called Santino at Sweden's Furuvik Zoo. For several years, Santino would run around and yell every day at around 11:00 A.M. as part of show of dominance typical of male chimps. Santino would also occasionally throw rocks at visitors. In the morning, he would prepare for his rock throwing by removing rocks from the moat around his enclosure and also chip away at concrete rocks to form throwing disks which were gathered into a pile ready for use.[83]

Primates also engage in intra-species violence; chimpanzees have been found to go on raiding parties of neighboring groups, killing adult members in a quest for territory and access to females. According to Harvard University anthropologist Richard Wrangham, an imbalance of power is one of the best predictors of violence between two groups of primates. "Chimps from one troop invariably attack individuals from a rival troop when the attackers have an overwhelming number advantage and hence a minimal risk of death or injury."[84]

Despite the intense competition for achieving and maintaining alpha male status and the general competition among males for access to females in estrus, there is strong cooperation among males of a community in protecting it from attacks by other chimpanzee communities or other species. Goodall found that a group of males on patrol would visit the peripheral areas of their community at least once a week.[85] Encounters with chimpanzees from the neighboring community would not lead to actual fighting when there was more than one male in the other group, although there may be wild charging displays.

> It is when two or more males encounter a lone stranger, or a couple of stranger females with infants, that fierce and brutal attacks take place. Indeed, if patrolling males hear the calls of an infant in some outlying part of their range and suspect the presence of a mother from a neighboring community, they sometimes stalk her, persisting for an hour or more in their attempt to hunt her down. And, if they are successful, they will attack. A stranger male may be attacked also, but during the course of our years of research at Gombe, we have observed only two, relatively mild, attacks on males from neighboring communities, as compared to eighteen severe assaults on stranger females.... It seems, then, that the attacks are an expression of the hatred that is roused in the chimpanzees of one community by the sight of a member of another.[86]

Goodall documented a "four-year-war" that started in 1974 when six adult males, an adolescent, and three adult females with their young split off from the main Kasekela community that was left with eight adult males and twelve females and their young. After a couple of years, each group formed a distinct community with its own territory. The new community, called the "Kahama community," took over the southern part of the original Kasekela community. For a year, the two communities did not engage in fighting but would hurl "noisy insults at each other" then retreat to the safety of their territory. Then the first attack occurred when a patrol of six Kasekela males came upon a young male of the Kahama community and viciously assaulted the Kahama male who was never seen again and presumed dead. "Over the next four years, four more assaults of this sort were witnessed."[87] At the end of the four years, the Kahama community was completely wiped out, most, if not all, killed by the Kasekela males. Additionally, during this period, there was intercommunity violence in which a mother and daughter team in the Kasekela community attacked other females with young and cannibalized as many as six infants.

The Kahama community chimpanzees, former members of the Kasekela community, were transformed from in-group members to out-group status based on their creation of an independent community. The malleability humans are capable of as to who belongs to a community and who does not, seems to be a genetic trait developed several millions of years ago in our primate ancestors. Goodall notes that the human capacity to "dehumanize" out-group members, which can lead to "the atrocities of war," can be seen in chimpanzees who "dechimpized" out-group victims of their aggression.[88] "Noncommunity members may be attacked so fiercely that they die from their wounds," in attacks, Goodall observes, that are "usually seen when a chimpanzee is trying to kill an adult prey animal—an animal of another species."[89]

De Waal recorded violent chimpanzee politics in a colony of 23 chimpanzees living at the Arnhem Zoo in the Netherlands.[90] The colony "was structured as a dominance hierarchy established on the basis of winning or losing in aggressive interactions.... Even though males were rivals, they formed strong male-male bonds, and members of both sexes joined complex coalitions and mediated disputes."[91] A political struggle of the three dominant males involved intrigue that could easily supply the plot for a successful murder drama. The leading dominant male, Nikkie, was a weak leader who, without the support of his older and crafty ally, Yeroen, could be beaten in a fight by the pretender to the throne, Luit. The manipulative Yeroen, although not the dominant male, through his alliance with Nikkie, was able to be the most successful with the female chimps. Tired of being manipulated by Yeroen, Nikkie and Luit joined forces and jointly dominated the colony. Yeroen became increasingly frustrated because Luit's sexual success, which came at the expense of Yeroen and which his former ally, Nikkie, did not attempt to limit. A fight resulted among the three in which Nikkie and Yeroen were seriously injured, leaving Luit as the dominant male. A couple of months of harmony returned to the colony although there was some tension among the males. Then, Nikkie and Yeroen, the allies turned enemies, restored their alliance and ganged up on

Luit. Luit was viciously attacked: his toes were bitten off, his testicles were missing, and there were gashes over much of his body. Luit died the next day.

> Parallels to the violence that engulfed Nikkie, Yeroen, and Luit in the Arnhem colony can be seen in many, if not most, human societies. Indeed, disputes occur frequently in contemporary human hunter-gatherer societies, and, especially when men compete for women, disputes escalate into violence.... From 1920 to 1955, murder rates among the! Kung Bushmen of southern Africa were twenty to eighty times higher than recent murder rates in industrial countries, and the Yahgan "canoe nomads" of Tierra del Fuego had a murder rate ten times that of the United States in the late twentieth century. There is little reason to doubt that such levels of violence also occurred widely in prehistoric hunter-gatherer societies.[92]

According to Harvard psychologist Steven Pinker, levels of violence prior to the advent of nation states about 10,000 years ago were much higher with at least 30 percent of the members of tribal societies dying as the result of group violence.[93] Edward O. Wilson believes that "intertribal aggression...is common enough to be regarded as a general characteristic of hunter-gatherer social behavior."[94] Territoriality and male dominance strategies in reproduction are the two principal causes of aggression in primates, including humans. In particular, male aggression in reproductive strategies is seen in the majority of animal species. Wilson observes,

> In most species, assertiveness is the most profitable male strategy. During the full period of time it takes to bring a fetus to term, from fertilization of the egg to the birth of the infant, one male can fertilize many females but a female can be fertilized by only one male. Thus, if males are able to court one female after another, some will be big winners and others will be absolute losers, while virtually all healthy females will succeed in being fertilized. It pays males to be aggressive, hasty, fickle, and undiscriminating. In theory, it is more profitable for females to be coy, to hold back until they identify males with the best genes. In species that rear young, it is also important for females to select males who are more likely to stay with them after insemination. Human beings obey this biological principle faithfully.[95]

In human males, aggression is inextricably intertwined with reproductive strategies; from seeking dominance over other males within the community to the conquering of territories to eliminate potential competitors and gain access to more females. The females of a particular band, tribe, or other societal group that identify as an in-group represent the genetic safekeeping of the particular in-group and are therefore zealously guarded. A pregnant female invests much time and energy in bringing the child to term, and once born, many years invested, usually with her mate, in nurturing and protecting the child. A female will always know who her child is but males will always suffer insecurity over parentage. Because of this huge investment, males have a particular interest in ensuring the child is their own. Males, as well as keeping a watchful eye over their particular mate or mates, collectively, as members of the same in-group, keep a watchful eye over the females of their group. In the vast majority of our existence as humans living in hunter-gatherer societies, these in-group females were relatives who shared many more genes than females from other groups. Females from out-groups are also sought by males for the opportunity they present for passing on the males' genes.

Individual and collective male aggression directed at females as a means to control whose genes will be impregnated is a worldwide epidemic. While our cultural rules prohibit rape and in the vast majority of places during the vast majority of times it is not tolerated, there are certain situational variables such as war or individual personal variables such as psychopathy that allow this genetic tendency to flourish. Since the beginnings of recorded history, rape has accompanied warfare; from wars fought in ancient Greece and Rome to wars in Bosnia-Herzegovina (estimated 20,000 to 50,000 rapes) and Kosovo (estimated 30 percent-50 percent of women of child bearing age raped) during the last decade of the twentieth century. In a biblical account of war found in the Old Testament, Numbers 31, Moses sends 12,000 Israelites to war against the Midianites. "And they warred against the Midianites, as the Lord commanded Moses; and they slew all the males."[96] Of the women and children taken captive, all were ordered killed by Moses except the virgins.

In a prelude to the Nazi barbarism of World War II, Japan went to war with China in the summer of 1937 after spending several years preparing for military domination of East Asia. After Shanghai finally fell in November 1937, taking much longer than anticipated, the Japanese imperial army set it sights on the Nanking, the capital city of Nationalist China.

> When the city fell on December 13, 1937, Japanese soldiers began an orgy of cruelty seldom if ever matched in world history. Tens of thousands of young men were rounded up and herded to the outer areas of the city, where they were mowed down by machine guns, used for bayonet practice, or soaked with gasoline and burned alive.... Years later, experts at the International Military Tribunal of the Far East estimated that more than 260,000 noncombatants died at the hands of Japanese soldiers at Nanking in late 1937 and early 1938, though some experts have placed the figure at well over 350,000.[97]

In addition to murder and torture, Japanese soldiers engaged in the systematic rape of at least 20,000 women and as many as 80,000 by some estimates. In the single worst instance of wartime rape, the Pakistan army, during a nine-month period in 1971, waged war against a rebellion in what was then East Pakistan. During the rebellion for an independent nation that later became Bangladesh, the Pakistan army raped an estimated 200,000 to 400,000 women. Rape is also a weapon used during genocides. During the Rwandan genocide of 1994, in which 800,000 were murdered in a mere four months, Hutu leaders ordered their troops to rape Tutsi women as part of their genocidal campaign.

War presents opportunity not only for territorial conquest but for genetic conquest as well. Is the fact that wars are fought mostly by young unmarried males due only to their general fitness and lack of attachment or is their also a sexual conquest motive? An analysis of the Y chromosome (that determines male gender and is passed down from father to son) suggests that 16 million men worldwide and 8 percent of Asian men are descended from Genghis Khan.[98] Research by Lei Chang of the Chinese University of Hong Kong Department of Educational Psychology sought to show a mating-warring association among young heterosexual men in four experiments.[99] When exposed to attractive, as compared to unattractive, opposite-sex photographs, the men were significantly more likely to endorse war-supporting statements. This same mating effect was not found in answering questions on trade conflict. When the men were primed by images of attractive women, they were significantly faster in responding to images or words of war than those primed by unattractive faces or national flags. The study authors see these results as "supporting the view that sexual selection provides an ultimate explanation for the origins of human warfare." Through rape of females in conquered territories, the victims' bodies, a resource for reproductive success from a male standpoint, are exploited to pass on the conquerors genes. This dark side to male human nature continues to plague the world both in individual relationships and collectively as part of war and genocide.

Sexual violence perpetrated by men against women is a worldwide epidemic. According to the UN Commission on the Status of Women (2000), globally, at least one in three women and girls is beaten or sexually abused in her lifetime. "Honor killings," involving the murder of women and girls for violation of a local sexual based taboo, take the lives of thousands of young women every year, mainly in North Africa, Western Asia, and parts of South Asia according to the United Nations Population Fund. Worldwide, up to 70 percent of female murder victims are killed by their male partners and one in five women (20 percent) will be a victim of rape or attempted rape according to the World Health Organization.

The vestiges of polygyny and the alpha male are rife in American culture. "Conservative estimates are that 60 percent of men and 40 percent of women will have an extramarital affair."[100] Fifty percent of all marriages in the United States will end in divorce.[101] Several United States presidents, from Thomas Jefferson to William Jefferson Clinton, have engaged in extramarital affairs. If we further examine American cultural icons and leaders, what we find is almost an epidemic of highly successful and driven males who have risked their fame and fortune on sex outside of marriage. Here are some recent examples: In 2008, New York Governor Eliot Spitzer resigned from office after he was caught on a federal wiretap arranging to meet a prostitute at a Washington, D.C. hotel. In 2009, South Carolina Governor Mark Sanford, married with four children, secretly went to Argentina to meet his "soul mate" during his affair with a forty-one-year-old

Argentinean woman. In 2010, Tiger Woods, whom many believe to be the greatest golf player of all time and who was married with two small children, was identified by several women as having had sexual relations with them. Woods issued a public apology for his "irresponsible and selfish behavior" and was divorced shortly after. Talk show host David Letterman revealed on his show that he had been involved in sexual relationships with women on his staff and apologized to his wife saying she had been "horribly hurt by my behavior." U.S. senator from North Carolina and presidential candidate John Edwards admitted to an affair with a campaign videographer and, after previous denials, to fathering a child with the woman. Arnold Schwarzenegger, actor and Governor of California, fathered a child with the family's housekeeper while married to Maria Shriver and kept the child a secret during his two terms as governor. Schwarzenegger revealed the affair to his wife after leaving office in January 2011 and the couple separated in May of that year. In statement released to the *Los Angeles Times,* Schwarzenegger stated, "There are no excuses and I take full responsibility for the hurt I have caused."

The question is often asked why such high status men, who have worked so hard to reach their fame or fortune, risk so much to engage in extramarital sex, but the reality is that such men are primarily driven to achieve success specifically to have the most mating opportunities with the most desirable women. Women who have a genetic predisposition to seek monogamous relationships with men who are committed to supporting child rearing are also genetically predisposed to take part in polygynous relationships with high status men who have the resources to support them despite having multiple partners. So there is no shortage of partners for the successful high status male. Even in cultures like Western culture that support monogamous relationships*, people such as *Playboy* founder Hugh Hefner have found a way to make polygyny seem acceptable and, particularly for men, desirable. Hefner has merely found a way to engage overtly in polygyny that most men in monogamous cultures secretly (and some not so secretly) desire for themselves.

Through our several million years hominid history as hunter-gatherers, monogamous relationships provided an advantage in successful offspring and the ability of males to acquire sufficient resources to support multiple families was limited so monogamy became the principal family structure. Limiting mating for males to one female also helped to keep the peace in these hunter-gatherer bands by assuring each male mating opportunities that would otherwise be limited if a few high status males were allowed to dominate. Despite monogamy being viewed as pro-feminist, from a genetic standpoint, it is actually a reproductive strategy that favors men.[102] But polygyny still resisted genetic extinction; during times of abundance, those successful alpha males who could acquire sufficient resources still reverted to the genetic mandate of seeking multiple partners as well as women who reverted to their genetic mandate to share. The result is that we are left genetically

---

* The support of monogamy is accomplished in part through laws that make polygyny and adultery a criminal offense. In the U.S., all states criminalize polygyny (usually referred to as bigamy) and about two dozen states make adultery a criminal offense, although rarely prosecuted.

with conflicting mandates as to male-female bonding, with the general rule being monogamy but with polygyny allowable to resource-rich alpha males.

The moral code adopted by Western culture is designed to enforce the general genetic predisposition for monogamy and to punish polygyny. This code is a dilemma for high status males and those who think they are. Men who wish to conform to established norms for behavior and also to be highly successful will be highly conflicted and most will give in to the genetic-based desire for multiple partners. While monogamy should be promoted, we should not demonize or be unduly harsh on those who fail to conform. Those who agree to monogamy by entering into marriage and have sexual relations outside of marriage and those unmarried who have affairs with married partners should be subject to contempt and have to make restitution for harm caused. But their punishment should be based on their inability to exercise impulse control that resulted in breaking a serious trust and not because of being inherently evil.*

Taxonomy: What is Human?

Taxonomy is the system of biological classifications of all species. In Chapter Three, we were introduced to the largest classification of "domains" that included bacteria, archaea, and eukarya. Under the taxonomic classifications, and therefore the way scientists look at people, "human" and "homo sapiens" are not the same. A look at the taxonomy of people continuing from eukarya will reveal the difference:

Kingdom	Animalia
Phylum	Chordata
Class	Mammalia
Order	Primates
Family	Hominidae
Genus	Homo
Species	Sapiens

So, when we talk about "humans," we are, in more scientific terms, referring to a "family" of numerous "hominid" species that evolved from primates about 6 million years ago and whose only surviving progeny are us (homo sapiens).

---

* The view on illicit affairs is not intended to condone the lies and cover-up frequently seen when public officials of significant office are caught. This is a separate harm that deserves full punishment and is probably a more serious harm than the affair itself when perpetrated by such public figures.

The First Humans

The first humans (or hominids) were a group of species that inhabited East Africa called the *australopithecines*. These were ape-like creatures whose most distinguishing difference from the apes was bipedal locomotion. One of the most famous fossil finds of early human ancestors was made in Ethiopia in 1974 of a skeleton of an individual given the nickname "Lucy"*. Lucy was a member of the species *Australopithecus afarensis* that lived some 3.5 million years ago. Australopithecines like Lucy had small brains (about 500 cc[†]) only slightly larger than chimpanzees (about 400 cc) and much smaller than modern humans (average 1350 cc). Based on their large cheek teeth, they were most likely vegetarians.[103] The males were twice the size of females, similar to gorillas, indicating competition among males for access to females and *polygyny* in which one male controls access to several females.[104] In his book, *Origins Reconsidered*, paleoanthropologist Richard Leakey considers these early hominids as really no more than bipedal apes living lives similar to modern savannah baboons. Yet, because of their bipedal nature, Leakey prefers the term "human" for these early hominids.

> So important to our later evolutionary history was the freeing of our hands that my preference is to use the term "human" for the first bipedal apes.... I'm not saying that once the bipedal apes had evolved, you and I were evolutionary inevitabilities, because evolution doesn't work like that. Nor am I suggesting that the earliest bipedal apes had the same intellectual powers or outlook as we do. Of course they didn't. All I am suggesting is that the origin of a bipedal form of locomotion was so fundamental a change, so replete with profound evolutionary potential, that we should recognize the roots of our humanity where they really are.[105]

The Handyman

The first member of our genus Homo was the species *Homo habilis,* who lived from about 2.5 million years ago to about 1.7 million years ago. Because of their ability to make and use stone tools, the nickname "handyman" was coined. The Latin origin of the name *Homo habilis* means "dexterous man." While some paleoanthropologists may disagree with the humanness of the australopithecines, *Homo habilis* marks the transition to traits that most, if not all, would agree are early signs of our unique human nature. They key to these newly evolving uniquely human traits was the appearance of larger brains. "Habilines mark the place in our history where the brain, that most dramatic of human peculiarities, starts to expand. Or, more accurately, starts to expand beyond the normal size of the already large brains of other apes." [106]

These early stone tools, called Oldowan technology based on the Oldowan Gorge in East Africa where many have been found, are difficult to produce,

---

*   The Beatles song "Lucy in the Sky with Diamonds" was playing in the camp the day of the discovery.

†   Cubic centimeters

requiring "strong intuitive knowledge of three-dimensional geometry as well as sophisticated motor skills."[107] *Homo habilis* marked the beginning of the hunter-gatherer lifestyle, a way of life that "would shape the human body and the human mind for more than two million years."[108] The males are now only about 20 percent larger than females, similar to the difference in size to modern humans, which indicates a dramatic shift in the social structure of the bands of hunter-gatherers. The more equal size of males and females indicates less competition among the males and mostly monogamous pairings. Unlike modern baboon troops (and probably australopithecines), mature males of the genus Homo stayed home, rather than adopting a new troop and, therefore, the troops contained closely related males. Because of the reduced competition amongst the males and their genetic closeness, there was increased cooperation within the troop.

The Turkana Boy

In a discovery of equal fame and importance as the discovery of Lucy, a team headed by Richard Leakey in August 1984 found the nearly complete fossilized skeleton of an adolescent boy who died in a shallow lagoon on the western side of Lake Turkana about 1.5 million years ago. The Turkana Boy was a member of the species *Homo erectus*', the species directly ancestral to *Homo sapiens*. Leakey regards *Homo erectus* as a "pivotal point in human evolutionary history; in a very real way, it is the harbinger of humanity. If we are to understand the origin of humanity, we have to understand *Homo erectus*."[109] Leakey clearly had been touched emotionally by the humanity of Turkana Boy; he begins his book, *Origins Reconsidered,* with a highly descriptive fictionalized but accurate account, insofar as hunter-gatherer behavior, of the death of the Turkana Boy.

> They had set out early, this band of six purposeful individuals, striding across rolling, grassy terrain punctuated here and there by flat-topped acacia trees....
>
> Everyone had heard the saber-toothed cats during the night, repeated choruses of throaty moans, a sure sign of a hunt in progress. Even though the band felt itself relatively safe at its riverside camp a mile from the lake, there was always tension when saber-toothed cats were near. Only a year ago, a child had been attacked when he strayed from the watchful eyes of his mother and her companions. Returning hunters, the same group of men who were setting out this day, arrived just in time to drive the predator away. But the boy had died some days later from the loss of blood and the kind of rampant infection that can be so deadly in the tropics. Not surprisingly, this morning's

---

* There is some disagreement among paleoanthropologists as to whether the Turkana Boy was a member of *Homo erectus* or another closely related species *Homo ergaster* and whether Homo ergaster is a distinct species. In deference to the discoverer, Richard Leakey, we adopt his classification of the Turkana Boy being a *Homo erectus*.

discussions urged extra care on the women and their offspring, gathering tubers and nuts near the camp, and the men on their hunt. These men, too, were predators.

A herd of large antelope with sleek brown hides and corkscrew horns was the day's target.... Brothers and cousins all, including the youngest boy. Despite his youth, he was tall, slender, and muscular, his face broad, marked by a low, sloping forehead and prominent brow ridges, like those of his kin. It was to be his first hunting foray. And his last....

On their way, the hunters had spotted a group of large primates, bipeds like themselves, but bulkier and with massive jaws. These bipedal primates weren't hunters; they foraged for plant foods, including tough fruits on the trees and bushes of the woodland and patches of forest. They scurried away when they saw the hunting band approach....

Later, the hunting band saw a tight herd of a kind of elephant, with enormous, elaborate tusks. The hunters would have gladly scavenged a newly dead carcass, but none was apparent. As it was, these animals were too big, too risky to tackle as prey. The antelope would be a surer, safer target.... When the herd came into view through an acacia grove that screened the hunting band, a strategy was formulated. Someone indicated a cache of rocks that had been made nearby, rocks suitable for making the stone knives and axes necessary for butchering a carcass....

Whatever it was that happened, the boy suddenly found himself running, running blindly, a long gash on his thigh bleeding profusely but, curiously, with no pain. Not yet, anyway.

Weak from the loss of blood, the boy became frightened as darkness fell....

One day passed, then another. Where was everybody? Why didn't they come? If only he could get to the lake, he would feel better in its cooling waters....

The boy did make it to the lake's edge, a shallow lagoon with lush grass all around, reeds growing from the bottom. Crawling, he hauled his ravaged body into the soothing water, the fever close to claiming its victim. For a short while, he did feel better, calmer, very sleepy. [110]

Leakey even expresses a connection felt through viewing the fossil remains of *Homo erectus*: "When I hold a Homo erectus cranium in my hand and look at it full face, I get a strong feeling of being in the presence of something distinctly human. It is the first point in human history at which a real humanness impresses itself so forcefully."[111] Professor Paul Ehrlich of Stanford University presents the humanness of *Homo erectus* in a slightly different way:

If a carefully groomed and dressed *Australopithecus africanus* were to show up at your dinner party, you quite likely would think Mr. Australopithecus was a curiously slender, upright ape that another guest had brought along from the local zoo. In contrast, a similarly cleaned-up *Homo erectus* seated at the dinner table, with a brain volume of about 1,100 cubic centimeters (cc), would be judged a very strange looking individual but unmistakably human. Even though your modern adult guests would have brains that averaged some 20 percent larger, Mr. Erectus would not look strikingly pinheaded.[112]

Homo erectus had a brain that was more than double size of the first bipedal apes, the *Australopithecines*, and nearly the size of modern humans. This large brain, which required cooling, and the exposure to the sun while foraging in the savannas lead *Homo erectus* to lose most of its fur and acquire an abundance of heat-dissipating sweat glands.[113] *Homo erectus* further refined tool making (Acheulean technology) and discovered the use of fire. They engaged in hunting of animals resulting in a dietary change that included meat, a new food source high in calories, proteins and fat need to support their growing brains. While the human brain constitutes only 2 percent of body weight, it consumes 20 percent of the energy used by the body. They were first hominid to migrate out of Africa by a million years ago with fossil remains having been found in western Asia and East Asia.

Leakey believes that with the increase of brain size in *Homo erectus,* there was "the real beginning of the burgeoning of compassion, morality, and conscious awareness that today we cherish as marks of humanity."[114] The fictional narrative above concerning the death of the Turkana Boy contains hints of a complex social life, including the division of labor by the sexes, an extended nurturing period of the young, the transmission of culture, cooperation, planning, sharing of food, and some form of rudimentary language ability. This account is based in part on the discovery of a 1.5 million-year-old Homo erectus campsite, called Site 50, on a river bank twelve miles east of Lake Turkana that resembles camp sites of hunter-gatherer people of today. This hunter-gatherer way of life that evolved over two million years ago and persists even to this day, "with all the elements of humanness that go with it, was a key event in our evolution."[115]

Mitochondrial Eve and Y Chromosome Adam

Based on studies in molecular genetics, modern human beings (Homo sapiens) evolved in Africa about 140,000 years ago and migrated out of Africa about 70,000 years ago, spreading to all continents and replacing all earlier hominids. This was the second migration out of Africa of hominids; the first being the migration of *Homo erectus* a million years ago. The key piece of genetic evidence for the origin of modern humans resulted from the analysis of the mitochondrial DNA of different living human populations. In the last chapter, we saw that eukaryotic cells formed the third domain of life that included all multicellular life such as plants and animals. Within these eukaryotic cells is a nucleus with chromosomal DNA and, in non-plant life, an energy-producing organelle called mitochondria. Mitochondria were once free bacteria that took up residence inside cells about 2 billion years ago "where they have been reproducing nonsexually by simple division, ever since. They have lost many of their bacterial qualities and most of their DNA, but they retain enough to be useful to geneticists."[116] Mitochondria are always inherited maternally and the DNA mutates at a regular and fairly rapid pace and therefore acts like a molecular clock. By comparing the genetic variations in the mitochondrial DNA of different populations, a determination can be made of when and where modern humans evolved. The mitochondrial DNA in all living humans can be traced to a single female who lived in Africa about 200,000 years ago—our *Mitochondrial Eve*. Likewise, the Y-Chromosome which is inherited by males always from the father mutates at a regular pace and also acts like a molecular clock. All living human males can trace their Y-Chromosome to a male who lived about 60,000 years ago—our *Y-Chromosome Adam*. Unlike the Biblical Adam and Eve, our Mitochondrial Eve and Y-Chromosome Adam were not a couple.

What about the Neanderthals?

There was an intermediate species between Homo erectus and modern humans, the *Archaic Homo Sapiens* that lived from about 900,000 years ago to about 100,000 years ago. In addition to modern humans, the *Archaics* were progenitors of another species known as the Neanderthals who lived in Europe and the Middle East from about 130,000 years ago to about 28,000 years ago. Until their extinction, the Neanderthals were contemporaries of modern humans who emigrated to Europe and the Middle East. Neanderthals were cold-adapted people who occupied Europe during the last Ice Age. Their adaptations to a cold environment can be been seen in their stocky builds, short limbs, and enormous noses. Interestingly, the Neanderthals had larger brains than modern humans, yet their tools were not of the quality and variety of the contemporary modern humans and the best reason for their demise may simply have been their inability to adapt to extreme environments and rapid changes in environment. While it is not clear why the Neanderthal disappeared, there is no direct evidence of combat with modern humans. However, there was a small amount of interbreeding between Neanderthals and human beings. Genetic material collected form the bones of Neanderthals indicates that if your ancestry is from places other than sub-Saharan Africa, between one and four percent of your genes are Neanderthal. It seems, without substantial contact with the modern humans, they simply couldn't adapt as well and didn't survive.

The Great Leap Forward

Around 40,000 years ago a marvelous transition occurred that bespeaks of the capacity of our culture to transform our lives. This transformation of culture was termed by Jared Diamond the "Great Leap Forward." Prior to the Great Leap Forward, stone tools and weapons remained mostly unchanged for a million years. Suddenly, these tools became elaborate and a variety of new weapons appeared. Tools and weapons were now being made of materials other than stone such as bone and ivory and sewn clothing was invented. Probably, the most profound change was the appearance of artwork in the form of cave painting, statuettes, and jewelry.[117] Music arrived with the creation of musical instruments such as bone flutes.

> A disinterested observer taking the long view from another planet might see our modern culture, with its computers, supersonic planes, and space exploration, as an afterthought to the Great Leap Forward. On the very long geological timescale, all our modern achievements, from the Sistine Chapel to Special Relativity, from the *Goldberg Variations* to the Goldbach Conjecture˙, could be seen as almost contemporaneous with the Venus of Willendorf and the Lascaux Caves˙, all part of the same cultural revolution, all part of the blooming cultural upsurge that succeeded the long Lower Paleolithic stagnation.[118]

About 10,000 years ago, towards the end of the last Ice Age, in the Fertile Crescent between the Tigris and Euphrates rivers in what is present day Iraq, the agricultural revolution had begun. Agriculture spread over the next five thousand years across the planet and 'started a positive feedback system that put humanity on the road to sociopolitical complexity."[119] Farming and domestication of animals led to permanent settlements, a more sedentary lifestyle, and the growth of societies much larger than the largest hunter-gatherer group of perhaps 200. The ability to produce more food than was needed led to a division of labor and more complex social organization as "human societies underwent a sequence of changes through villages, clans, chiefdoms, and archaic states that led eventually to modern nation-states."[120] Since the agricultural revolution, our evolution "has been overwhelmingly cultural.... A major contemporary human problem...is that the rate of cultural evolution in science and technology has been extraordinarily high in contrast with the snail's pace of change in the social attitudes and political institutions that might channel the uses of technology in more beneficial directions."[121]

˙   The Goldbach Conjecture is a mathematical conjecture proposed in 1742 by the Prussian mathematician Christian Goldbach that has never been proved that every even integer greater than two can be expressed as the sum of two prime numbers, e.g., $6 = 3+3$ and $8 = 3+5$.

˙   The Venus of Willendorf is a statuette of a women carved in limestone discovered in Willendorf, Austria, made between 26,000 and 24,000 years ago. The Lascaux Caves are caves in southwest France that contained murals of mostly animals painted about 17,000 years ago.

Our Nature: Genetic and Cultural Evolution

> If there are lessons to be learned from our biological and cultural past, one
> would expect this longest epoch of our history [hunting and gathering] to be
> a principal textbook. Hunting and gathering was the basic hominid way of
> life for some 5 million years.... In contrast to the length of time our ancestors
> hunted and gathered, the first human lineages to take up agriculture did so
> only about 400 generations ago, and industrial societies have been around
> for only a dozen or so generations.... It is thus reasonable to assume that to
> whatever degree humanity has been shaped by genetic evolution, it has largely
> been to adapt to hunting and gathering—to the lifestyles of our preagriculture
> ancestors.[122]

Prior to the agricultural revolution, "there is no evidence of frequent
violence or warfare in human prehistory."[123]' We do not have a "warrior gene"
that drives us to conquest for the sake of conquest.[124] Based on the success of
hunter-gatherers through millions of years of cooperation, during the period
of the tripling of our brain size, our genetic blueprint predisposes us to
cooperative efforts and alliances.[125] It also predisposes us to have empathy for
one another. For more than 99 percent of human history, we lived in small
bands of about two to three dozen genetically close members. During this
period, "We can be fairly certain that most of the genetic evolution of human
social behavior occurred."[126] Unfortunately for *Homo sapiens* of today, as with
our hunter-gatherer ancestors, the genetic predisposition to cooperation and
empathy is limited to a relatively small number of *in-group* members. For
anyone not a member of our group, the desire for cooperation and empathy
will likely be reduced or not exist at all.

The milieu of our hunter-gatherer past has provided us a genetically-based
palette of emotional colors to deal effectively with one another: guilt, shame,
and embarrassment as internal controls to motivate each of us to comply with
our social responsibility to the group; sadness and distress to evoke empathy
from members of our group; happiness and pleasure evolved to reinforce
mutually beneficial behavior; disgust to help us avoid the unclean—including
substances and people who are morally offensive; fear, to identify threats to
survival and to prepare to flee; love, to promote pure altruism towards our
closest kin and our mate (who is key to our reproductive success).' We are also
genetically predisposed to use aggression as a means to solve certain threats to

---

' The extensive review of rates of violent death in various societies in various time periods by
Steven Pinker in his book *The Better Angels of Our Nature* indicates violence and warfare is
also a fairly consistent part of the hunter-gatherer societies with an average of about 15
percent of deaths due to warfare. So while hunter-gatherers were successful through internal
cooperation they readily could become violent against any outside group perceived as a
threat. The limited empathetic response to kinsman and mistrust and fear of outsiders
conspired to produce a steady source of conflict and aggression.

' Guilt, shame, embarrassment, and disgust are uniquely human emotions that evolved in
hominids to deal with our highly complex social systems.

survival and reproductive interests and cultural evolution, which, having overtaken genetic evolution, drives the aggressive means by which such threats are identified and overcome. Our emotional limbic system evolved the use of simple binary distinctions of us and them to identify threats and "We tend to fear deeply the actions of strangers and to solve conflict by aggression."[127] Anger helps us remove, in a forceful way, obstructions to our goals, but anger is brief, not designed to destroy or annihilate the object of anger. "Like most other mammals, human beings display a behavioral scale, a spectrum of responses that appear or disappear according to particular circumstances."[128]

Hate is a unique human experience that while emotionally based on threats to survival and reproductive interests, co-opts the neocortical brain's ability to ascribe meaning and ability to plan and strategize. Hate is specific to what we perceive as the harmful intentions of other people or groups. Although natural disasters and disease kill many more humans than the intentional harmful acts of people, we do not become obsessed with a hatred of hurricanes, tornadoes, and earthquakes, nor even things like cancer and heart disease. We work hard at protecting ourselves from these calamities, but we are not consumed by hate in the process of doing so. Hate evolved during our hunter-gatherer past to negate our natural empathy towards members of our group whose intentions have been determined to be a threat to our survival and reproductive interests. Once empathy is cancelled, the destruction of the threat, in this case a human being, is possible. Unlike anger, which is a temporary removal of an obstruction, hate can last a lifetime and become intergenerational and is committed to the annihilation of the person or group identified with the threat. The actions of another do not have to be personally experienced to give rise to hate; we can learn to hate through the experience of others whom we deem to part of our *in-group*. Because of our limbic system's tendency to make easy binary distinctions of people into an *in-group* or *out-group*, whole classes of people can be hated based on the perceived harmful intentions of just one. Thus, one who identified oneself as a Nazi in the 1930s and through World War II in Europe hated an entire class of people (Jews, Romany, communists, etc.) and either passively stood by or participated in the destruction of that whole class of people. The hatred can become so extreme that it becomes not "us versus them" but "me versus the world." One individual can perceive the whole world against himself or herself and hate the whole world, as Virginia Tech student Seung-Hui Cho did when he murdered thirty-two students and faculty on April 16, 2007. In his words, "You forced me into a corner and gave me only one option."

With the advent of agriculture, we adopted much larger sized sedentary societies that relied upon specific plots of land for food production and thus, defense and acquisition of territory became a cultural adaptation that reinforced the already existing genetic predisposition to defend land with abundant food sources.

"As societies evolved toward states, intercommunity violence continued to center mainly on control of territory and resources. It evolved culturally into a much more organized, even ritualized, kind of conflict involving incorporation of the productive capacities of subjugated peoples into the resource flow of the conquerors, and it became entwined with and justified by religious ritual and belief."[129]

In northeastern Syria in one of the earliest urban settlements called Brak, a mass grave of more than 100 people killed in a "ferocious battle or brutal mass murder on a scale unprecedented for such an early date" was discovered in 2006. "The corpses of the losers in the conflict were left for weeks to rot in the sun, then dragged and shoved into shallow pits. The winners carved pointed sticks out of some of their enemies' bones, slaughtered prize cows, feasted on roast beef, and tossed the scraps and plates on top of the decaying bodies."[130] Warfare has continued unabated through the millennia with increasing lethality, culminating in the most deadly century, the twentieth, in which at least 167 million people died as a result of war. How will humanity fare in the present century? "We have barely begun to solve the problem with which cultural evolution has presented us: how to live in large groups, perpetually intensifying our activities, creating technologies few can understand and even fewer can control, without sowing the seeds of our own destruction."[131]

The killings in Brak nearly four thousand years ago and major conflicts, wars, and genocides since then, too numerous to name, show more than simply the killing of an enemy. The brutality of the killing indicates the primitive ability *we all share* to completely dehumanize human beings classified as "them" and, when faced with a perceived existential threat, to sanction or participate directly in their merciless destruction. Our ability solve problems of potential conflict involving societies in the billions with devastating lethal technology is based on a mind equipped to handle conflict among societies of a few dozen people equipped with stone axes and spears. As evolutionary psychologists Leda Cosmides and John Toby state, "our modern skulls house a Stone Age mind."[132]

Chapter Five
Why We Hate—Why We Help

"While nothing is easier than to denounce the evildoer, nothing is more difficult than to understand him."

- Fyodor Mikhailovich Dostoevsky

What motivates a man to pack explosives into the sole of his shoes or secrete them in his underwear, climb aboard a passenger jet and attempt to blow it up? And, what makes a woman, and—increasingly throughout the world—a child, strap a bomb to their chest, walk into a crowded restaurant or hotel, and blow themselves up? For that matter, what makes anyone walk into a school full of children, pull out an automatic weapon, and kill innocent children as they flee or attempt to secrete themselves under the nearest desk? What makes millions of people participate in or standby idly while men, women, and children are slaughtered because of their religious beliefs, ethnic background, skin color, or other attached label?

Whenever we listen to the news and hear the latest tragedy involving innocent victims, whether it's a local homicide or an international act of terrorism, we exclaim loudly to the nearest listener: "How could this happen? What monster could have done this?" We empathize with the victims whom we view as a part of our *in-group* and we mourn the loss of innocent lives. We follow the event closely to get a glimpse of the murderer and we expect to see, literally, at some level of consciousness, an ugly Ogre with grossly distorted features, including horns and a tail. We do this as humans because we can't imagine, even for a moment in time, that one human being like us could commit such an unspeakable act against another. Ultimately, we realize that the answer to the question is even more frightening than an Ogre: It is ourselves.

We, as human beings, are capable of the most heinous, despicable acts against our own kind, including genocide.

Hate is a devastating emotion; it is the opposite of empathy and uniquely human, reserved in its true form for application against other humans. Hate is not like anger; anger dissipates fairly quickly in a matter seconds or minutes[133] and is usually tied to a specific event or trigger[134]. Anger can even be reasonably interpreted and resolved without violence or bloodshed if the brain's prefrontal cortex, responsible for impulse control[135], has a chance to react. Hate is all-consuming and is tied to the most basic emotions and primitive instincts of survival and reproduction in humans. Research psychologist Paul Ekman, one of the world's foremost researchers on emotion, considers hatred not to be an emotion because it lasts too long and, although "heavily invested with anger...not the same as anger."[136] Ekman states that "hatred is usually long-standing and focused on a specific person....[and] can fester, taking over the hating person's life so he or she becomes preoccupied with the hated person."[137] The Greek philosopher, Aristotle, poignantly expressed the difference between anger and hate in his Rhetoric dated 350 B.C.E.:

> Much may happen to make the angry man pity those who offend him, but the hater under no circumstances wishes to pity a man he has once hated: for the one would have the offenders suffer for what they have done; the other would have them cease to exist.

More recently, author Rush W. Dozier Jr. expressed that "Hate is the nuclear weapon of the mind. Its detonation can blow apart the social order and plunge nations into war and genocide."[138] When acted on, hate most often results in tragedy. Hate is a byproduct of primitive human development and more specifically, how the human brain has grown and developed over the course of human evolution since the split from the common ancestor with the chimpanzee about 6 million years ago. To prevent genocide and to truly understand how one human can commit such acts of abuse and cruelty to another, we must first understand the human brain and how it functions.

The human brain is an extremely complex organ (perhaps *the* most complex machine in the universe) that has grown and developed at a remarkable pace in evolutionary terms over the last few millions of years, enabling mankind to survive on planet earth and to (mostly) coexist with one another and hold dominion over all other organisms and species. What we also know, and quite frankly try sometimes to forget or deny, is that the human brain also enables each one of us to become a killing machine, a homicidal terrorist, or someone capable of participating in genocide. To accept this fact is to take the first step towards understanding what enables a normal human being, without psychological defects, to commit deliberate and planned violence. In the end, it is the only path that will enable our global society to root out terrorism and other organized campaigns of destruction and prevent genocide.

To help us understand the concept that all of us, as part of our human condition, are capable of killing and committing other unspeakable acts, let's look at what makes us tick, the human brain.

The human brain has been developing at an amazingly fast pace in evolutionary terms for millions of years, from our nearest common ancestor with chimpanzees, to the most primitive hominids, to the earliest nomadic tribes of hunter gatherers and cave dwellers, to the "civilized" man of today. The earliest hominids, *Australopithecus*, had a brain size of about 400 cubic centimeters, slightly larger than the great apes. The size of the human brain of today is about 1,350 cubic centimeters. In less than 4 million years, the human brain tripled in size. Although the brain has developed from these ancient times leading to the advanced cognitive abilities and emotions used to exist in modern times, psychologists and neurological experts believe the brain of today retains most of its primitive form and functions from epochs long before the rise of civilization. These primitive parts of the human brain are sometimes called the "limbic system" and "reptilian brain" and are also referred to collectively as the "reptomammalian brain."[139] These primitive parts of the brain have the sole function of survival and reproduction not unlike the brain in all other animals. It is where the origin for the "fight-or-flight" responses dwell and are released from. It is the first part of the brain to perceive and react to threats, even before conscious awareness.[140] It initiates these primitive responses automatically on a subconscious level.

Several experiments have been conducted to test the brain's ability to perceive and react to unconscious stimuli, much like when we jump or shout when we are startled by a sudden noise or a movement across our path. One such experiment was conducted by Swedish researchers Arne Ohman and Joaquim J. F. Soares and dealt with phobias—intense, irrational fears of specific objects or situations that cannot be voluntarily controlled by the person nor reasoned away.[141] Thus, phobias are thought to arise unconsciously as a form of extreme anxiety through preconscious, automatic information-processing mechanisms that cannot be intentionally controlled. In essence, the experiments set out to show that conscious awareness of the fear-provoking stimulus is not necessary for producing physiological response reactions.

The experiment essentially looked like this: Men in white laboratory coats smile and nod imperceptibly at each other while the man strapped to the chair sits practically motionless staring intently at the screen in front of him. To the casual observer, this scene might have been misinterpreted as a truth-telling session or some type of torture. It was neither. The man strapped to the chair was seated perfectly upright at a tiny desk; his attention was intently focused on a small square box set in the middle of the desktop. The box looked like a cross between a television set and a radar screen. Timed images would be flashed onto the screen, including flowers, mushrooms, spiders, and snakes. In a pretest, the subjects selected to participate in this experiment were shown to have an uncontrollable fear (phobia) of spiders and snakes. Images flowed gracefully across the screen; colorful sunsets, spectacular mountain vistas, and even a marching band strutting in front of a crowd in a crowded football stadium. The man blinked off and on almost imperceptibly as he sat staring at the screen. The two men standing directly behind a short distance away monitored a similar looking box that had wires extending from the back. The wires from this box draped across the table in front of the two men and ran a short distance down to the tile floor and across its short span to attach to the man seated comfortably upright a few feet in front. Once the wires reached the man's chair, they appeared to climb up the back of the chair and attach themselves to the seated prey. They grasped him around the chest, ran down his arms, and attached to his fingertips with little black caps that looked like sewing thimbles. The man had his hands lightly resting on the small table top in front of the screen and his eyes remained steadily focused on the screen, almost as if he was aware of the caps on his fingertips and was willing himself to ignore them.

The two men in lab coats remained in a somewhat rigid posture but they both seemed to rock ever so slightly back and forth as if they were listening together to some strange, quiet melody. Together, they stood staring at the small box in front of them in excited anticipation that was palpable in the room. One could tell from the steady nods and the smiles the two men exchanged in regular intervals that the box was giving the correct answers or at least the answers they had hoped for. There was a tiny camera mounted on top of the small box in front of the man in the chair. The tiny camera was focused intently on the man's face, recording every eye blink, furrowed brow, or tiny bead of sweat that was brought about unconsciously by the unseen images in front of him. This quiet little scene went on several minutes and ended abruptly when both screens simultaneously faded to black. The man quickly stood upright while the attendants in white lab coats unceremoniously detached the wires from his hands. The man stood slowly and stretched his arms to the sky while flexing his fingers vigorously as if he were shaking a thimble from the tips of his finger. He turned around awkwardly and set off in a direct line to a desk adjacent to the exit door. He smiled at the attendant seated beside the door, turned and nodded to the two men in the white coats, and picked up his check as he briskly left the room.

If this were a sporting event, the two doctors in attendance would have exchanged high fives. They had worked to develop their hypothesis over the last two years and even in this early stage of experimentation, it appears that the evidence supports the contention that the primitive reptilian brain is alive and well in modern man. In this experiment, the man sitting motionless in front of the computer console had been questioned prior to the experiment. He was pointedly asked what his biggest fear was and he told the researchers that he loathed spiders and snakes; in fact, he said just the sight of a spider or snake made his skin crawl. Using this information, the test was set. The man sat motionless in front of the screen attentive to the soothing scene before him. He was blissfully unaware of the fact that single frame photos of spiders and snakes were scrolled randomly across the screen. These images were flashed on the screen so fast that the conscious mind could not see them but, the unconscious mind, the mind of someone who "loathed" them as vile creatures, clearly saw the images and transmitted the danger warning to the body.

The casual observer of this experiment would not be able to perceive the man's reaction to this subliminal event, but the computer diagnostics and the camera captured it as if it were projected in three dimensional Technicolor. While the subjects did not consciously perceive the flashing images of spiders and snakes, their subconscious mind did, releasing a flood of hormones that radically altered their physical and mental state.

The primitive brain functions in humans today the same as it did hundreds of thousands of years ago. These primitive response and control areas of the human brain work unconsciously to quickly identify and respond to perceived threats, just as it did millennia ago to keep the cavemen alive. The primitive humans across the globe were hunters and gatherers that collected in small bands or tribes. Their sole "purpose" was to survive from day to day and reproduce to carry on the species. The word "purpose" here does not mean a conscious and deliberative choice made to survive but simply the manifestation of the genetic-based mandate or instinct to continue living and reproducing. The first evidence of a conscious purpose to living is perhaps seen in Cro-Magnons starting about 40,000 years with the appearance of standardized stone tools, jewelry, statues, musical instruments, and cave paintings such as the painted life-sized bulls and horses in the Lascaux Cave of southwestern France. The primitive brains in these hunter-gatherers functioned in this environment in a way designed solely to protect them from harm by recognizing threats and initiating a response to these threats, and to draw them towards things that would enhance survival and reproduction through emotions such as happiness and pleasure. Primitive sensory perceptions from the environment that stimulate the fight-or-flight response in the face of danger were a major part of a primitive human's existence. They functioned on pure survival instincts protecting their tribes and bands in order to reproduce to ensure the survival of the species. As the human brain developed over millions of years, it slowly increased the capacity for empathy and to attach meaning to thoughts, ideas, and events. Although the modern human brain has developed the capacity for higher level thinking, empathy, and understanding and to cope and reason, it still contains the primitive brain that dwells deep within and functions the same as it did during the Ice Age. This primitive brain is the origin of our ability to hate, allowing us to override our natural tendency for peaceful coexistence when one among us betrays us or when threatened by an out-group.

Hunters-gatherers were all that existed in the world for countless millennia. These primitive humans lived out their harsh existence in small groups, usually less than 150, and they survived in an environment that was constantly threatening with real and perceived dangers. The brain of these early humans functioned on a very basic level. The brain was, at this stage of development, keenly in tune with ever-present dangers fulfilling its genetic and instinctual mandate for survival and reproduction. It worked much of the time on an unconscious level to provide warnings in advance of danger. It functioned in such a way as to interpret what was observed through the senses at an unconscious level to alert the body that there was danger present or lurking nearby. The primitive human bands had many enemies, including poisonous snakes, predatory animals, and warring factions and the primitive brain was adapted to ensure safety from these threats.

The modern brain encapsulates the primitive brain and, according to one theory, the human brain is actually three brains in one. The "Triune Brain" consists of the reptilian system, the limbic system, and the "neocortex" or "new brain." While many neuroscientists will find this description overly simplistic, it serves as a useful model for understanding the genesis of deliberate and planned aggression. In order to truly understand the genesis of hate and how mankind can house the capacity for committing the most shocking and repulsive acts imaginable, we must understand how the human brain functions, specifically the interactions between these "three brains," each with their own functions and rules that can sometimes be in conflict. According to Paul MacLean, the former director of the laboratory of the Brain and Behavior at the United States Institute of Mental Health, the three parts of the brain perform separate and distinct functions but interact substantially.

This interaction, specifically from the most primitive cores of the brain with the neocortex, is what enables political leaders to convince nations to go to war and seek the destruction of another nation or the annihilation of a whole population. The basic recipe for placing a society on the path to planned aggression is the identification of a threat to survival or reproductive interests (limbic system provocation) and the identification of a group responsible for the threat or interfering with the ability to overcome the threat (cortical reasoning followed by planning activity). There are numerous variables we will discuss later that factor into the scope of the aggression, such as obedience to authority and dehumanization of the out-group, but identification of an existential threat and a human cause forms the basis of hate and the violence that follows. This interaction between primitive cores of the brain and the neocortex also allows terrorists to enlist new recruits to wage a "holy war" against the "infidels" or to manipulate, through pure terror, the minds of their enemies, weakening their resolve to fight. Through the manipulation of primal fears and identification of a responsible out-group, terrorists can motivate their adherents to extreme violence and alter the policy of an entire nation through one act of terrorism, as occurred in the bombings of four commuter trains in Madrid, Spain, in March 2004, killing 191 and wounding 1,800 three days before Spain's general election. The election resulted in the ouster of the party in power, expected by most political analysts to stay in power, and the election of a new Socialist Party-controlled government led by a prime minister who immediately announced his intention to withdraw Spanish troops from Iraq only four days after the terrorist attack. By May 21, 2004 all Spanish troops, about 1,400, were out of Iraq.

The experiment above evidences the fact that the primitive core or reptilian brain exists on a separate level to identify threats and initiate a response of fight-or-flight, which is a most basic instinct in humans. Research also shows these primitive areas are connected to the higher order executive functioning areas of the brain, meaning that evocation of primitive fears cannot only cause immediate instinctual reactions such as anger, but can also bring about a long-term, consciously planned and rationalized course of action to eliminate the threat fueled by hate.

The reptilian system consists of the brain stem and the cerebellum; its purpose or function is the physical survival of the body. This portion of the brain is the oldest section in terms of development and houses the most basic human functions. It is responsible for life-sustaining functions, including digestion, reproduction, breathing, and initiating fight-or-flight response when faced with perceived threats or danger. The important characteristic of the reptilian brain for our purpose is to grasp that this portion of the human brain initiates actions on a subconscious level, automatic responses to stimuli that represent real or perceived threats.[142] The behaviors that are invoked by the reptilian brain are automatic; they have a ritualistic quality and are highly resistant to change. Think about the last time you were startled unexpectedly by a person hiding in a nearby closet or perhaps by a small animal that ran across in front of you as you were walking along a path at the river's edge. When this happened, you reacted instinctively in any number of ways: You might have jumped back in fear or screamed; you may have even stood motionless or ran. All these actions were precipitated by an event that was sudden and unexpected, and your responses were initiated at a subconscious level by the primitive brain. In addition to the outward reactions to this sudden event, the brain was instantly initiating some core responses to keep you safe and out of harm's way. Your pupils may have dilated to allow for more light to enter, your blood pressure and heart rate may have become elevated in preparation for fight-or-flight, your auditory and other senses may have been slightly diminished as blood flow is routed to the brain and large muscles to prepare for escape or battle. These are the same responses as seen in the spider and snake experiment.

In his book, *Emotional Intelligence*, Daniel Goleman calls this automatic brain response a "neural hijacking," in which the limbic section of the brain proclaims an emergency and recruits the rest of the brain to instantly respond. This hijacking is instantaneous and triggers an automatic, primitive survival response before the "thinking brain" has a chance to digest what is happening and fashion a response of its own. Joseph LeDoux's work on emotions and the brain reveals to us that the design of the brain that allows sensory signals from the eyes or ears to travel first in the brain to the thalamus, and then, across a signal synapse to the amygdala, the emotion-generating component of the brain.[143] In effect, this allows the amygdala to respond even before the more advanced portions of the brain are able to receive, review, and respond to the threat.

Although the reptilian system is considered a distinct section of the brain that carries out these primitive instinctual functions, it is closely linked with the other two brain systems. One of these is the limbic system. This part of the brain is the second to evolve and it is the center of emotion; it includes the amygdale, which mediates emotional response, and the hippocampus, which mediates memory. These centers serve to associate events with emotion and work to store memory for long-term recall of events. The hippocampus allows for memory storage to take place from repeated and deliberate study and from commonplace experiences and for placement of memories into a contextual setting.[144] The amygdala is a key to our understanding the terrorist as it arouses feelings such as fear, joy, anger, and hatred. This section of the brain links emotions with behavior and is also attached to activities related to primitive behaviors such as our needs and desires for food, sex, and bonding. Through the amygdala and the reptilian brain, people experience the most basic and primitive drives—what psychologists sometimes refer to as the "four Fs: Fight, Flight, Food, and Reproduction'."

It is within these two sections of the brain that humans deal with the environment and other humans on a most primitive and reactive basis. These two sections of the brain have a profound effect on our decision making— "even though we humans like to think of ourselves as being able to make non-emotional decisions, emotions play a part in all decisions."[145] These two brain systems, based on the need for quick decision making in survival-related situations, lock us into the *binary* of *us vs. them* thinking: When the limbic and reptilian parts of the brain classify other people as "them," we are devoid of most positive emotions, particularly empathy, towards the *out-group*. "Social psychologists have shown that group loyalty and hostility emerge with predictable ease. The process begins with groups' categorizing into Us and Them. It is called *in-group—out-group bias* and is universal and ineradicable."[146]

If we are to survive this experiment called life, we must have empathy towards *all* our fellow man. When people function solely within the framework of the negative emotions of the reptilian brain and the limbic system, we lose our capacity for empathy for all except a limited class of people we identify with.

The third portion of the human brain is the neocortex. This is the largest and most recently evolved part of the brain and the part that is responsible for consciousness and our most sophisticated capabilities. It is responsible for our logical thinking constructs and our ability to plan for future events. It also is responsible for speech and language, voluntary movements, and sensory perception.[147] This is our thinking brain; it is where we attach meaning to events and perceptions and it is inextricably linked to our primitive reptilian

---

[.] This is not a typo but a bit of psychologist humor.

and limbic systems. The neocortex is the high order functioning portion of the brain and although it is directly linked to the two other systems, it works to apply logic and advanced thinking to emotions aroused in the primitive brain cores.[148]

According to Rush Dozier, Jr., author of *Why We Hate*, "The human limbic system poses a special danger because of its extensive connections to the neocortex, allowing us to fuse hatred and violence with the highest capacity of the human mind: Meaning...our limbic system has evolved a powerful tendency to blindly interpret any meaning system that we deeply believe in as substantially enhancing our survival and reproduction."[149] This is powerful stuff. This is why we believe hate to be more than simply an emotional state but an *emotional-cognitive state* in which meaning, planning, and feeling are combined for the special purpose of eliminating other people deemed to be a threat to our survival and reproductive interests. Once a person or group is deemed by the limbic system to be one of "them" and not "us," the capacity for empathy—the source of our motivation to help another person—is limited or eliminated. If that person or group is perceived as a threat to survival or reproductive interests, hate easily fills the empathy gap. As we shall see in the next chapter, if leaders sufficiently dehumanize the hated out-group and convince their followers that the out-group is responsible for, or contributing to, an existential crisis, destructive violence including war and genocide are likely.

Empathy

Imagine:

> A runaway trolley is hurtling down the tracks toward five people who will be killed if it proceeds on its present course. You can save these five people by diverting the trolley onto a different set of tracks, one that has only one person on it, but if you do this, that person will be killed. Is it morally permissible to turn the trolley and thus prevent five deaths at the cost of one?

> Once again, the trolley is headed for five people. You are standing next to a large man on a footbridge spanning the tracks. The only way to save the five people is to push this man off the footbridge and into the path of the trolley. Is this morally permissible?[150]

According to Harvard University Professor of Psychology Joshua D. Greene, most people believe it is morally permissible to divert the trolley onto the different set of tracks to save the five people at the cost of the one. However, most people also believe it is not morally permissible to push the man onto the tracks in order to save the five people. In both situations, the harm and benefit are the same yet the circumstances produce a different result for most people. Greene posits a theory of moral judgment that the response to the trolley dilemma is controlled by "the operations of at least two distinct psychological/neural systems."[151] One system, based in the frontal lobes of the neocortex, is based on reason and is relatively unemotional. The other system is the emotional limbic brain that uses moral intuition influenced by deeply ingrained instincts with a strong genetic foundation. The rationality of saving five lives at the expense of one is appealing to the neocortical part of the brain, which involved moral decision making process and the lack of interaction with the victim in the first scenario limits the influence of the emotional limbic brain.

Greene conducted a brain imaging study of participants faced with a "personal moral dilemma," such as the trolley dilemma scenario involving pushing a person onto the tracks to save five others, and an "impersonal moral dilemma," such as the trolley dilemma scenario involving diverting the trolley to a different set of tracks resulting in the death of one to save the lives of five others.[152] Greene "found that judgments in response to 'personal' moral dilemmas, compared with 'impersonal' ones, involved greater activity in brain areas that are associated with emotion and social cognition."[153] He notes that "there is a growing consensus that moral judgments are based largely on intuition—'gut feeling' about what is right and wrong in particular cases."[154] Greene has a hypothesis, which we share, that altruistic instincts developed in an environment in which we were up close and personal to those in need and, therefore, the trigger for self-sacrifice is proximity. He notes that "We evolved in an environment in which we could help nearby desperate people but not distant strangers."[155] For those who are out of sight, the impulse to aid is dormant even though the conscious mind is aware of the suffering. "Thus," according to Greene, "evolution may have given us heartstrings that are tuggable, but not from afar."[156]

So, for most people, the response seems natural that it is morally permissible to save the five lives at the expense of the one in the trolley-diverting scenario; more lives will be saved and primitive instinctual resistance to killing fellow humans is limited by lack of contact with the victim. In the second scenario, despite the utilitarianism of saving the five lives at the expense of one, the strong emotional resistance to killing is evoked due to the decision maker having to physically push the person onto the tracks. The term "psychological distance" can be interpreted to mean the emotional distance from the human qualities of another. The person who is killed by the train that is diverted by the pulling of the lever is unseen and unknown to the person pulling the lever. Their humanity is conceptual and the psychological distance is therefore great. Psychological distance is an emotional process; a concept of a human being, while understood by the neocortical thinking brain, does not have much effect on the emotional limbic brain. The emotional brain needs to see, hear, touch, and have intimacy with another human being to make a strong connection with the person and close the gap of psychological distance.

The emotional process of connection with another is a physical process involving the physical senses and physical sensations. Research at the University of Southern California Brain and Creativity Institute and Rossier

School of Education involved telling participants stories designed to evoke compassion and admiration for virtue.[157] Participants reported that they felt physical sensations in response to the stories. These feelings or "pangs" of emotion were detected as well in brain scans of the participants. One participant reported feeling like there was a "balloon or something under my sternum, inflating and moving up and out." The participant, while thinking about the sensation, considered his own relationship with his parents and expressed a desire to show more gratitude towards his parents. The researcher Mary Helen Immordino's hypothesis, as indicated by the results of the research, is that physical feelings or emotional reactions in the body may sometimes prompt introspection, and can ultimately promote moral choices and motivation to help or emulate others. She notes that humans are an "intensely social species" and that there is now biological evidence that so-called "gut feelings" are a real part of social emotions that play a role in moral decisions.

We believe that empathy is the foundation for the desire to help others outside of immediate kin and that, through a similar physical process, the suffering of the other is actually experienced as one's own or one's near kin's suffering. Once felt, the motivation to act is basically the same motivation one would feel to help one's self. Because of our evolutionary history of existing for the vast majority of our past in small bands, the triggering of this empathetic process requires physical closeness and identification of the other as part of the in-group. Robert Wright in *The Moral Animal* observes that "the design work was done in a social environment quite different from the current environment. We live in cities and suburbs and watch TV and drink beer, all the while being pushed and pulled by feelings designed to propagate our genes in a small hunter-gatherer population."[158] In terms of the triggering of empathy and other moral sentiments, Wright notes that these "sentiments are used with brutal flexibility, switched on and off in keeping with self-interest; and how naturally oblivious we often are to this switching."[159] Empathy, for those distant or unknown to us, or for those labeled as not part of the in-group, is difficult and requires strong conscious effort. Wright observes that we find in the mind "a binary moral landscape, comprising an in-group that deserves consideration and an out-group that deserves exploitation."[160] In a sense, this type of empathy for out-groups requiring conscious effort is a sort of artificial empathy that we have named *neocortical empathy*. If you were to read the hundreds of "tweets" posted by the Dalai Lama on the social networking website, Twitter [www.twitter.com], you will find most have an underlying message that seeks to create empathy where it may not exist or be weak, i.e., trying to create neocortical empathy. Today, August 15, 2011, at 11:10 am, as we write, the last tweet by the Dalai Lama is: "Love and compassion arising with a clear recognition of the importance and right of others will reach even those who would do you harm."

Our belief that the source of motivation to help others, i.e. altruistic motivation, outside of our immediate kin is based on empathic emotion is supported in psychological research and is known as the *empathy-altruism hypothesis*.[161] The leading proponent of the empathy-altruism hypothesis is social psychologist Professor C. Daniel Batson, Ph.D., of the University of Kansas. While the dominant view in psychology, biology, and social sciences is that helpful behavior towards others is ultimately self-serving or *egoistic*, Batson believes that empathic-based altruism is truly motivated by the ultimate goal of helping another and not benefit for the self, although both motivations may exist at the same time.[162] Batson cites that "over thirty experiments have now been conducted to test the empathy-altruism hypothesis against various egoistic alternatives, that is, against hypotheses claiming that the motivation produced by empathy is directed toward the ultimate goal of obtaining some self-benefit. With remarkable consistency, results of these experiments have supported the empathy-altruism hypothesis...[leading] to the suggestion that we psychologists need to change our view of human motivation and, indeed, of human nature."[163]

We agree with Batson and further assert that because of the strong evolutionary advantage of pro-social behavior to hominids over the past several million years, empathic emotion evolved in support of reciprocal altruism by essentially hijacking the neural circuitry involved in self-preservation so that another's distress became our own. As we have already seen in nature, natural selection does not generally create new systems but adapts existing systems to the needs of natural selection pressures.

Neuroscientists have even uncovered the neurological process by which such empathic feeling occurs through activation of special neuron cells in the brain known as *mirror neurons*. These brain cells "fire not only when we perform a particular action, but also when we watch someone else perform that same action. Neuroscientists believe this 'mirroring' is the mechanism by which we can 'read' the minds of others and empathize with them. It's how we 'feel' someone's pain."[164] Studies have shown that the same neuronal networks involved in experiencing disgust, pain, and touch are activated by merely observing another person who is experiencing such emotion or sensation. Vittorio Gallese, M.D., of the Department of Neuroscience, University of Parma, is one of the discoverers of mirror neurons in humans and believes "mirroring could be a basic functional principle of our brain."[165] According to Gallese, "our capacity to empathize with others might be mediated by embodied simulation mechanisms, that is, by the activation of the same neural circuits underpinning our own agentive, emotional, and sensory experiences."[166] In other words, in order to understand another, we simulate their state of mind and, when that other person is in a state of distress, we experience that distress as our own, which motivates us to relieve the distress. We are truly wired in our brains to walk a mile in another's shoes.

Empathy is the key to our morality as it guides our response to the needs of others. Morality itself can be seen as a type of struggle between the impulses of egoistic behavior versus altruistic behavior. Pushing us towards altruism is empathy, which is embodied in a rule many philosophers such as Confucius,

Isocrates, Thomas Hobbes, Baruch Spinoza, and John Stuart Mill, believe the first moral principle—the Golden Rule. The Golden Rule—"thou shalt love thy neighbor as thyself" (Lev. 19:18)—is universal and found in all the world's major religions and in the writings of influential thinkers throughout recorded history. The key to our survival as a species lies in empathy and it is no wonder that religious/philosophical leaders such as the Dalai Lama are preoccupied with it. Our survival as a species also required the need to negate empathy when threatened by other humans and thus the ability for top-down ability to control it, including the ability to actively seek the destruction of other humans through the antithesis of empathy—hate. In modern globalized society, hate has the advantage—there are a lot more reasons to be suspicious of and mistrustful of others than to embrace others. Empathy requires close contact and familiarization with others; hate does not. Our primitive emotional brains evolved a capacity for empathy for groups usually no larger than a few dozen people. There is even research by Adam Waytz of the Northwestern University Kellogg School of Management and Nicholas Epley of the University of Chicago that suggests that people who are socially connected tend to be less able to empathize with more distant others and can more easily dehumanize more distant others.[167] The need for social connection was compared by the authors of the study to the need for food. People who are hungry seek food as people who are socially disconnected seek to connect with others. However, people whose hunger is satisfied will be less motivated to seek out food and, similarly, people who are socially connected will be less motivated to seek out social connections. We believe that because of the small size of our ancestral social network as hunter-gatherers, our appetite for social connection is easily filled by a small circle of family and friends. Once this need is satisfied, empathy for others becomes more difficult.

Hate is limitless in its scope and easily provoked, while empathy is limited in scope and generally requires identification with the other as part of the in-group. As primate researcher Frans B.M. de Waal of Emory University notes, "Empathy is fragile…. Among our close animal relatives, it is switched on by events within their community, such as a youngster in distress, but it is just as easily switched off with regard to outsiders."[168] De Waal tells us, "Our evolutionary background makes it hard to identify with outsiders. We've evolved to hate our enemies, to ignore people we barely know, and to distrust anybody who doesn't look like us. This is the challenge of our time: globalization by a tribal species."[169] We can easily at times hate the whole world yet how many times do we go out of our way for a single person outside of our small in-group?

Our ability to empathize is limited and can easily be manipulated to limit or negate its effects. Recent studies "show that empathy is a highly flexible phenomenon" with responses being "malleable with respect to a number of factors—such as…the interpersonal relationship between empathizer and other, or the perspective adopted during observation of the other."[170] While experiencing the emotions of others is automatic through a "bottom-up" process, executive functions of the brain "in the prefrontal and cingulate cortex serve to regulate both cognition and emotion through selective attention and self-regulation…and in return controls the lower level by providing top-down feedback."[171] In his book, *Why Empathy Matters*, J.D Trout, professor of philosophy and psychology at Loyola University, observes:

> When the person suffering is similar to us, empathy really ramps up: we experience stronger physiological arousal, report identifying more with the suffering person, and report feeling worse while waiting for the painful stimulus than subjects observing the same pain administered to someone not similar to them. We are even more willing to pay a personal cost to help when suffering individuals are similar to us.[172]

One study clearly showed how a person's attitude toward another can affect whether an empathetic response would be generated.[173] Male and female participants in the study played a game with confederates who would play both fairly and unfairly. Brain scans using fMRI (functional magnetic resonance imaging) were then taken of the participants while they observed the confederates receiving pain. Participants of both sexes experienced empathy-related activation in pain-related brain areas towards the fair players. However, in men, empathy responses were significantly reduced when observing an unfair player receive pain. There was also, in men observing the unfair players receive pain, an increased activation in reward-related areas, correlated with an expressed desire for revenge.

In the book, *The Science of Evil*, author Simon Baron-Cohen, professor of developmental psychopathology at the University of Cambridge, asserts that "empathy is one of the most valuable resources in our world" and its erosion "is an important global issue related to the health of our communities, be they small (like families) or big (like nations)."[174] Baron-Cohen even goes so far as to believe that "evil" can be substituted with the concept of "empathy erosion," which may result from corrosive emotions like revenge and hatred or from permanent psychological conditions such as psychopathy.[175] In other words, what we call "evil" in the world is, in essence, the result of human action or inaction *permitted by the absence of empathy*.

According to Baron-Cohen, "Unempathetic acts are simply the tail end of a bell curve, found in every population on the planet…. We all lie somewhere on an empathy spectrum. People said to be evil or cruel are simply at one extreme of the empathy spectrum."[176] The other extreme are those who are highly empathetic who are constantly concerned with other's feelings and who are extremely generous, helpful, and supportive. Based on fMRI, it is generally accepted in neuroscience that there are "at least ten interconnected brain regions" involved in empathy that, according to Baron-Cohen, form an "empathy circuit" that shapes an individual's position on the empathy bell curve.[177] Many of these areas involve the more highly evolved parts of the cortical brain such as the medial prefrontal cortex, a "hub for social information processing" involved in evaluated others' thoughts and feelings, and the orbito-frontal cortex involved in impulse control.[178] Significantly, the center of the emotional brain, the amygdala, is also part of this "empathy circuit."[179] It is interesting to note that there is also research that indicates a "hate circuit" is functional in the brain that also involves the highly evolved cortical areas of the brain, including the parts of the frontal cortex involved in the planning and execution of motor acts and in the prediction of acts by others.[180] The "hate circuit" as described in the research by Semir Zeki of the University College London, Wellcome Laboratory of Neurobiology, does not, however, include activation of the key parts of the emotional limbic brain, the amygdala and hippocampus.[181]

We believe the first step on the path to destructive behavior in psychologically normal people is the shutting down of empathy based on an emotional decision that a person or group is a threat to some core survival or reproductive interest. They are no longer members of the in-group and as Baron-Cohen describes, are treated as objects, not people.[182] Once there is no emotional relevance of another person or group and they lose their human qualities, hate can easily fill the gap as an unemotional process of elimination of the threat. We also believe that empathy, despite the individual's overall position on the empathy bell curve as normal, can be selective. For people of moderate empathy, meaning most of us, we have the ability to shut down empathy for a select person or group based on that person or group's level of threat to our core interests of survival and reproduction and their psychological distance from us. For low empathy people, they already are capable generally of mistreating others and for the high empathy people, only the most extreme and immediate threat can override their concern for others and inability to harm others. An example of the selective nature of empathy is seen in many of the Nazi physicians who performed the most cruel and gruesome experiments on prisoners at the Auschwitz-Birkenau death camps. Most of these physicians were found by Dr. Robert J. Lifton in his book, *The Nazi Doctors: Medical Killing and the Psychology of Genocide,* to be normally caring and supportive of their family and friends while at the same time committing atrocities as part of a process he referred to as "compartmentalization."

Because of the ability of empathy to be reduced and negated by both internal factors, such as bias against unfamiliar groups or different racial groups, and external factors such as cultural expectations, obedience to authority figures, or a present crisis, it is a weak and ineffective barrier to the conflict and aggression of modern globalized society. Empathy is even ineffective to motivate us, in the industrialized and relatively wealthy nations, to effectively respond to worldwide crises involving disease, droughts, and famine. Although we may believe we have definitive moral foundations, the reality is that our morality concerning others (as most of morality is concerned with) is heavily influenced by contextual variables such as how far away the person is in terms of psychological distance and how we perceive others as a threat to our interests. In *The Descent of Man*, Darwin expressed the need for our empathy to expand its influence beyond what our natural instincts have prepared us to include:

> As man advances in civilisation, and small tribes are united into larger communities, the simplest reason would tell each individual that he ought to extend his social instincts and sympathies to all members of the same nation, though personally unknown to him. This point being once reached, there is only an artificial barrier to prevent his sympathies extending to the men of all nations and races.

In the century that followed his words, humanity witnessed its most violent century, in terms of actual numbers of causalities, in its existence in which more than 175 million died during wars and conflicts due to deliberate and planned aggression. The expansion of empathy beyond what natural selection has prepared us has not come as easy as Darwin expected, nor should we expect it to arise easily in this century.

We cannot rely upon our natural empathy and must, as the Dalai Lama tweets, develop a deliberate, conscious empathy towards all.

Chapter Six
The Cycle of Violence

We hate some persons because we do not know them;
and will not know them because we hate them.

- Charles Caleb Colton

The AK47 rifle has a distinctive sound when it spits bullets angrily in rapid fire succession. Named after its inventor, Mikhail Kalashnikov, the AK47 is regarded as one the most reliable battle rifles ever produced. Around the world today, there are over 30 million of these killing machines in circulation. The AK47 is the preferred weapon of the Russian military and it has lived up to its well-earned reputation. The "AK," as it is sometimes referred to, performed particularly well on this day when hell descended upon the tiny settlement of Novye Aldi. Lying on the outskirts of Grozny and at the foot of the Caucasus Mountains, Novye Aldi found itself trapped in conflict as the marshaled forces of the Russian Federation began their *Zachistka* operations. After several days of intense battle, the first wave of soldiers assigned to "mop up" duties entered the city, battle weary, looking to move swiftly through the city and flesh out any remaining pockets of resistance. As the force methodically and deliberately wound its way through the streets, they were keenly aware that the second wave, not of their kind, was right on their heels. The second wave came into the city on February 5, 2000, and spit hellfire from their AK47s slung tight against their chests. They cursed the living and showed no mercy or discrimination in their delivery of death. They displayed an unmatched brutality without flinching as they slaughtered any human standing in their path. There was a name to describe the massacre that followed: *Bespedrel*, which loosely translates to "no limits." On this day, there was no limit to the atrocities that would take place. The brutality inflicted upon and witnessed by the Chechen population were so extreme that the federation forces themselves used the term *Bespedrel* to describe the events. Kill, rape, brutalize, and leave nothing in your wake. There was no limit to the pain, suffering, and death that was inflicted upon the people of this village.

What started as an attempt by Russian forces to suppress a rebel uprising became a scorched earth policy that killed scores of innocent people. The war in Chechnya was about geography, it was about culture, it was about ethnicity and about differences between groups of people. It was the culmination of hate that had been carefully cultivated into the minds of the killers that allowed them to kill so ruthlessly and violently without empathy or purpose beyond what was apparent to the victim's population—*annihilation*. Hate, at its climax, affords the killer the detachment from reality, needed to continue the onslaught without concern for the dead and dying. Hate imbeds an "us vs. them" cognitive process in the killer that makes the victims less than human and thus allows killing without limits. On this day, the Chechen rebels wore green bandanas with "Allah Akbar," etched across the front, displaying their cause for the entire world to see. For years, the conflict ebbed and flowed with both sides laying claim to episodes of extreme atrocity and cruelty.

The Chechen conflict spanned across the first and second war and is responsible for hundreds of unspeakable atrocities against people of the region. This conflict is regarded by the international community as particularly brutal. Neither side of this issue had clean hands as the atrocities swung like a pendulum back and forth. The Chechen terrorists committed many unspeakable horrors against innocent people to further their goals. The most notorious Chechen terrorist, Shaymil Basayev, conducted a particularly brutal reign of terror. Basayev orchestrated some of the most devastating attacks against Russia. He has been connected to the seizure of a hospital in Budyonnovsk in southern Russia in 1995, and of a theatre in 2002, which led to nearly 200 deaths as Russian forces filled the theatre with noxious chemicals in effort to end the siege. He is also the mastermind behind the notorious seizure of the school in Beslan, where nearly half of the 331 deaths were school children. The Beslan massacre began when Chechen terrorists, demanding a free republic from Russia, seized the school and ushered children and teachers in the gymnasium. The seizure was carried out in part by a group called the Sabotage Battalion of Chechen Martyrs. The group took a total of 1,100 hostages and was well prepared to defend their position and ultimately sacrifice themselves and as many of the hostages they could for their cause.

The Chechen conflict clearly illustrates the devastating consequences of human hatred. Like other mass killings throughout the years, the Chechen conflict is a result of binary thinking; an "us vs. them" mentality with an all or nothing perspective on the dispute. Deep-seated hatred can result from generations of conflict or from recent events that cause disagreement, which most often traces its roots to earlier conflicts. Conflict and, ultimately, genocide, can sprout from what objectively appear as insignificant events to the international community. The seeds of hatred, once planted in the human brain, can, with proper nourishment, grow into active support of genocide. Whole populations may come to the conclusion that individual and in-group survival relies upon the annihilation of another population. Hatred, when orchestrated as part of a plan designed to respond to an existential threat by respected leaders, has mobilized hundreds and thousands of people to kill indiscriminately. Hatred is the most intense and long-lasting form of primitive hostility according to Dozier, and when hatred takes hold of a large segment of the population, it can have devastating results.

Throughout history, there have been epic battles and isolated conflicts, often resulting in scores of tragedy and death. In the twentieth century alone, it is widely accepted that there have been nineteen epic events classified as either ethnic cleansing or genocide. Although the term "genocide" did not exist before 1944, systematic mass murder of populations has occurred throughout history. Today, there is still some debate as to how to characterize the Armenian atrocities committed by the Turks, circa. 1915. The debate should not be framed in terms of how to characterize the slaughter of millions of people. Rather it should be, "How did this and other atrocities happen?" "Why are there still such atrocities occurring today?" And most important, "How do we stop today's brutal killings and prevent future atrocities?" Like the Russian-Chechen wars, the Armenian Genocide was religious and ethnic based. When populations are dissimilar in religious beliefs and ethnic backgrounds and they share common borders, fringe elements on either side can mass support and create an "us vs. them" mentality, which can spark conflict, escalate to war, which can ultimately result in genocide. Such conflicts often span across generations, with only brief rest periods occurring between atrocities.

There are many well-documented accounts of human slaughter dating back as far as 416 B.C., with the Athenian siege of Milos, to the more recent ethnic cleansing of Bosnian Muslims in Sarajevo, where Radovan Karadzic, president of the illegitimate Bosnian Serb Republic, was quoted as saying, "Serbs and Muslims are like cats and dogs. They cannot live together in peace. It is impossible." It seems every time an atrocity occurs, the world shudders, holds it collective breath, and sighs, "How could this have happened?" And yet it does, over and over again. Other recent examples of genocide include a case in Rwanda where, in 1994, an estimated 800,000 people were killed in less than 100 days. The slaughter was mainly of ethnic Tutsis at the hands of the ethnic Hutus. The history of hate between the Tutsis and the Hutus dates back centuries to a time when the Tutsis, a cattle-raising people from the upper Nile region, infiltrated the area and won dominance over the Hutus, already living off the land as a peaceful, agricultural people. In 1916, Belgian colonists arrived, and applied a classification system to the two tribes. The Belgians considered the Tutsis to be superior to the Hutus and the Tutsis enjoyed the status by securing better jobs and educational opportunities than their neighboring Hutus. The resentment among Hutus built up over the years and in 1959, more than 20,000 Tutsis were killed at the hands of the Hutus in a violent backlash, which many called the "winds of destruction." Shortly thereafter, Belgium granted Rwanda independence and, suddenly, it was the Hutus who gained control. The friction from these events remained over the years, finally culminating in the unbelievable atrocities of 1994. At one point in this escalation of slaughter, the Hutus offered their Tutsis victims the option to purchase a bullet to save them from being butchered by machetes or clubbed to death. It is of critical importance to the discussion of Hate and Terror to note that the Tutsis and Hutus are very similar in that they live in the same densely populated area, speak the same language, and look similar—except that the Tutsis are often taller and thinner that Hutus. Thus, the seeds of hate can be sown by a group that has similar attributes as another and the results are the same merciless slaughter of innocent people.

As we view the many accounts of the slaughter of innocents over time, including the ethnic cleansings and the genocides, it is hard to fathom as truth what Brigadier General S.L.A. Marshall, a military historian of WWII, is quoted as stating in his book, *Men Against Fire*. Marshall tells us that "The average healthy individual has such an inner usually unrealized resistance towards killing a fellow man that he will not of his own volition take a [human] life if it is possible to turn away from that responsibility." General Marshall was speaking about the history of military conflict and throughout history, it has been shown that given the opportunity in a life or death situation to turn away from killing, soldiers will not fire the fatal shot or inflict the fatal blow. How do we reconcile this body of work that points directly to man's extreme resistance to killing another human, with the unspeakable atrocities documented throughout the ages, including the genocide carried out by history's most infamous dictator, Adolph Hitler?

The Nazi Holocaust is the world's most documented genocide; survivors of brutal death camps like Auschwitz and Dachau continue to provide living testimony to the horrors inflicted upon a whole population. The story of the Nazi Holocaust, told in pictures, writings, and survivor accounts, is an extremely gruesome tale that often evokes visceral reactions when told. Universally, when speaking of the Holocaust, the question comes up, "How could this happen?" And in asking that question, it often evokes and equally disturbing question, "How could a nation, continent, and a world stand idly by?" As a race, we, as human beings, must stare into the face of horror and directly confront the individuals who took arms to unarmed civilians, forced executions en-masse by marching thousands of innocent people into gas chambers, and committed any number of unspeakable atrocities, apparently without hesitation or remorse. We stood by, mostly silent, but knowing—and that is the second devastating tragedy.

Even before his expressed hatred of the Jews was codified in *Mein Kampf*, Hitler was spreading the seeds of hatred and anti-Semitism across Germany and the region. Efforts to foment hatred against a group and to ultimately dehumanize a population start with characterizations of members of the group as comparable to objects that evoke disgust. The Nazi propaganda machine was "expert" at such portrayals by comparing Jews to "vermin." By mastering the techniques of teaching hate and the widespread characterizations of the Jewish people as subhuman, Hitler and his goose-stepping hate mongers began the steady march of Jews towards annihilation.

The genesis of such atrocities can begin when one person or group associates another person or group, in this case the Jews, with objects that evoke the primitive emotion of disgust. When this happens, the acceptance of the group as being immoral and worthy of hate is much easier and almost inevitable. Once established, there is a direct emotional link in the mind between visceral disgust of unpleasant objects and disgust for the morally repugnant. Research conducted at the University of Toronto showed a link between disgust related to poison and disease and moral disgust.[183] In this research, facial expressions made when participants tasted unpleasant liquids and looked at photographs of disgusting objects such as dirty toilets were compared to the participant's facial expressions made when they were treated unfairly in a laboratory game. Results showed that people make similar facial expressions in response to both primitive forms of disgust based on repugnant objects and moral disgust based on being treated unfairly by another. Lead author Hannah Chapman commented that the "research shows the involvement of disgust in morality, suggesting that moral judgment may depend as much on simple emotional processes as complex thought." Research involving brain scans using fMRI of people viewing faces of hated people and faces for whom there were neutral feelings showed activation during viewing of the hated faces of a unique pattern in brain. Part of this circuit for hate in the brain was activation of the right putamen, "a structure that has also been implicated in the perception of contempt and disgust."[184] It seems that disgust is the emotion of genocide and that when one group begins to express propaganda that characterizes another group as objects of disgust, we should be prepared to intervene.

In preparation for the eventual planned annihilation of Europe's Jews, the Nazis produced a film in 1940 called *Der Ewige Jude* (The Eternal Jew) that made a direct comparison of Jews to rats, including images of hordes of rats followed directly by images of Jews in the ghettos of Warsaw, Poland. The narrator states the rats are "cunning, cowardly, and cruel, and usually appear in massive hordes. They represent elements of sneakiness and subterranean destruction among animals just as the Jews do among mankind." By associating a group of people with objects of visceral disgust, moral disgust becomes an easy step to take. As we generally have no reservations about exterminating disgusting rats that threaten our home (although there are a small minority who would have reservations), we generally have the capacity to become at least indifferent to the demise of a group we find morally disgusting who pose a threat to us and, at most, we will participate in their destruction.

As we have seen previously, every human being is capable of unspeakable horrors given the right circumstances and training or indoctrination. In the face of unspeakable evil, we know that human beings are not unlike other species in that they have an innate resistance toward killing their own species. This is based on hundreds of millions of years of natural selection favoring the social nature of mammals and, in particular for humans, our capacity towards empathy. What leads to the path of killing and slaughter is a primitive brain function that allows for a person to regard another as less than human and thus easy to kill. This process stars with an "us vs. them" way of binary thinking, appealing to the powerful survival instincts of the limbic brain that pervades individual thought and permeates collectively across groups and large segments of society. The process of dehumanization of others, relatively easy when the other has already been classified as "them" by the limbic brain and morally disgusting, completely obliterates the one emotion that is critical to preventing senseless killing: *Empathy*. The Nazi genocide machine is a fantastic study in limbic brain binary thinking, moral disgust, dehumanization, and of the resultant ease of preparing one group of people for the slaughter of another group of people. The period of Nazi Germany also shows us how binary thinking, moral disgust, and dehumanization led to the indifference of entire nations and the world.

So we will in chapter nine dissect this atrocity and look deep into the eyes of hate to help us understand the genesis of such events and help to understand how it happened in Nazi Germany as well as Rwanda, Chechnya, and across the globe throughout history. We will reach the disturbing conclusion that the answer lies within each one of us.

Distance: Physical and Psychological

The earth can be a formidable place and at times impenetrable, except to a few hearty souls such as the legendary warrior Hannibal, who braved the Alps with his army of foot soldiers and a herd of elephants to try and conquer Rome. Or the brave souls who developed and boarded the first submarine during our nation's Civil War. The submarine, called the H.L. Hunley, successfully negotiated itself beneath the surface to maneuver in position and sink the USS Housatonic off the coast of Charleston harbor. Geography has kept countries isolated from war for centuries and has also imposed severe restrictions on armies that try to defy the elements and wage war across oceans, deserts, and mountains to battle on foreign soil. America has enjoyed just such geographical separation from invasion over her short lifespan since the War of 1812, which ended when the Japanese military put "Operation Z" into motion on December 7, 1941. The infamous attack on Pearl Harbor was the first attack on American soil in modern times and, up until the World trade Center bombings, the deadliest attack on American soil. Pearl Harbor was clear and convincing evidence to America that her borders were not impenetrable and geography, her best ally, had been defeated. America had been breached. In ancient times, geography played a much larger role in securing countries' borders and the people of a nation. As time marched forward, populations began to create distance by erecting walls, castles, forts, and other defensive structures, none as grand as the Great Wall of China. By some estimates, the Great Wall spans nearly 5,600 miles. The wall was erected in attempt to defend the northern border of China from invasion since the fifth century B.C. Geography can alienate cultures and societies; it can also place populations close together so that differences can be exacerbated, anger and hostility can rise up, and killing can take place at either side's convenience. Such is the nature of geography and its impact on war across history.

Distance and separation is of great importance as factors leading to war and atrocity not only because they can establish limiting boundaries between warring factions, but distance and separation also exacerbate differences in language and culture. Language barriers exist that can alienate populations even today. Separation, for our purposes, includes the example set above but, most importantly, it is comprised of that emotional distance that exists between two human beings. When we examine closely the capacity for humans to kill, research shows that, like other species, humans must overcome extreme internal resistance to kill another human being. Thus, when we reference distance and separation, we reference our physical distance and separation from others but, more importantly, our emotional distance that creates barriers to empathy.

It has been shown time and time again that it is easier to overcome man's reluctance to killing another if physical distance is increased. In his book, *On Killing*, Lieutenant Colonel Dave Grossman provides, by way of combat veteran testimony, the intense trauma most men experience who are called upon to kill at close range while staring at an adversary. Conversely, he sites examples of how, when the distance is increased, the repugnance and reluctance to kill may decrease also.

Unlike physical distance, psychological distance is not apparent on the surface to the untrained eye. Psychological distance, as we refer to it here, means the amount of emotional distance from another's humanity. More specifically, we can, as humans, relate to other members of our species as something other than human when they appear different from or are unfamiliar to us, especially when we feel threatened by the other group. We have abundant evidence through history that points to this ability to look at people and populations as not one of "us" but one of "them." In the most egregious of these instances, we have seen how one group of people may look upon another group and fail to acknowledge them as human. To this end, Hitler's propaganda machine began in the early years to call Jews a people of robbers and that Jews are a foreign people. Later, Hitler and his followers reached a critical point where Jews weren't even looked upon as human, but rather as *untermenschen*, or less than human. The creation of this psychological distance allows people to justify or rationalize a hostile act, even killing, once that threshold is crossed. Americans are not immune to this. We have many examples from our history, including the dehumanization of the Indians to the way we trained for war in recent conflicts by calling our enemies (including noncombatants) names like "gooks, slopes, towel heads" and the like. This has the effect of creating psychological distance for our soldiers that may help enable them to kill without serious concern, but it also has the repulsive downside that can cause whole societies to dehumanize, discriminate, and mistreat an entire population.

Chapter Seven
The Capacity for Evil

Evil is knowing better, but willingly doing worse.

- Philip Zimbardo

For centuries, society has recognized and been victimized by those with the capacity to kill with impunity and without conscience. In the early 1800s, psychiatrists called this affliction "moral insanity." By the end of the century, the term used was "psychopathic personality." Today, we also use the term, "sociopath." This term and the person it describes shield us from one of our deepest anxieties. Surely, no "sane person" could possibly commit any of the cruel and inhuman acts of barbarism that we were witness to. No human being could twist our sense of humanity to the extreme such that these atrocities are a natural result. "Sociopath," "psycho," "animal," and other such words are salve spread across an open wound that provides only temporary relief for our deepest anxieties. Newspaper and television accounts of mass murders and horrific events, when witnessed, can only lead to one conclusion: "The person who did this must be insane." For we, as civilized humans living together in a civilized society, cannot reconcile the evil we see prominently displayed across newspapers and in brilliant colors on our sixty-inch plasma televisions with any of our friends, neighbors, or any other acquaintance in our social circles. And as a parallel to this disbelief, we often discover that just below the surface, in small letters beneath the stark headlines and graphic photos, is a description of an average neighbor who "was by all accounts a nice guy, a hard worker who kept to himself and stopped to say hello when he was out raking in his yard."

We will continue to witness the daily killings that are overexposed in the media in addition to the millions upon millions of people slaughtered in ethnic cleansings, genocides, war, and other atrocities over the ages that are buried in our collective memories. Yet, trying to fathom the unthinkable and trying to come to grips with these facts causes us to come to the erroneous conclusion that such extreme atrocities must have been the handiwork of sociopaths or an evil soul. We bury the truth even as we are faced with the stark reality of our capacity as humans to kill.

"Sociopaths," in truth, make up a very small percentage of the world's population, somewhere between 1 and 4 percent. This number also includes the population that is diagnosed with Antisocial Personality Disorder, characterized by a lack of regard for the moral and legal standards of the local culture. The persons described as such may have the propensity to kill upon compulsion and without remorse, or they may limit their antisocial behavior to petty crimes and recklessness. This limited number of truly pathological "evil" people as compared to the magnitude of destruction wrought through wars and genocide leads us to a disturbing conclusion: All humans, notwithstanding an innate resistance to killing another human being, possess, under the right set of circumstances, the capacity to willingly kill after rational deliberation. All of us have the capacity to become temporary selective sociopaths when a particular person or group presents us with an existential threat, real or contrived, and such person or group has been sufficiently dehumanized.

Linsly-Chittenden Hall stands stoically on the Old Campus at Yale University situated on the West Side of New Haven Connecticut. This hallowed building is where Dr. Stanley Milgram conducted his now famous research experiments on obedience to authority. The genesis for this experiment was the controversial and highly publicized trial of Adolf Eichmann. Eichmann, a member of the Nazi party, served the Third Reich very well by assuming the leading role in the deportation of European Jews to death camps. The world sat transfixed to this "trial of the century," and wondered aloud, "How could this apparently normal man send millions of Jews to their death?" The "banality of evil" is the term that social philosopher Hannah Arendt used to describe the life of Eichmann and his nondescript business-like attitude towards the atrocities he committed.

Arendt detailed the Eichmann trial in her 1963 book, *Eichmann in Jerusalem: A Report on the Banality of Evil* and received international scorn for suggesting that Eichmann was a normal, functional bureaucrat and not a sadistic, psychotic monster who could not possibly function as a normal member of society. Eichmann stated emphatically, as so many other Nazi leaders had stated upon arrest and interrogation, "I was only following orders." Eichmann had also spent many sessions with multiple psychiatrists who all came to the same disturbing conclusion: Eichmann the "monster" was certified as "normal" in every respect. In fact, one of the examining psychiatrists emphatically stated that Eichmann was "more normal, at any rate, than I am after having examined him." Another had found that Eichmann's whole psychological outlook, his attitude toward his family and friends was "not only normal but most desirable." And finally, in Arendt's conclusion, she states, "The trouble with Eichmann was precisely that so many were like him, and that the many were neither perverted nor sadistic, that they were, and still are, terribly and terrifyingly normal."

This striking realization is a mere codification of the centuries of historical data that point conclusively to the fact that normal individuals across the globe are largely responsible for the terrorist acts, senseless violence, and even genocide inflicted upon societies. In truth, the question for society remains: Why did someone, apparently normal in intellect and mental capacity, commit acts that were repulsive to every accepted standard of human decency and morality? Did he and others act in self-preservation under compulsion of death or under other such oppressive conditions that he was left with no choice? As we shall see, a major factor leading to such acts of atrocity is obedience to authority without such compulsion as the threat of death. To help us understand this seemingly incomprehensible statement of fact, we will look to Dr. Stanley Milgram.

Dr. Milgram's landmark experiments set out to prove that average people and not sociopaths can, and do, commit acts that are counter to moral standards and beliefs given the right circumstances and under "obedience to authority." In essence, this experiment was targeting the age-old issue "Whether one should obey when commands conflict with conscience." To test his theory, Dr. Milgram conducted a set of experiments using volunteers from New Haven, Connecticut. Although many experiments use students as subjects, Dr. Milgram was concerned that the students would represent too homogenous a body; they were nearly all in their teens or early twenties, they were highly intelligent, and some had familiarity with psychological experimentation. So, it was decided that the volunteers would be selected from the nearly 300,000 people of the New Haven community. The volunteers were paid for their participation in a "study of memory and learning" and the group of volunteers ranged in education from one who had not completed high school to those who had advanced educational and professional degrees. The occupational makeup of the group included skilled and unskilled laborers, white collar workers, and business professionals. The volunteers were brought into the Interaction Laboratory of Yale University. The experiment required three people to perform. Two of the participants were actually collaborators in the experiment, briefed prior to the start of the experiment for playing their designated roles of "experimenter" and "learner." The third participant was not a role player and as such was the actual subject of the experiment in the role of "teacher." The "teacher" was led to believe he or she is merely assisting in a memory experiment involving the "learner" as the subject of the experiment when in fact the "teacher" was the real subject of the experiment. The experiment began by designating one of the participants a "teacher" and the other a "learner." These designations appeared to be randomly assigned; however, the participant designated as the "learner" was in reality one of the preselected active role players. The other active role player was the official-looking person in the grey lab coat, the "experimenter" who was in control of the experiment. The "teacher," the actual subject of the experiment, was led to believe he or she was randomly selected for that role. Prior to beginning the experiment, a drawing was conducted to see which participant will be the "learner" and which will be the "teacher." The drawing was rigged so that a new "teacher" is cycled through every test and the "learner," as an active role player, remains constant. This outcome was achieved simply by placing two slips of paper in a bucket to be drawn at random by the two participants. Both slips of paper had the word "teacher" written on it, guaranteeing the outcome (since the preselected role playing "learner" merely ignored his slip of paper that stated "teacher" and pretended he drew the "learner" designation).

The experiment was designed to observe how normal human beings react to authority figures when asked to do something that conflicts with his or her conscience, something that is repulsive and against set standards of morality. The premise for the experiment was a simple word match game whereby the "teacher" recites pairs of words to the learner who must memorize them and, when asked, must try to recall the correct matching pairs based on a choice of four possible correct matching pairs. For each wrong answer, the "learner" was administered an electric shock by the "teacher," the electric shock increased incrementally in strength.

The experiment began by having the learner (a role-playing collaborator in the real experiment) escorted to an adjacent room where he was hooked up by electrical wires to an electric shock machine. The teacher was brought along to observe the hook-up and even received an actual electric shock as a sample of the punishment he or she was about to administer. The experimenter explained to both teacher and learner that the shocks may be extremely painful; however, they will not cause permanent tissue damage. The learner, with the wires attached to his arms, then remains out of sight from the teacher, who returned to his or her position in the other room (proximity of teacher to learner is varied in other test phases). Unbeknownst to the teacher, the learner will not actually receive any form of shock when the teacher toggles the switch to shock the learner, because the machine is a nonfunctioning prop for the experiment. In fact, the learner, once the teacher leaves the room, will get up and leave and the responses to the questions from the teacher in the other room will be in the form a recording.

The teacher then sat in front of a large box, the shock initiator, which has a series of toggle switches arrayed in a straight line across the front. The shock initiator is designed, as believed by the teacher, to deliver a shock each time one of the toggle switches is depressed. Each toggle switch represents a corresponding number of volts that would be delivered to the learner when depressed by the teacher upon receiving an incorrect answer form the learner. The array of toggles starts with 15 volts and incrementally increases by 15 volts left to right up to a maximum of 450 volts. In addition, there are warnings written on the box that provide the teacher with an explicit description of what would happen to the learner if the switch were toggled. These warnings also increased in seriousness from left to right: "slight shock, moderate shock, strong shock, very strong shock, intense shock, extreme intensity shock, danger: severe shock XXX."

The experiment was a very simple conceptual design that required the teacher to toggle a switch and thus deliver a shock in increasing strength to the learner every time the learner answered a question wrong. The questions were designed so that the learner would provide the wrong answer most of the time.

Prior to conducting experiment, several graduate students were asked what percent of teachers in this experiment would go ahead to the end and deliver a shock that could prove fatal by toggling the switch marked "XXX" at the high end of the voltage array. This would equate to a corresponding shock containing 450 volts of electricity. The graduate students were in general agreement that perhaps 1 to 2 percent of the individuals would in fact deliver a potentially fatal shock. If this question was asked broadly today, we feel a similar response of 1 to 2 percent would be given, reflecting a vast disconnect by the majority of the population that believes we are, as normal functioning human beings, incapable of acts that intentionally cause an innocent person to suffer grave injury or die. Most of us want to believe that only 1 to 2 percent of the population would be willing to administer this type of injury on another human. This concept generally aligns with the fact that approximately 1-4 percent of the population are sociopaths.

The teacher and learner were in separate rooms but close enough to clearly hear the questions and responses. Close enough also to hear cries of pain from the learner upon receiving a shock. The teacher begins the simple word association test that is designed to elicit wrong answers. If the answer to the question is incorrect, the teacher toggles the switch that delivers a shock to the learner in the amount of volts inscribed above the toggle switch. To add to the reality and trauma of the event, the learner (actually a recording of the learner) upon the toggle switch being thrown, would give an audible grunt as if in pain from the shock he had received from the teacher. Every time a question was answered incorrectly, a stronger shock was delivered and an increasingly intense scream of pain was heard from the other room. At different points in the question and answer routine, the learner would object to the experiment, state he has a heart condition, and express his desire to quit. When this happened, the experimenter in the lab coat would calmly tell the teacher to continue on with the experiment. Many of the participants in fact continued on delivering shocks despite the verbal protests, the screams of pain, and the clear and present danger to life that were the apparent result of their actions. Oftentimes, the teachers would verbalize their concerns about continuing on in the process and after reassuring words from the experimenter, would increase the voltage and deliver the shock.

In the end, incredibly, 65 percent of the teachers in this experiment willingly delivered a shock in the severe range that was considered to be extremely dangerous or even fatal to a human being. The only compulsion they suffered was the obedience to the authority figure in charge of the experiment.

Similarly, the combat soldier facing the enemy on the frontline levels his weapon to sight in his enemy and hesitates to pull the trigger. History has shown us he is reluctant to pull the trigger to kill another human being but the mere order to fire from his sergeant is enough for the soldier to overcome his doubts and take a life. This task of killing gets easier and the hesitation disappears in relation to increasing spatial and psychological distance from the enemy combatant. Milgram modified the test parameters to measure the effect of proximity on the teacher's willingness to deliver a shock to the learner. He accomplished this by situating the learner in the same room a few feet from the subject; thus, the teacher could hear and see the responses to his or her shocks. Another modification to test proximity put the teacher and learner in the same room next to each other and required the learner to place his hand on a shock plate to receive the shock. At the 150-volt level, the learner would refuse to place his hand on the shock plate, thus requiring the teacher to physically place the subject's hand on the shock plate to receive the shock. Amazingly, under circumstances that require the teacher to physically place the learner's hand onto a shock plate, 30 percent delivered a shock at the maximum level, and the median shock level for this portion of the experiment where teachers refused to continue was nearly 270 volts, or the "intense shock" level. Think for a moment what this tells us about obedience to authority. When told by an authority figure to grab someone's hand, place it in contact with a metal plate and toggle a swatch to give them a shock of 450 volts that is extremely painful and possibly fatal, 30 percent of the participants complied. And when the learner was in another room, out of sight from the teacher, the 450-volt shock was delivered by a staggering 65 percent of the teachers.

We have clear and convincing evidence that, given the right circumstances, in this case obedience to authority, a human can and will commit acts of extreme cruelty upon another human. Understandably, this experiment caused great concern regarding the ethics of carrying out a test of human morality in such a manner and, as disturbing as the context may be, this experiment has been replicated in various parts of the world with similarly disturbing results. Our lessons in inhumanity have been taught through the ages and through countless experiments, including Dr. Stanley Milgram's "shocking" experiments. Such experiments provide us with the validation some have needed as to our capacity to deliberately inflict harm on an innocent person under the right social pressures. This validation is key to moving towards a true, "final solution" to senseless violence and killing because it provides a firm, scientific basis for what history has taught us for generations: given the right motivations, circumstances and conditions, all humans harbor the capacity for purposeful destruction of others.

We have seen many examples of the human capacity for evil. We have also seen the workings of the primitive mind and its innate ability to respond to real or perceived threats. It is time now to examine how we tend to treat others in captivity. We historically have looked upon our captives and prisoners with abject contempt, as mere objects unworthy of care, compassion, and any semblance of decency. Through the ages, there have been many prisons and prison camps, jails and holding facilities where guards, assigned to keep good order, often violated the rules of human decency and, in some cases, committed atrocities upon their captives. No prison camps are as infamous as the death camps of Nazi Germany. But to show the naked truth about our capacity to brutalize those in our custody, we need not sink to the lowest level of depravation and explore such hell holes as Dachau, Auschwitz-Birkenau, Treblinka, or Sobibor. To understand the nature of humans to abuse and brutalize fellow humans, we need look no further that our own backyard.

The place we speak of is a makeshift detention facility built specifically for one purpose—housing criminals. All the trappings of a good prison are present and in place. There are prison cells with bars across the doors and not a window to be found to let light inside the darkened rooms. The solitary confinement area or "hole" is the size of a closet, about two feet wide and two feet deep, barely enough room for a person to stand erect. The recreation area, called the "yard" is nothing more than a hallway for the prisoners to stretch their legs on short, confined walks. This prison is a perfectly constructed asylum that takes away privacy and individual freedoms. It is a model facility where even the sense of time is taken away with not one clock visible and nothing but bare walls and covered windows that provide the captives with a very limited sense of the hour of the day or even if it was day or night.

Once arrested by the police and transported to the prison in handcuffs, the prisoners are brought into the prison blindfolded, not knowing where they are or what lies in wait for them inside. They are all marched in a straight line under the guard's command into the heart of the facility where they are systematically processed into the prison. They are stripped naked and searched in full view of the guards and immediately sprayed down like animals in a process called "delousing," to be sure they don't have any germs or lice that may infect others. Some of the guards make offhand remarks about the prisoner's penis size or unevenly hanging testicles, which elicit nervous laughter. After the intake process, all the prisoners are given a "uniform," which is no more than a smock to wear over their exposed flesh. In this prison, they wear a women's nylon stocking over their head to conceal their hair and, finally, a heavy chain is placed tight around the prisoners' right ankles, bolted on, and worn at all times, even in their fitful attempts to sleep.

The guards at this prison receive no specific training on prisoner detention, although they are obligated to keep good order within the prison at all times. The guards work day and night to watch over the prisoners. They are free to make up their own set of rules, including decisions on discipline, when and as needed, for the maintenance of security and good order. The guards are instructed to take precautions for their own safety and that their job is worthy of considerable attention to the dangers it may entail. The guards are rotated through three shifts over a twenty-four-hour period and quickly learn how to deliver punishment to keep the prisoners in line.

In this prison, minor punishments are doled out for real or perceived infractions and quickly turn to into blatant prisoner abuse as guards try and one-up each other's punishments. Oftentimes, prisoners are ordered to engage in physical activity such as pushups in the form of punishment. Prisoners are also routinely rousted from their beds in the middle of the night for specious head counts at the guards' beckon call. At times, the guards push and shove the prisoners. On one occasion, the guards have the prisoners bend over, exposing their bare backsides and tell the other prisoners to get behind them and "hump them like camels." Sexual innuendo and references pervade punishments that are given randomly with seemingly no purpose or adherence to standards. Often, the prisoners are separated with sacks placed over their heads to keep them from any communication or observation of their surroundings. With sack over their heads, they are ushered out to the yard in a single file, chained like the infamous chain gangs seen years past alongside the highway cutting grass or picking up litter.

Stripped naked, deloused, blindfolded, and subjected to physical abuse, some of these prisoners opted out of the *experiment*. That's correct, the description above is not of one of the most recognizable prison systems of our times, Abu Ghraib; rather, it is a prison erected in 1971 in the hallowed halls of Stanford University. The Stanford Prison Experiment, like the Stanley Milgram Obedience to Authority experiment, caused ripples through the world of psychology and sociology and forced us to rethink our core beliefs about basic human nature.

The Stanford Prison Experiment, conducted in the summer of 1971, was designed to see what happens when good people are put into a bad place. Is the basic human condition good or evil? Amazingly, the experiment was planned to run for two weeks, but it only lasted just six days as the guards became more abusive and sadistic towards the prisoners and the prisoners showed signs of clinical depression and extreme stress. To select the participants in this experiment, an ad was placed in two local newspapers and about 100 respondents applied. The 100 respondents were whittled down through interviews and psychological assessments to a final group of twenty-four. All were healthy male college students of average intelligence.

The selection process to determine who would be a guard and who would be a prisoner was done randomly by the toss of a coin. It should be noted that all the participants had originally expressed a desire to be a prisoner for the duration of the experiment. These randomly assigned, middle class college students took to their roles with fervor. The guards worked hard to keep good order and the prisoners did all they could to avoid punishment and abuse. This all took place in a sterile environment under the watchful eyes of the observers and became all too real, all too fast, even for the principal investigator, Philip Zimbardo, who got caught up in his role as the prison warden. In the end, the experiment, originally planned to run for two weeks, was abruptly halted after just six days. Much has been written about the Stanford Prison Experiment, in fact, as was suggested by Zimbardo in his book, *The Lucifer Effect*, we logged onto the Google website, typed in the word "experiment," and the Stanford Prison Experiment was listed as the second-ranked website in the world.

There are many conclusions we can reach about human nature and our ability to objectively control our actions and emotions in certain dependent situations. Like the Milgram Obedience Experiment, the Stanford Prison Experiment paints a very vivid picture of the human capacity for evil. Zimbardo writes:

> The Stanford Prison Experiment, along with other social science research, reveals a message we do not mean to accept: that most of us can undergo significant character transformations when we are caught up in the crucible of social forces. What we imagine we would do when we are outside that crucible may bear little resemblance to who we become and what we are capable of doing once we are inside its network....this lesson should have been taught repeatedly by the behavioral transformation of Nazi concentration camp guards, and of those in destructive cults, such as Jim Jones's Peoples Temple.... The genocide and atrocities committed in Bosnia, Kosovo, Rwanda, Burundi, and recently in Sudan's Darfur region, also provide strong evidence of people surrendering their humanity and compassion.... Any deed that any human being has ever committed, however horrible, is possible for any of us."

Conclusions drawn from this experiment and put forth thus far seem to focus on the surroundings or prison environment as the de facto cause of the psychological damage brought about in this experiment. Although the environment is a major factor in this eventuality, as we have seen, there is ample evidence of other factors that affect our capacity as humans to commit these abuses. Understanding all these factors is the key to unlocking the door of peace.

Let us now fast forward to a place and time far removed from the heart of Silicon Valley and the quiet, bucolic campus of Stanford University. Abu Ghraib Prison is located about 22 miles west of Baghdad, within the Sunni triangle, in the heart of war-torn Iraq. To some, Abu Ghraib, meaning the "Place of Ravens," is appropriately named after an "ill omen." Abu Ghraib Prison was originally built by British contractors in the 1950s. The prison had a long and sordid history even before coalition forces rebuilt the crumbling structure to house military prisoners and terrorist suspects from the Iraq War. During Saddam Hussein's reign in Iraq, the western media dubbed the prison, "Saddam Hussein's Torture Central." It is the place where Saddam ordered twice-weekly public executions of "dissidents." For the people of Iraq, Abu Ghraib Prison was the symbol of an evil regime, a place where many friends, family members, and neighbors were brought to and never returned from.

In early 2003, U.S. forces took control of the infamous prison and put it back on the map as an infamous place once again. The rebuilt prison was under the command of an army reserve brigadier general and members of the 372nd

Military Police Company were assigned day-to-day operations as prison guards. The members of this unit were, by all accounts, given no operational guidelines, policies, or even specific instructions on how to accomplish this task—a recipe for disaster. The prison population consisted of Iraqi citizens who were charged with crimes against coalition forces and those who had been picked up in house sweeps or at military checkpoints for "suspicious activity." The population also included whole families who were kept for interrogation. In addition, there were persons brought in without any identification or description, being held by other federal agencies for interrogation. CIA, FBI, contract personnel, and other civilian and federal law enforcement personnel streamed in and out of the prison, often with unnamed or unidentified prisoners in tow, held for further interrogation. The untrained, poorly supervised prison guards intermingled with these shadowy interrogators, who oftentimes lavished them with praise for their ability to "soften up" prisoners for interrogation.

What happened at Abu Ghraib over a short span of time shocked the world. Military leaders expressed disgust and disbelief as the pictures of abuse surfaced on major news outlets across the globe. These same leaders were quick to conclude and exclaim to the entire world that a "few bad apples" were responsible for the abuse and they would be held accountable.

The abuses committed at Abu Ghraib prison at the hands of United States military personnel were indeed shocking, disturbing, and inhumane; however, given the environment these untrained, unsupervised men and women were placed into, the outcome should not have been unexpected. Young men and women were left in charge of an overcrowded prison, in a combat zone in a foreign land. The prisoners were terrorists and unlawful combatants believed responsible for the deaths of innocent civilians and American soldiers. Very few had any corrections experience, certainly not the type of prison experience that could prepare them for Abu Ghraib and its unique prison population. There were no formal rules or regulations to use for guidance or instruction, and the military failed to provide direct supervision and oversight of these men and women as they attempted to carry out their undefined mission. In addition, there was constant pressure exerted on the guards from interrogators, who bore no responsibility for the safety of the prisoners, to "soften them up" for interrogations. This was a situation ripe for abuse. As Zimbardo states, the Abu Ghraib Prison scandal was not the result of a few bad apples but a "bad barrel." As shown in the Stanford Prison Experiment and Milgram Obedience Experiment, normal, functioning human beings can, and will, commit morally repulsive acts when certain environmental influences are present, particularly when whatever authority figure is present defaults on its responsibility to maintain basic moral and ethical conditions or, in the worst case, sanctions and encourages inhumane treatment.

Chapter Eight
Bias to Atrocity

He is a man with tens of thousands of blind followers.
It is my business to make some of those blind followers see.

- Abraham Lincoln

Bias involves automatic stereotypic associations of the unconscious mind. Bias is a deeply rooted survival instinct that is part of normal human development. The bias that leads to atrocity usually starts innocently as an unconscious negative bias that we do not consciously seek and its effects—avoidance and discrimination—are not our conscious intention.

Unconscious bias is rooted in our limbic system, which stereotypes based on perceived threats. "Scores of studies now support the essentially automatic aspect of stereotyping."[185] This negative bias, on the subconscious level, automatically identifies an individual, group, gender, religion, nationality, ethnicity, or race as dangerous and to be avoided. This automatic stereotyping by the limbic system results in a tendency to avoid the subjects of bias or to take actions against individuals based on the unconscious belief that they are dangerous, bad, or otherwise a threat to us. Brain imaging studies have shown "amygdala activation in response to pictures of unfamiliar out-group faces, indicating what may be primitive emotional prejudices."[186] It is the amygdala, part of the limbic system, which generates our negative emotions.

Unconscious negative bias manifests subtlety through the actions or inactions of the offender. Contemporary examples of this include racial profiling by police, unfair lending practices, as well as housing and employment discrimination. These contemporary issues cause great tension between those expressing this bias and the individual or group that is subjected to it. Historically, unconscious negative bias has been the first step in the progression to segregation, war, and even genocide. In America, we have struggled with bias since the days of the earliest settlers. The treatment of Native Americans is a long, sordid chapter in our history that paints a clear picture of how bias can cause us to create schisms between cultures that can lead to disharmony, hatred, and war. Another prominent example of the dark path that unconscious negative bias can take us down occurred two months after the Japanese attack on Pearl Harbor, when President Roosevelt signed Executive Order 9066. This now infamous order authorized the internment of over one hundred thousand of American citizens of Japanese ancestry as well as resident aliens from Japan. In addition, American citizens of Italian or German descent were also rounded up and interned but in much smaller numbers. This overtly racist action was deemed necessary and appropriate to protect "American citizens." Its constitutionality was eventually challenged and upheld by the United States Supreme Court (See Toyosaburo Korematsu v. United States, 323 U.S. 214 [1944]). This Supreme Court decision has not been overturned and still stands as the law of the land today.

Forty-three years later, the congress and the president, recognizing the unjust treatment received by Japanese American citizens as a result of Executive Order 9066, enacted the Civil Liberties Act of 1988. This act acknowledged the injustice of the internments and also authorized the payment of reparations to the affected families. In addition to congressional passage of the act, President Ronald Reagan sent a letter to each family stating in part, "In passing the Civil Liberties Act of 1988, we acknowledge the wrongs of the past.... In retrospect, we understand that the nation's actions were rooted deeply in racial prejudice, wartime hysteria, and lack of political leadership."

As a nation, the United States looked back in time at the outrageous treatment of those interned during the war. Through a clear lens—by this we mean high order thinking—it became obvious to all, especially our political leaders, that this was a decision based in prejudice, made "acceptable" by wartime hysteria. The question for all of us as a nation and as a global society is a simple one: Given a similar set of circumstances today, would our nation or any nation for that matter, and its leaders, make similar decisions based on a limbic, primitive brain response that is initially fueled by unconscious bias? Suffering another devastating terrorist attack such as the attack on the world Trade Center in New York City and the Pentagon, would the president issue an executive order similarly interning Muslim American citizens during the pendency of the war on terror? Reflecting on events that have transpired since the attack, the answer certainly appears elusive and not so simple. Since the attacks of 9/11, the United States has enacted many pieces of legislation designed specifically to equip our federal, state, and local authorities with the tools they need to thwart terrorists within our borders and throughout the world. Specifically, we should consider the post 9/11 law known as the "Uniting and Strengthening America by Providing Appropriate Tools Required to Intercept and Obstruct Terrorism Act" (P.A.T.R.I.O.T.). This legislation was passed shortly after the 9/11 attacks and dramatically increased the capabilities of federal, state, and local law enforcement to search, without a warrant, phone records, financial records, and other data that had been rigorously guarded by the constitution prior to the passage of the act. Many civil rights groups claim this law to be an infringement on protected civil liberties and believe it opens the door to unwarranted invasions of privacy and activities protected by the First Amendment.

This limbic system bias is also partly responsible for an apparent paradox in today's society: As a whole, members of society condemn overt prejudice in the strongest terms and yet acts of blatant racism still occur. Research by York University (Toronto), University of British Columbia, and Yale University suggests that "Although people predicted that they would be very upset by a racist act, when people actually experienced this event, they showed relatively little emotional distress."[187] According to the study, "People overestimated the degree to which a racist comment would provoke social rejection of the racist. These findings suggest that racism may persevere in part because people who anticipate feeling upset and believe that they will take action may actually respond with indifference when faced with an act of racism." We feel that this indifference is due to the fact that there is an unconscious bias working in advance to influence our reactions and to dampen our anticipated conscious rejection of overt racism. This bias is promoted and put forth by our primitive limbic system and sets the table for our actions following the perceived event. On the road to atrocity, this indifference in the face of overt racism is a major milestone. This indifference, if not confronted, will lead towards desensitization, dehumanization, deindividuation, and directly to the next step on the road to atrocity. In order to negate this primitive unconscious bias, we must counter this bias with our neocortical, higher order thinking, including *neocortical empathy*—the deliberate conscious effort to see and experience the humanness of another person.

Unconscious bias is the first step on the road to atrocity. It is a product of our primitive brain's hard wiring and prepares for us a fertile soil for the planting of the next step—*hate*. Holocaust survivor and Nobel Peace Prize winner, Elie Wiesel, spoke of the extreme power of hate in his essay titled, "We Choose Honor." Wiesel, a Holocaust survivor, states, "Hatred is the root of evil everywhere. Racial hatred, ethnic hatred, political hatred, religious hatred. In its name, all seems permitted. For those who glorify hatred, as terrorists do, the end justifies all means, including the most despicable ones. If they could, fanatics of violence would slaughter all those who do not adhere to their ideological or religious principles." Elie Wiesel wrote this essay shortly after the September 11 attacks on the World Trade Center in New York City and Pentagon to remind the world what hate leads to.

Hate, devastating for many reasons, begins within our brain's limbic system. The limbic system acts primitively to identify individuals of different groups, religions, nationalities, and ethnicities as dangerous and a direct threat to our survival and reproductive interests. Once classified by the brain as a threat, use of force, aggression, and violence is justified to remove the perceived threat. In *step-two*, we now have the limbic system working in conjunction with the neocortical brain that ascribes meaning to this threat identification. As explained by Rush W. Dozier, Jr., "The human limbic system poses a special danger because of its extensive connections to the neocortex, allowing us to fuse hatred and violence with the highest capacity of the human mind: meaning."[188] Dozier goes on to say, "Meaning, rather than instinct, is so overwhelmingly important to our species…that our limbic system has evolved a powerful tendency to blindly interpret any meaning system that we deeply believe in as substantially enhancing our survival and reproduction."[189] When this happens, devastating consequences can result. Corruption of our meaning system is like planting a nuclear weapon inside the mind. Terrorist leaders can carefully craft a meaning system, such as their extremist ideology, in a way that can radicalize hundreds and thousands of individuals to believe another group is worthy of destruction. When hate starts to pervade our meaning system, we witness such signs as overt racism, religious intolerance, unprovoked aggression or violence, and a total lack of empathy and indifference to suffering to the target of the hate.

With a head start through our unconscious bias and the attachment of meaning to hate, many extremists and fanatics easily weave a web of intolerance and rejection as they work to teach hate. Teaching hate is particularly effective on children and young adults who do not possess strong impulse control and are easily indoctrinated into the culture of hate. Studies have shown that the brain's frontal lobe area is the last part of the brain to fully develop in humans. This impulse control area is still developing and maturing in adolescents, sometimes into their early twenties. Conversely, the primitive limbic system is matured by the time a child reaches the age of five. As we know from our educational systems, children's minds are like sponges, absorbing everything they see and hear. Rest assured that if we know it, the terrorists know it, too.

A particularly striking example of this paradigm in effect is witnessed in this disturbing interview on Jaam-e Jam television, Iran.[190] This interview takes place during the "Jerusalem Day Parade" on September 25, 2008:

Interviewer: "What's your boy's name, and how old is he?"
Father: "Soheli is one year old."
Interviewer: "Why did you bring him along?"
Father: "In order to inject into his blood loathing for Israel from an early age."
Interviewer: (Now speaking to an eight-year-old boy) "What is your name, my boy?"
Boy: "Mohammad" (Holding sign).
Interviewer: "Your sign says, 'Death to Israel.' Why did you come here today?"
Boy: "In order to…."
Interviewer: "To say, 'Death to Israel'? Go ahead."

Boy: "Death to Israel."

Interviewer: "Well done. It's very interesting that little children, like this girl and boy, are already experiencing the culture of unity and solidarity, alongside their parents and fellow citizens."

According to Dozier, "The hater sees someone, first and foremost, as a stereotype. Unique individual qualities are of little or no importance.... Hatred can be expressed in many ways, depending on the circumstances: through anger, rage, contempt, mockery, disgust, avoidance, indignation, or stony silence."

It is interesting to discover how deeply rooted the emotion of hatred is in our brain system. Researchers at the University College of London have identified a "hate circuit" in the brain. Subjects were undergoing MRI brain scans (which show brain activity) while being shown pictures of a hated person and pictures of neutral people that were familiar to the subject.[191] When shown the pictures of hated persons, the brain activated areas of the cortex and sub-cortex evidencing high order thinking. In particular, areas of the frontal cortex were activated that involve judgment, reasoning, predicting the actions of others, and motor planning. At the same time, the anger and fear emotion-generating amygdala and hippocampus areas of the brain were not activated. Also not activated was the orbitofrontal cortex involved in impulse control. Activity was also shown in the putamen, a part of the subcortical system involved in the perception of contempt and disgust and conditions in which cognitive planning is required to trigger a motor act. Lastly, activation also included the insula, which is involved in the expressions of disgust and the appraisal of disagreeable stimuli. What is interesting to note is that the activation of the putamen and insula correspond closely to the activation of the same areas seen in romantic love.

While the patterns differ for hate and romantic love insofar as the cortex, the linkage of hate and romantic love in activation of the putamen and insula, "may account for why love and hate are so closely linked to each other in life."[192] The study authors believe "that in the context of hate, the hater may want to exercise judgment in calculating moves to harm, injure, or otherwise extract revenge."[193] This observation appears to validate the concept of attaching meaning to hate. In essence, when humans attach hate to a meaning system, it involves the high order thinking process and works to eliminate the source of the hatred, whether it be a person, nation, or entire racial or religious group.

The study also provides preliminary neurological evidence for the differentiated levels of culpability for unlawful killing under the criminal law in the United States. Voluntary manslaughter or the killing of another in "the heat of passion" is the least culpable form of killing, which recognizes the power of emotional limbic thinking to override the more reasoned, analytic, and restrained deliberative process involving the "thinking" neocortical brain. The laws punish most severely, including up to death in certain jurisdictions, murder "in cold blood," or murder committed with "deliberately premeditated malice aforethought." This type of murder, most commonly referred to as "murder in the first degree," is subject to the greatest punishment meted out by the judicial system, specifically because the killing was done after the individual had time to think about and deliberate his or her conduct. The phrase "in cold blood" also is descriptive of the neurological findings in the study that show the lack of activation of the limbic system areas involved in the generation of emotion but activation of areas of the frontal lobes involved in planning. There is much anecdotal evidence that when persons are engaged in carrying out deadly violence, there seems to be a lack of emotive content and even a calmness while the person is still able to concentrate and focus on completing the task at hand. The Israelis, probably the most experienced in dealing with suicide bombers, have referred to suicide bombers in the final steps of the act as "the walking dead" because of their calmness and lack of emotion.

Dr. Ariel Merari, head of the Center for Political Violence at Tel Aviv University, has studied every suicide bombing in the Middle East for an eighteen-year period, beginning with the bombing of the U.S. Marine barracks in Beirut, Lebanon, in 1983. Merari says the only abnormal thing about the suicide bomber is, at a certain point, a total absence of fear. Merari states, "I don't know of a single case of a person who is really psychotic. And still, this absolute absence of fear, I doubt it is a general personality characteristic. I doubt that this person under any circumstances would be fearless."[194]

Nineteen-year-old Palestinian Murad Tawalbi, from a refugee camp near the West Bank town of Jenin, was arrested on his way to blow himself up in a crowded marketplace. He was recruited by his older brother. "He wasn't trying to make me wear an explosive belt. He was giving me a ticket to heaven. Because he loves me, he wants me to become a martyr. Because martyrdom is the most exalted thing in our religion. Not just anyone gets the chance to become a martyr.... I was very happy. I was waiting for the time to come. I was counting the seconds before I went down. I felt very calm, as if nothing were happening.... I was just thinking about saving the Palestinian people. That's all. I never felt so calm in my life. It was the will of God."[195]

Merari's research and Tawalbi's story show, in additional to the paradoxical calmness associated with planned hate-inspired murder, how hate and other situational variables can drive healthy normal people to commit acts of mass murder and suicide. Tawalbi's mission, as hard as it is to see for us, was, if it is possible to analyze in a truly detached manner, an act of altruism. Many, if not the vast majority of people outside his culture, would not accept the notion of the mission as altruistic and most likely vigorously object to such a notion. It is this resistance to a detached and analytic view of purposeful and deliberate aggression by our opponents that is one of the greatest impediments to our ability to understand and prevent such acts. Just as we Westerners are hated by groups such as extremist Islamic terror groups, we hate them. Just as such extremist groups fail to see out point of view and engage in empathy, so do we. Although the conduct of targeting civilians in suicide bombings is morally wrong, the people involved in promoting and carrying out such acts are completely righteous about their conduct and not only believe it is justified but an imperative for their existence.

In Tawalbi's case, the natural resistance to killing was overcome by hate and dehumanization of the Israelis, an existential crisis—the survival of his in-group, sanctioning by political and religious authority, and to an appeal to his self-esteem. Tawalbi's instinct for survival was overcome by an appeal to kin altruism, the survival of his kinsmen, and therefore, many of his genes from an evolutionary biological perspective, and by his belief in the survival of his soul and entry in Paradise. Tawalbi illustrates the relative ease involved, during a perceived existential crisis, in programing normal people to commit acts of violence and mass murder motivated by altruism and sense of duty to one's in-group. Behind every war and genocide are the masses of people like Tawalbi—average and psychologically normal people in the midst of a crisis driven by hate and other situational variables to violence or at least to indifference towards the suffering of the out-group identified as the source of the crisis. Sometimes, the aggression results from a personal existential crisis directed at a particular person, as in the case of Clara Harris.

During the evening of July 24, 2002, in Houston, Texas, Clara Harris and her stepdaughter, Lindsey, were driving in Clara's Mercedes Benz looking for Clara's husband, David Harris.[196] That morning, David had sworn to Clara that he would end an affair with his former office coworker, Gail Bridges. Clara had hired a private detective and discovered the affair. She was intent on winning him back and during the week before that evening, had visited a tanning salon, beauty shop, and gym and consulted with a plastic surgeon about breast implants. According to Lindsay, Clara made herself "real pretty so Dad would want her and not Gail." That evening, Clara found David in the lobby of a hotel with Gail, hand-in-hand—the same hotel where they were married a decade earlier. Clara went "ballistic" and attacked Gail, ripping off Gail's blouse and wrestling her to the ground. David separated the two women and a clerk escorted Clara out of the hotel.

It was then that Clara Harris became strangely calm, according to her stepdaughter, Lindsey, who accompanied her out of the hotel. Clara silently got into her Mercedes, and her tears stopped flowing. Clara was cool and composed as she suddenly stomped on the accelerator and rammed the car into her husband. She ran over him again and again.[197]

It appears Clara's rage was fueled by her limbic system based on a threat to her reproductive fitness, one of the prime directives of the emotional brain. If her husband, David, preferred Gail, then it meant, in her mind, that she was inferior as a potential mate to David. When her attempts to make herself more desirable failed, her response to the provocation of seeing David and Gail together was now uncontrolled and resulted in extreme anger. When the anger dissipated, hate quickly took control and its neural circuitry profoundly altered her behavior and thinking. David was a threat to her basic needs of reproductive fitness and would be eliminated—coolly, calmly, and deliberately.

There is no shortage of irony when the human mind reconciles the conflict between the powerful limbic brain impulses of survival and reproductive fitness with reality. The destruction of David, the threat to Clara's overriding need to be reproductively fit, destroyed the very person with whom she desired to share her reproductive fitness. Her emotional brain could not accept the rejection by David which translated into a rejection of her reproductive fitness. Her cognitive mind rationalized the threat not as being the result of her own shortcomings but as the result of an affront by David which had to be eliminated.

Hate is sufficient to allow for an individual to believe it is imperative to eliminate another person based upon a threat to survival or reproductive fitness directly attributable to the other person. For an individual to believe that it is imperative to eliminate a whole class of people with the destruction of members of the class justified simply by being a member class, without any specific conduct by members of the class directed against the individual, something more than hate is needed. That something is the *dehumanization* of members of a whole class of human beings.

The third step in the road to atrocity is when hate combines with dehumanization. Once the group that has been the subject of hate has been dehumanized, actual violence against members of the group can often become routine. This is the stage when binary, "us versus them" thinking takes over the consciousness. The results are usually catastrophic. A complete lack of empathy towards the victims is present at this stage, and victims are looked upon as less than human; mere objects to be disposed of.

Zimbardo tells us, "Dehumanization is one of the central processes in the transformation of ordinary, normal people into indifferent or even wanton perpetrators of evil." When we dehumanize, we are acknowledging to ourselves as individuals and collectively as a group that the person standing in front of us is "not human." As incredible as this may sound, history is replete with examples of atrocity and genocide, all of which embrace the concept of dehumanization. This process of dehumanization is critical for those in power to effectively gain the participation of those needed to carry out the killings, and those needed to stand idly by. In one of the most brutal examples of mass slaughter, during the "Rape of Nanking," the Japanese imperial army marched into China's capital city and proceeded to murder 300,000 soldiers and civilians over a six-week period. Film footage taken by occupying Japanese soldiers show unspeakable horrors: soldiers practicing their bayonet strikes on civilians, decapitating them and displaying their heads as trophies. Eyewitness accounts were so outrageous in their depiction that the Americans were in disbelief. A Japanese general was reported to say that it was easy for his soldiers to brutally massacre civilians because "We thought of them as things, not like us." Dehumanization allowed the entire Japanese imperial army to slaughter soldiers and civilians alike without hesitation and without empathy.

Nazi propaganda had as a major goal the dehumanization of the Jewish race. The efforts to foment hatred started with the characterization of members of the group as comparable to objects that evoke disgust and hatred. The Nazis compared Jews to "vermin" or "parasites." Similarly, Islamic extremists label Westerners, Christians, and Jews as "sons of apes and pigs." In 1944, a Nazi newspaper, *Der Sturmer*, was written, "Life is not worth living when one does not resist the parasite, never satisfied as it creeps about, we must and we will win." Also, a Nazi pamphlet from the same year was titled "The Jew as the world parasite." There were also propaganda films created to dehumanize the Jewish population, including a 1940 documentary film titled *The Eternal Jew.* This film was the inspiration of Joseph Goebbels, the Minister of Propaganda, and it showed footage of Jewish ghettos in Poland from 1939. This film was an extreme vilification of Jews, designed to evoke strong reactions of disgust and hatred in effort to dehumanize the Jewish population, most notably through the comparison to rats. Unfortunately, this type of propaganda and attempted dehumanization exists today; witness the Egyptian cleric Sheik Said Al-Afini on Al-Rahma television in a broadcast in Egypt on January 17, 2009: ["The Jews] are the offspring of snakes and vipers...we hate them...the Jews are behind all the ruin and destruction in the world."[198]

The same dehumanization process has occurred throughout the ages in countless atrocities. Perhaps the single most important factor for us to remember is that this dehumanization process must occur if mass killings, ethnic cleansings, and genocides are to take place. As a global society, we must be ever vigilant and guard against it. We must fully understand that it begins with our human fallibility, our unconscious bias. This unconscious bias can quickly turn to hate and then to dehumanization. More importantly, we must remain critically aware that the emotion of hate, coupled with the dehumanization of a group or population, can quickly turn to mass murder and genocide. Without this dehumanization process occurring, there can be no genocide. For, without it, we as humans will tend to empathize with the victims and thus treat them in a more just, humane manner.

The final step from Bias to Atrocity is at the point where the hate and dehumanization of a group or entire population moves rapidly toward mass destruction. At this point, real or perceived existential threats are attributed by the "us" group to the "them" group. This crisis is often manipulated by the authority figures to induce action. This is *level-four* or the final level. An existential crisis can be experienced by an individual, group, or even a whole nation. For the individual or group, this is the ultimate "me/us versus them" crisis in which an entire class of people, already hated and dehumanized, are rationalized by the meaning-based neocortical brain as a direct threat to survival or reproduction or the equivalent such as racial, ethnic, national or religious identity, self-esteem, or the ability to earn a living. The "us" group feels trapped, with no way out and no alternative but to eliminate the threat.

In its final extreme form, death of the "them" group is the desired result, as the need for objective physical survival is replaced by the need to end the threat to the higher order subjective survival interest. The results are deadly acts of terrorism without regard to the identity of the victims, suicide bombings, mass shootings, workplace violence, ethnic cleansing, and genocide. The atrocity and devastation is enhanced when it is sanctioned or promoted by an authority figure, entity, or government. And, as we have shown, it can also be enhanced through physical or psychological distance between the perpetrators of the violence and the victims.

The following table (9-1) represents a scoring system for rating the likelihood of genocide or for other deliberate organized in-group campaigns for the complete destruction of a designated out-group. The scoring system is based on a scale from 0 to 100, with a higher score indicating a greater probability of genocide or similar destruction of an out-group. The table assigns sub-score for each of the four steps to genocide—bias, hate, dehumanization, and existential crisis—and a final score is reached by totaling each of the four sub-scores. The sub-scores are assigned based on an evaluation of the degree to which the in-group has experienced, perpetrated, or is subjected to each of the four steps to genocide: The higher the sub-score, the higher degree to which the in-group has experienced, perpetrated, or is subjected to each of the four steps to genocide.

RATING	NEGATIVE BIAS	HATE	DEHUMANIZATION	EXISTENTIAL CRISIS	TOTAL
	Pervasive history of negative bias by the in-group against the target out-group	Pervasive history of in-group blaming target out-group for threats to in-group	Respected authority figure(s) or media of in-group has engaged in propaganda campaign to dehumanize target out-group	General threat to in-group such as war, political crisis, or economic crisis impending or occurring where out-group complicit or threatens success	
Non-Existent	0	0	0	0	
Very Mild	2-3	4-7	6-11	8-15	
Mild	4-5	8-11	12-17	16-23	
Moderate	6-7	12-15	18-23	24-31	
Strong	8-9	16-19	24-29	32-39	
Extreme	10	20	30	40	
SCORE					

Table 9-1. Scoring the Likelihood of Genocide

The next table (9-2) assigns the overall rating and classification of the likelihood of genocide or for other deliberate organized in-group campaigns for the complete destruction of a designated out-group. Using the total score from Table 9-1, the society or in-group is placed into one of eleven classifications based on the likelihood of genocide or out-group destruction from *improbable* to *imminent—virtually certain*. Each classification also contains a description of the types of mistreatment typically experienced by the out-group.

SCORE	LIKELIHOOD OF ORGANIZED DESTRUCTIVE BEHAVIOR AGAINST OUT-GROUP
0-5	*Improbable.* Due to inherent natural bias no diverse community or society larger than a hundred or so people can achieve this score.
6-20	*Remote.* Isolated and infrequent discriminatory practices in law enforcement, housing, employment, medical care, and lending. Rare forms of individual violence such as hate crimes.
21-30	*Very Low.* Isolated but regularly occurring discriminatory practices in law enforcement, housing, employment, medical care, and lending. Rare forms of individual violence such as hate crimes.
31-40	*Low.* Mildly pervasive discrimination exists in the form of discriminatory practices in law enforcement, housing, employment, medical care, and lending. Isolated but persistently occurring forms of individual violence such as hate crimes.
41-50	*Low-Moderate.* Moderately pervasive discrimination exists in the form of discriminatory practices in law enforcement, housing, employment, medical care, and lending. Low but significant levels of individual violence, such as hate crimes.
51-60	*Moderate.* Highly pervasive discrimination exists in the form of discriminatory practices in law enforcement, housing, employment, medical care, and lending. Regularly occurring individual violence such as hate crimes. Government unlikely to intercede except in extreme cases of violence.
61-70	*High-Moderate.* Highly pervasive discrimination exists in the form of discriminatory practices in law enforcement, housing, employment, medical care, and lending. Regularly occurring individual violence such as hate crimes. Low but significant outbreaks of small groups engaging in organized violence and destructive behavior. Government indifference to discrimination and violence. Small segments of government support and take part in violence.
71-80	*Strong.* Completely pervasive discrimination exists in the form of discriminatory practices in law enforcement, housing, employment, medical care, and lending. Regularly occurring individual violence such as hate crimes. Moderate and significant outbreaks of small groups engaging in organized violence and destructive behavior. Government policy supports discrimination and is indifferent to violence. Small segments of government support and take part in violence.
81-90	*Very Strong.* Completely pervasive discrimination exists in the form of discriminatory practices in law enforcement, housing, employment, medical care, and lending. Regularly occurring individual violence, such as hate crimes. Regular and significant outbreaks of small groups engaging in organized violence and destructive behavior. Government policy supports discrimination and is indifferent to violence. Large segments of government support and take part in violence.
91-94	*Imminent.* Completely pervasive discrimination exists in the form of discriminatory practices in law enforcement, housing, employment, medical care, and lending. Regularly occurring individual violence such as hate crimes. Regular and significant outbreaks of small groups engaging in organized violence and destructive behavior. Government policy supports discrimination and violence. Large segments of government support and take part in violence.
95-100	*Imminent—Virtually Certain.* Campaign to completely destroy out-group sanctioned—mass murder, genocide, and war.

Table 9-2. Rating the Likelihood of Genocide or Organized Destructive Behavior and Typical Mistreatment of the Out-Group

As an example, in the following table (9-3), we score the United States concerning minority groups of African-Americans and Latinos:

RATING	NEGATIVE BIAS	HATE	DEHUMANIZATION	EXISTENTIAL CRISIS	TOTAL
	Pervasive history of negative bias by the in-group against the target out-group	Pervasive history of in-group blaming target out-group for threats to in-group	Respected authority figure(s) or media of in-group has engaged in propaganda campaign to dehumanize target out-group	General threat to in-group such as war, political crisis, or economic crisis impending or occurring where out-group complicit or threatens success	
Non-Existent				0	
Very Mild					
Mild			14		
Moderate		14			
Strong	8				
Extreme					
SCORE	8	14	14	0	36

Table 9-3. Scoring of African-American and Latinos in the United States.

Based on this scoring, the classification for the African-American and Latino groups in the United States is *Low*, meaning that that likelihood of an organized campaign of destructive violence is low but that mild forms of widespread societal discrimination exist, with isolated acts of individual violence such as hate crimes. This is an overall estimation for the entire nation for two large racial groups; tables can be constructed for more specific groups in more specific areas. We note that given the present fears in the United States based on the perception of the lack of control over illegal immigration and violence and loss of economic opportunity associated with illegal immigration, Latinos are at risk of even higher violence and discrimination. This higher risk would result from an additional score from the *existential crisis* category. Other groups that are at risk of scoring higher than the present score for African-Americans and Latinos are Muslims, Arabs, Middle and Near Easterners, and South Asians. Another large-scale attack against the United States based on extremist Islamic terrorism would create a high score in the existential *crisis* category for these groups.

These two tables provide a road map for assessing the progress of a society or group towards genocide or mass murder and a means for predicting the likelihood of such violence. We now have the tools for accurate assessment and prediction: Prevention, whether at the community, sub-state, national, or global level, is attainable and the failure to engage in preventive steps inexcusable.

The path from bias to atrocity is clearly marked and as we look across the globe today, we see specific regions that are currently on this path. We have provided the steps here as an attempt to intercede and reverse the course, for history has taught us what the result will be if we don't.

Chapter Nine
The Final Solution

The Wannsee Conference and Protocol

On January 20, 1942, in the picturesque lakeside Berlin suburb of Wannsee, a meeting was convened by SS Obergruppenfuhrer (Lt. General) Reinhard Heydrich, chief of the Reich Main Security Office (RSHA), at the request of Reichsmarschall Herman Goering, to develop a plan for the "final solution to the Jewish question." In a stately three-story villa surrounded by well-manicured gardens, Heydrich assembled fourteen high-level Nazi government and military officials over an hour-and-a-half midday buffet luncheon to finalize the commitment to the annihilation of the 11 million Jews of Europe. Despite the careful use of euphemistic language, e.g., "the final solution," in the protocol (minutes), the desired results from the Wannsee Conference were clear:

> Able-bodied Jews, separated according to sex, will be taken in large work columns to these areas for work on roads, in the course of which action doubtless a large portion will be eliminated by natural causes. The possible final remnant will, since it will undoubtedly consist of the most resistant portion, have to be treated accordingly, because it is the product of natural selection and would, if released, act as the seed of a new Jewish revival…. In the course of the practical execution of the final solution, Europe will be combed through from west to east.

From this paragraph in the protocol, the complete dehumanization of Jews is readily apparent through the use of the pronoun "it" (German "es") to refer to the Jews and through a reference to the murder of Jews as though a treatment for a parasitic infection. This reference to the Jews as some sort of disease is also consistent with the Nazi campaign to associate Jews with objects that evoke the emotion of disgust. Disgust, as we have seen, is the emotional reaction to something resulting in the complete revulsion to and rejection of the object of disgust. Treatment of a group of people as objects of disgust historically precedes genocide.

At the close of the conference, more than 80 percent of the eventual victims of the Holocaust were still living; thirteen months later, about 80 percent were dead.[199] At the time of this meeting, the commitment to Hitler's diabolical plan for the annihilation of the Jews had already been made and its implementation was well underway. The *Einsatzgruppen* were paramilitary units formed under SS Reichsfuhrer Heinrich Himmler and Heydrich in the summer of 1941. Himmler, one of Hitler's most trusted officials, was one the most powerful men in the Nazi regime. He controlled the entire security apparatus, including the police forces, Gestapo, and SS (*Schutzstaffel*). There were four Einsatzgruppen units created, each composed of 600 to 1000 men who were mostly from the Waffen-SS (the military arm of the SS) and German police forces. Each of these units (lettered A, B, C, and D) was specifically directed to follow the advancing German Wehrmacht (Army) into Eastern Europe and Russia and to "liquidate" Jews, Romany (Gypsies), and Communist political operatives.

About one and a half million mostly Jews were murdered mostly in the Ukraine and the Baltic states of Latvia, Estonia, and Lithuania by or under the direction of the Einsatzgruppen. The vast majority of these murders were committed by lining up victims in front of mass graves and shooting the victims, either by being machine gunned down or individually shot in the neck at the base of the skull. In an example of the sheer brutality and depravity of these operations 33,771 people, virtually the entire Jewish population of Kiev, were murdered in two days from September 29 to 30, 1941, in Babi Yar, Ukraine, by Einsatzgruppen C, aided by Ukrainian paramilitary units. Jewish residents who were ordered to appear for "resettlement" had their belongings taken, led to a ravine, ordered to strip naked, and lined up at the edge of the ravine where they were machine gunned down.

Adam Grolsch, a radio operator in the Wehrmacht on the Russian front, observed the mass murder of Jews in Pinsk, Belarus, in October 1942. In two days, 25,000 men, women, and children would perish at the hands of the SS and local paramilitary units.

> Back then, the Ukrainians and the White Russians didn't like the Jews either. They hounded them and hated them just as much as the Nazis did, just not in this way. In short, I then set out with a friend, and with my own eyes saw how the people there were slaughtered; in two days, 25,000 men, women, and children, and in the most beastly way. I saw how they had to undress in front of the tank traps and many other things. And the absolute worst thing I saw was how this man took a screaming baby and beat it headfirst against a wall until it was dead.

Of course, the Germans were the ones who ordered this, but the ones who carried out the orders were mostly Russians: Cossacks, Lithuanians, and Latvians. The auxiliary troops provided the force, but that doesn't relieve the Germans of responsibility. One called them Hilfswillige [voluntary helpers], or Hiwis for short. They were mostly Lithuanians, Latvians, and Estonians, and they carried out the worst jobs for us, the dirty work....

They had dug it all out and there were all these corpses. Then they had to undress. Mothers were still carrying their children, usually in one arm. Then they would go up there and they shot them. I saw everything, everything....

It was horrifying. What an experience that was! I just thought to myself, Something like this just can't happen.[200]

After his discomfort in watching the execution of 100 by mass shooting in Minsk in the late summer of 1941 and due to reports of suicides and mental breakdowns of the Einsatzgruppen taking part in the atrocities, Himmler ordered that a more "humane" way be found to commit the executions. Victims were then placed in vans, which were driven around while exhaust was piped in, which suffocated the victims through the effects of carbon monoxide. This method of killing was found not to be efficient and was soon replaced by the most efficient means available, the mass gassings by hydrogen cyanide gas (Zyklon B) in extermination camps, in which three to four million Jews were murdered from 1941 to 1945 in infamous places such as Auschwitz, Chelmo, Treblinka, Sobibor, and Majdanek.

The methods for industrialized killing with poison gas were already perfected during a euthanasia program ordered by Hitler on September 1, 1939, for "the mentally ill, handicapped, and other 'burdensome life forms'"[201]. A special department in the Fuhrer's Chancellery known as T-4 carried this secret euthanasia program, known as *Aktion T-4,* for two years until, after its existence was leaked, a public outcry halted it. "But the expertise thus acquired was not to be wasted. It was now to be used outside Germany, on other victims."[202] The halting of Aktion T-4 tells us that the German public could, if it chose, exert pressure on the government to refrain from abhorrent conduct. Mentally ill and handicapped Germans were considered part of the *in-group* and their plight evoked empathy from the public and probably from the vast majority of government officials aware of it. Jews, Romany, and eastern European communists were not part of the *in-group* and were subject to devaluation, resulting in little or no empathy for their plight. In particular, there was a prevalent anti-Semitism in Central and Eastern Europe, where Jews were subjected to a virulent and vicious propaganda campaign by the Nazis.

Before the Wannsee Conference began, more than half a million Jews had already been murdered by the Einsatzgruppen and the gas chambers in Chelmo were already being used for mass murder under the guidance of former Aktion T-4 officials. The genocide was well underway and participants at the Wannsee Conference were not surprised as to the ultimate goals of the "final solution." The conference was more about Heydrich asserting his overriding authority over the various ministries in regards to the "final solution" and to entangle a wide assortment of high-ranking officials as being responsible for the consequences of the "final solution" should Germany lose the war. In December 1941, the Wehrmacht suffered its first defeat by failing to take Moscow and the outcome of the war was now far from being certain.

Otto Ohlendorf, commander of Einsatzgruppen D and close associate of Himmler, testifying at the Nuremberg trial, stated that Himmler assembled the Einsatzgruppen and personally gave the liquidation order "and pointed out that the leaders and men who were taking part in the liquidation bore no responsibility for the execution of this order. *The responsibility was his, alone, and the Fuhrer's*" [Italics added.]. Wilhelm Keitel, a defendant at the Nuremburg trial, who served as the chief of staff of the German High Command, stated, "We all believed so much in him [Hitler], and we all stand to take all the blame and the shame. He gave us the orders. He kept saying that *it was all his responsibility*" [Italics added.]. Keitel was found guilty of war crimes and crimes against humanity by the International Military Tribunal and sentenced to death by hanging, which was executed on October 16, 1946. The acceptance of responsibility by authority figures was a key factor we saw in the Milgram Obedience Experiment that enhanced an individual's ability to minimize his or her own moral reservations. As Milgram observed based on his Obedience Experiment, "The most common adjustment of thought in the obedient subject is for him to see himself as not responsible for his own actions. He divests himself of responsibility by attributing all initiative to the experimenter."[203] This acceptance of responsibility by the highest leaders of the state made to a highly authoritarian group combined with a general anti-Semitism or indifference to the Jews and the exigencies of war sealed the fate of the Jews and other "undesirable" groups.

Hannah Arendt, author of the acclaimed book, *Eichmann in Jerusalem: A Report on the Banality of Evil*, describes Himmler as the "member of the Nazi hierarchy most gifted at solving problems of conscience." Arendt shows Himmler's ability to allay feelings of guilt and empathy and to encourage the fulfillment of the "final solution" through quotes of speeches by Himmler to commanders of the Einsatzgruppen and SS: "To have stuck it out and, apart from exceptions caused by human weakness, to have remained decent, that is what has made us hard. This is a page of glory in our history which has never been written and is never to be written."[204]

Himmler represents arguably the most Machiavellian personality of the entire Nazi hierarchy, even greater than Hitler, in his capacity to enlist tens of thousands of people into the systematic murder of defenseless and compliant millions. Through his desire to prove himself to Hitler and thus cement his position, in true Machiavellian fashion, as the second most powerful person in the German Reich, Himmler was able to neutralize whatever shreds of humanity were left in his followers to serve his own narcissistic needs for power. Himmler quickly rose to lead the SS in the early thirties, and, along with Goering, persuaded Hitler to agree to the elimination of the leadership of the rival *Sturmabteilung* (SA) organization on June 30, 1934, in an incident known as the *Night of the Long Knives*. The SA, known as the "brown shirts," were the first paramilitary group associated with Hitler and National Socialism and were key to the early success of the National Socialist German Worker's (Nazi) Party. The leader of the SA, Ernst Rohm, was a close friend and loyal supporter of Hitler in the early days of the Nazi Party and it was with reluctance that Hitler authorized his execution.

Himmler molded the SS into an elite organization founded on its members' loyalty to Hitler and the Nazi party, racial purity and superior status as guardians of the Aryan master race. With Rohm and the SA out of the way and, through a power sharing agreement with his main rival Goering, Himmler, by 1936, had complete control of the security apparatus and eagerly nourished Hitler's pathological hatred of the Jews.

Himmler's empathy deficit was extraordinary and allowed him, using one of his favorite words, to "ruthlessly" annihilate individuals or groups who stood in the way, whether it was his pursuit of the Nazi ideology of a racially pure Aryan race, communists and other political enemies of the state, or his personal insecurities concerning "the temptations of homosexuality to which he himself had been subject to in the past."[205] Himmler's anti-Semitism, although adopted as a young adult, was not the group he most fervently sought to persecute prior to the November pogrom of 1938. Prior to this time "it is impossible to find any lengthy anti-Semitic statements by Himmler. He mostly treated the question of the Jews cursorily and often in a stereotypical manner along with other enemies, and without spending any time on them."[206] While Himmler eagerly adopted Hitler's plan for the destruction of Europe's Jews, "he was bent on the destruction of Christianity"[207] which he described as the "the destroyer of every nation."[208] Prior to World War II, Himmler was also preoccupied with "the fight against abortion and homosexuality."[209] For Himmler "it was vital to combat homosexuality, for otherwise 'it would be the end of Germany, the end of the Teutonic world.'"[210]

Himmler's final Machiavellian act was to betray Hitler in April 1945 in a desperate attempt to save his own skin. By late 1944, he already ordered the exterminations of Jews to stop and to destroy evidence of the "final solution." He now sought to negotiate surrender to the Allied forces in the West, seeking to unite forces with the Americans and British against the Soviets. When this failed, he attempted to negotiate a complete surrender to Eisenhower—who wanted nothing to do with him—in return for his immunity from prosecution. His complete self-serving and despicable nature was obvious to everyone except himself: He was shunned by his own military, even being declared a traitor by Hitler, and hunted by the Allies as a war criminal. Following the surrender of Germany, Himmler assumed a false identity and attempted to elude the Allied forces, but he was captured by the British Army, who soon recognized his true identity, on May 22, 1945. Rather than face the music, he committed suicide by means of a potassium cyanide capsule.

Himmler's demise reminds one of the pitiful demise of President Saddam Hussein of Iraq, another narcissistic Machiavellian, who was hunted down by Coalition Forces after the fall of his Ba'ath Party government in April 2003. On the run for eight months, the disheveled and fully bearded Hussein was captured on December 14, 2003 hiding in a hole in the ground under a two-room mud shack on a sheep farm near his ancestral home of Tikrit. His first words to his captors were, "I am Saddam Hussein. I am the president of Iraq and I want to negotiate." Both Himmler and Hussein, despite utter defeat and condemnation, both continued to delude themselves as to their own importance and belief that they would be welcomed by their enemies. Despite these strong pathological defects, these two men controlled the destinies of millions and caused unimaginable death, destruction, and misery.

Both Himmler's boss, Hitler, and his key underlings, Heydrich and Eichmann, all suffered from some form of insecurity based on their own or others' perception that they had Jewish blood and, true to his Machiavellian nature, Himmler exploited this. Hitler's father, Alois Hitler, was born in 1837 as the illegitimate son of Maria Schickelgruber. The father of Alois, Hitler's paternal grandfather, has never been conclusively established. One theory, now considered highly unlikely, that Hitler was aware of, and was in circulation before World War II, was that Maria worked for the Jewish Frankenberger family in Graz, Austria, at the time of Alois's birth and that a nineteen year-old son of the family was the father. In the society he created, which required proof of Aryan ancestry going back several generations for full citizenship, Hitler's missing grandfather and the possibility he was Jewish, however remote, must have caused considerable insecurity and fueled his hatred towards Jews. William Paterson University Professor of Psychology Neil J. Kressel observes that "Anti-Semitism, for Hitler, was no mere tool, no popularity building device, no Machiavellian trick (though he occasionally downplayed his hostility when it served the interests of the party)."

> Hitler's hatred of Jews and his racial imperialism were not tactics in his drive to power; they were *the reason why* he sought power in the first place. If there was any one thing in which Hitler truly believed, it was anti-Semitism....

> And when Germany lay in ruins, Hitler consoled himself that, at least against the Jews, the war had been won.[211]

Like Hitler, Himmler's key subordinate in the implementation of the "final solution," Heydrich, also suffered from insecurity about his ancestry. As a child, Heydrich grew up in a home of harsh discipline and was bullied by schoolmates because of rumors of his Jewish ancestry. As an eighteen-year-old cadet in the German Navy who not only was rumored to be Jewish but also was tall and skinny with a high-pitched voice, Heydrich again became an easy target for bullying. The connection between bullied children and antisocial behavior is now well established in psychology,[212] and to whatever extent

Heydrich suffered from antisocial personality disorder, his experiences nurtured this tendency as well providing a convenient cause to blame for his suffering—the Jews.

Heydrich was a talented musician and athlete, highly ambitious and driven to excel. Joining the SS in 1931 at age twenty-seven provided Heydrich with the ideal environment to blossom into a complete Machiavellian: The SS provided a fertile environment for the growth of narcissism of its members by admiring and praising its adherents' superior status as pure members of the Aryan master race, by providing devalued groups such as Jews to victimize, and by providing its members godlike powers over the lives of others, including the power of life and death. This power is perhaps most vividly seen in the selection process at the extermination camps as described by Victor Frankl, the Austrian psychiatrist sent to Auschwitz in October 1944:

> We did not realize the meaning behind the scene that was to follow presently. We were told to leave our luggage in the train and to fall into two lines—women on one side, men on the other—in order to file past a senior SS officer.... He was a tall man who looked slim and fit in his spotless uniform.... He had assumed an attitude of careless ease, supporting his right elbow with his left hand. His right hand was lifted, and with the forefinger of that hand, he pointed very leisurely to the right or to the left. None of us had the slightest idea of the sinister meaning behind that little movement of a man's finger, pointing now to the right and now to the left, but far more frequently to the left.... It was the first selection, the first verdict made on our existence or nonexistence. For the great majority of our transport, about 90 percent, it meant death. Their sentence was carried out within the next few hours. Those who were sent to the left were marched from the station straight to the crematorium.[213]

Professor Elie Wiesel of Boston University, winner of the Nobel Peace Prize, also describes in terrifyingly similar terms the selection process at Auschwitz where he was sent with his family as a fifteen-year-old from Hungary in 1944:

> We continued to walk until we came to a crossroads. Standing in the middle of it was, though I didn't know it then, Dr. Mengele, the notorious Dr. Mengele. He looked like the typical SS officer: a cruel, though not unintelligent, face, complete with monocle. He was holding a conductor's baton and was surrounded by officers. The baton was moving constantly, sometimes to the right, sometimes to the left.... Not far from us, flames, huge flames, were rising from a ditch. Something was being burned there. A truck drew close and unloaded its hold: small children. Babies! Yes, I did see this, with my own eyes...children thrown into the flames.[214]

Heydrich quickly rose through the ranks of the SS. Before he turned thirty, he was promoted to the rank of brigadier general and controlled the feared, even amongst loyal Nazis, SS Security Service known as the SD

(*Sicherheitsdienst*). Here, Heydrich's treachery was allowed to thrive: he oversaw a vast network of informers and spies and constructed dossiers on party members that could be used to intimidate, exploit, and extort. Despite his success, Heydrich was always plagued by the persistent rumors of his possible Jewish ancestry, which both Hitler and Himmler were aware and which was exploited by them. Hitler described Heydrich as "very dangerous…whose gifts the movement had to retain…he would eternally be grateful to us that we had kept him and not expelled him and would obey blindly." Hitler and Himmler found the ideal man to orchestrate the "final solution": a treacherous, narcissistic Machiavellian willing to do anything to prove himself to his masters, Hitler and Himmler; who was given complete license to destroy the group responsible in his mind for his greatest insecurities—the Jews. In a rare case of swift justice for the architects of the "final solution," Heydrich, serving as the Deputy Reich Protector of Bohemia and Moravia in Prague, was attacked on May 27, 1942, while driving in his open top Mercedes by two Czech agents trained by the British and sent to assassinate him. He died about a week later from his wounds, but the plans he set in motion at the Wannsee Conference for the annihilation of a whole race of people would faithfully be carried out by thousands and most faithfully by his able assistant, Adolf Eichmann.

One of the perpetrators of the worst act of domestic terrorism in the United States, Timothy McVeigh, shared many similarities with Heydrich. McVeigh demonized federal law enforcement for the FBI siege of a mountain cabin in Ruby Ridge, Idaho, in 1992 and the fifty-one-day siege of the Branch Davidian compound in Waco, Texas, that ended with the death of at least seventy-four on April 19, 1993. McVeigh, seeking revenge and to teach the federal government a lesson, detonated a rental truck loaded with nearly 5,000 pounds of explosives in front of the Alfred P. Murrah Federal Building in Oklahoma City on April 19, 1995, killing 168 and injuring over 500. While awaiting execution for his crimes, which took place on June 11, 2001, McVeigh was interviewed by *Buffalo News* reporter Lou Michel, resulting in forty-five hours of audio recordings of the interviews. These recordings provided a chilling look into the mind of a psychopathic killer.[215]

McVeigh's parents divorced when he was ten years old. He was raised by his father. According to McVeigh, "I know what love is, and I don't think I feel it towards my parents." Like Heydrich, McVeigh was a skinny kid who was the subject of bullying at school: "I think they started calling me 'noodle McVeigh…chicken McVeigh'…. 'Noodle' because I was as thin as a noodle." McVeigh, like Heydrich, joined the military, enlisting in the Army. Both McVeigh and Heydrich had military careers that started out promising but were cut short. McVeigh served in the Gulf War and was awarded the Bronze Star but, after the war, dropped out of a try-out for the Army Special Forces because he could not complete the physical fitness requirements. He left the Army shortly thereafter. Heydrich rose quickly to the rank of second lieutenant in the German Navy but was forced to resign his commission for unbecoming conduct.

McVeigh, like Heydrich, had narcissistic tendencies and a deficit in empathy. After leaving the Army, McVeigh, shattered emotionally by failed relationships, humiliating experiences of being bullied, and the failure to make the grade for Special Forces, was desperately looking for a cause to prove himself as strong and in control. Heydrich, too, was looking for a cause to satisfy his narcissistic needs but was fortunate to find an organization sanctioned by the state—the SS—that thrived on feeding its members' needs for power and domination, and thrived on the destruction of designated inferior groups. As a bonus to Heydrich, the principal group targeted for destruction—the Jews—were the very group he resented. McVeigh was attracted to right wing militia groups and survivalists whose principal values were the right to bear arms and non-interference from the government. McVeigh, however, lacked the charisma of Heydrich and was unable to become a leader in these movements. The best he could do was form a small conspiracy of three, which basically fell apart.

Although McVeigh attempts to justify the Oklahoma City bombing deaths as a militarily necessary counter-attack against the government to defend the freedoms of American citizens, his words reveal his true inner need to satisfy his narcissism at the expense of innocent people for whom he is incapable of empathy. McVeigh tells the families of those killed to "Get over it." While dismissing the pain of the families who lost loved ones, McVeigh makes a special point of making sure we know that he did not run away after igniting the fuse, telling us that "I did jog because I knew nobody was looking."

> Just for my own personal pride, I make sure I use the word "jog" there, 'cause I wasn't running in a panic or nothing. It was a conscious decision to jog.

> I was always in complete control.... I left a trail on purpose.... So, even if I wouldn't have been apprehended and had a trial, I would have still gained the benefit automatically of being identified.... There was a no lose situation.... I describe it as playing a game with them. I am playing the game with law enforcement and every day I laugh.

> There are steps leading down from the courthouse. And I had to concentrate on where the steps were going to be without dipping my head down and looking down because people would take dipping of my head down as a sign of defeat or something.

> I, in fact, may be, in a sense a groundbreaker in a new "suicide by cop."

> I knew my objective was state-assisted suicide, and when it happens, in your face motherfuckers. In other words, I'm manipulating the system for my own gain.

> In the crudest terms, 168 to 1 if you had on the scoreboard, right? So I sit here content that there's no way that they can beat me by executing me.

It is quite disturbing to hear his words and realize the devastation wrought by one individual willing to trade 168 lives merely to satisfy his need to prove he is not weak and powerless; that he is in control of his destiny, is the manipulator and not the manipulated, and that he looks upon lost lives not as people but as numbers. Lou Michel, coauthor of McVeigh's authorized biography *American Terrorist*, notes that being bullied "was one of the resentments that [McVeigh] harbored throughout his entire life; bullies, he hated bullies." After Waco, Michel observes, "It was the bully again, this time the horns were on the head of the federal government." His life was clearly troubled and it should be a lesson on the devastation that can result from people with high but fragile self-esteem and low empathy whose early lives are experienced in an environment of powerlessness, humiliation, and lack of control. Heydrich was such a person who was willing to trade the lives of millions for his own needs.

Present at the Wannsee Conference and responsible for transcribing the minutes or "protocol" was SS-Obersturmbannführer (Lt. Colonel) Adolf Eichmann, whom, we noted in chapter two, inspired Hannah Arendt to coin the phrase the "banality of evil." Eichmann was chief of the RSHA section IV B4 for Jewish Affairs serving directly under Heydrich. In this role, Eichmann directed the deportation of millions of Jews to death camps in Poland and the occupied Soviet Union.

Eichmann, like his boss, Heydrich, was teased by classmates who thought he was Jewish and did not complete his high school education. He then worked for his father and held a couple of sales jobs, the last being a district agent for Vacuum Oil Company AG, a subsidiary of Standard Oil. Eichmann enlisted in the SS in April 1932 and began active duty in November 1933 at the Dachau concentration camp in Germany, the first concentration camp for political prisoners of the Nazi régime. Eichmann had attracted the attention of Heydrich and Himmler while serving, beginning in 1934, in the Jewish section of the SD, the security service branch of the SS. He established himself as an expert in Jewish issues through a study of Jewish culture, in particular the issue of Zionism. In 1937, he visited Palestine to explore the possibility of mass emigration of Jews to Palestine, but was ordered out of the country by British authorities then in control of Palestine. After the annexation (*Anschluss*) of Austria by Germany in March of 1938, Eichmann was sent to Vienna where he established a Central Office for Jewish Emigration. The goal was the forced emigration of Jews from Austria, which would be financed by the Jews themselves, including the wealthy Jews assuming the costs of the emigration of Jews who could not afford to emigrate. Arendt writes:

> The assignment in Vienna was his [Eichmann's] first important job; his whole career, which had progressed rather slowly, was in the balance. He must have been frantic to make good, and his success was spectacular: in eight months, forty-five thousand Jews left Austria, whereas no more than nineteen thousand left Germany in the same period; in less than eighteen months,

Austria was "cleansed" of close to a hundred and fifty thousand people, roughly sixty per cent of its Jewish population...."[216]

Himmler and Heydrich found their man to implement the logistics of the "final solution" and put Eichmann in charge of the Gestapo Jewish Affairs section after the start of World War II in the fall of 1939. Up until this time, Eichmann, who craved bureaucratic advancement, was able to gain recognition for his efforts without facing any major moral dilemmas. The emigration of Jews, his specialty, was entirely consistent with the National Socialist agenda, to which he subscribed, and Jews of Austria seemed anxious to depart'. Shortly after the German invasion of Soviet-occupied territory in June 1941, Eichmann was informed by Heydrich of Hitler's order for the "physical extermination of the Jews" and he began visiting Einsatzgruppen extermination sites in occupied Eastern Europe. Like Himmler, Eichmann was physically sickened by exposure to the reality of brutal mass murder. In Eichmann's own words to his Israeli Police interrogator Captain Avner W. Less concerning an engine exhaust gassing operation:

> I was horrified. My nerves aren't strong enough.... I can't listen to such things...such things, without their affecting me. Even today, if I see someone with a deep cut, I have to look away. I could never have been a doctor. I still remember how I visualized the scene and began to tremble, as if I'd been through something, some terrible experience. The kind of thing that happens sometimes and afterwards you start to shake.[217]

There was no question in Eichmann's mind what the fate would be for the first mass deportations of Jews and Roma from Germany to the East he was responsible for in the autumn of 1941. Eichmann "for the first and last time" decided to violate orders to send the first shipment of 25,000 Jews and Roma to Russian territory, where the Einsatzgruppen would have executed them, and, instead, "directed the transport to the ghetto of Lodz where he knew that no preparations for extermination had yet been made."[218] No longer involved in emigration which did not raise matters of conscience, Eichmann faced, for the first time, decisions on following orders to deport Jews and Roma to the East to certain death and "for the first and last time" exercised his conscience to save lives and chose to disobey orders. He did get into considerable trouble for this decision but was soon forgiven by Himmler and Heydrich.[219] After this incident, Eichmann chose to suppress his humanity and to dutifully carry out the transports of millions to certain death in the occupied areas of Eastern Europe. Unlike Hitler, Himmler, and Heydrich, Eichmann was neither narcissistic nor suffering from any form of antisocial personality disorder and most likely did

---

* To the extent it was true that Jews of Austria sought to emigrate it was due mostly to the rampant discrimination and anti-Semitism that was present after the rise of the Nazi Party in the early 1930s.

not hate the Jews. He was, however, ambitious with a lackluster past and, for the first time, was achieving success and recognition. He had finally made it as a trusted member of the inner circle of the Nazi leadership and his duties, though troubling, were sanctioned by the ultimate authority and head of state—the Fuhrer. The only thing standing in the way was concern for the lives of Jews, Roma, homosexuals, and communists for whom Eichmann simply lacked empathy. In the social environment of Eichmann, the groups victimized by the Holocaust were already devalued and subject of pervasive negative bias, which is all it took for Eichmann and the vast majority of people in Germany and its aligned and occupied countries to have reduced or no empathy. What little empathy Eichmann had for Jews and other victims was easily subdued by Eichmann's overpowering need to be successful at something and be recognized in combination with sanctioning of respected authority. Moreover, and of equal importance, he never had to actually carryout a killing and was only one part in a process in which his activities were quite removed from the brutality of the killing. As the Milgram experiments, Trolley Dilemma experiments, and other psychological research shows, involvement in actions that lead to death become easier the further one is removed from the actual mechanisms for causing death.[20]

Eichmann, who explained he would have to look away rather than view a deep cut and, who, in his final plea after having been found guilty at his trial, stated he "would have put a bullet through [his] brain" rather than carry out an order to carry out a killing "to solve the conflict between conscience and duty," was able to resolve his conflict of conscience because he did not actually pull the trigger or release the gas. This was so even though in a legal and moral sense he was just as guilty had he been the person to pull the trigger or release the gas. Professor Neil J. Kressel observes that while participants in the Holocaust "shared a willingness to murder Jews, or assist in their murder, their motives differed substantially."

> Many who did not personally pull the trigger, or release the Zyklon-B gas, did not see themselves as perpetrators. The bureaucratic division of labor permitted them to see themselves as "doing their job" and to see others as "the killers."[221]

In addition to his ambition and obedience, this "psychological distance" from the acts of murder was the key factor to make it possible for Eichmann to abdicate his conscience, which his behavior at the start of deportations showed he possessed. For this abdication of conscience, Eichmann was found guilty of mass murder and rightfully sentenced to death by hanging.

On July 28, 1943, the city of Hamburg was subjected to a massive firebombing campaign by the British Royal Air Force, creating a firestorm that consumed an area of about four square miles and killed seventy thousand people, marking the introduction of new strategy to indiscriminately use massive aerial bombing on population centers. Lt. Colonel Dave Grossman in his book, *On Killing,* makes the following observations about this and other firebombing campaigns of the Allies:

> Seventy thousand people died at Hamburg the night the air caught fire. They were mostly women, children, and the elderly, since those of soldiering age were generally at the front. They died horrible deaths, burning and suffocating. If bomber crew members had had to turn a flamethrower on each one of the seventy thousand women and children, or worse yet slit each of their throats, the awfulness and trauma inherent in the act would have been of such a magnitude that it simply would not have happened. But when it is done from thousands of feet in the air, where screams cannot be heard and burning bodies cannot be seen, it is easy...
>
> Eighty thousand or so died in 1945 during a similar firebombing of Dresden. Two hundred and twenty-five thousand died in firestorms over Tokyo as a result of only two firebomb raids.... Throughout World War II, bomber crews on both sides killed millions of women, children, and elderly people, no different from their own wives, children, and parents. The pilots, navigators, bombardiers, and gunners in these aircraft were able to bring themselves to kill these civilians primarily through application of the mental leverage provided to them by the distance factor. Intellectually, they understood the horror of what they were doing. Emotionally, the distance involved permitted them to deny it.[222]

Grossman makes a key point in distinguishing between the intellectual and emotional awareness of mass killing. The Holocaust was presided over by highly intelligent members of the Nazi government. Eight of the fifteen attendees of the Wannsee Conference held doctorate degrees. All but one of the twenty-one defendants in the Trial of the Major War Criminals held before the International Military Tribunal in Nuremberg, Germany, during 1945-46 had Wechsler-Bellevue IQ Test scores above normal with nine defendants in the second highest category of "very high" intelligence (120 to 129) and another nine defendants in the highest category of "gifted" (130 and above). Despite this concentration of Nazi leaders with very high cognitive intelligence, they utterly failed to appreciate the moral implications of their actions. Our understanding the difference between cognitive intelligence—the ability to comprehend complex ideas and solve complex problems—and "emotional intelligence"—the ability to understand and control emotion and judge actions against basic moral values—is going to be the difference in whether or not the human species survives. The mechanism for inhibiting deadly violence is not an intellectual process but is based on an emotional process that identifies the other as being a human being like ourselves or like our family. The closer we are in terms of physical distance in the directness our actions physically cause injury, or in terms of identification of the other as part of our *in-group*, the more we empathize with the other person and the more difficult it becomes to cause injury or death. Without such empathy, the intellect can easily be convinced of the utility of behavior that condones or passively takes part in killing.

Like Eichmann, psychological distance from victims can permit us to rationalize the killing of others. In the twentieth century, in which political ideologies permitted one individual to have unchecked and absolute power over millions and in which technology permitted the killing of people over great distances with massive lethality, mass murder and genocide became inevitable. We, the people of all nations, are not intellectually capable of sufficiently recognizing the humanity of all peoples in order to prevent our destruction and our emotional capacity for empathy, the only reliable safeguard we have to check our aggression, is too primitive to guide us through the psychological distance and destructive power created by modern society. Would President Harry S. Truman, who authorized the use of atomic bombs dropped on Hiroshima and Nagasaki, been able to personally kill a single Japanese noncombatant citizen of either of those cities face to face with his own hands? Despite his presumed *inability* to personally kill even a single noncombatant, even if fully justified by the exigencies or war, Truman *was able* to authorize the use of atomic weapons against civilian population centers where it was certain they would incinerate tens of thousands of noncombatants and cause unimaginable suffering for many more. It is probable that Truman, if flying in one of the bombers, would have not even been able to press the button or pull the lever to actually release the atomic bomb. But dutiful soldiers who did *not* make the decision to use atomic weapons and who were simply following their orders and defending their nation were able to arm the weapons, fly the planes, and release them over Hiroshima and Nagasaki. Likewise, dutiful scientists, technicians, and military support staff were able to construct the atomic weapons, test them, and deliver them to the bombers. Truman's order to use the atomic bomb and his acceptance of responsibility, captured by the famous slogan, "the buck stops here'," allowed the participants in the atomic bombings to divest themselves of responsibility, giving them the needed psychological distance to take part in the bombings.

Was the use of atomic weapons on population centers in Japan and the equally destructive conventional bombings of Tokyo and German population centers such as Dresden and Hamburg during World War II by American and British forces justified? Or, were the military leaders of America and Britain guilty of judgment tainted by the influences of dehumanization, hate and revenge, deficient empathy, unconscious bias, psychological distance, and diffusion of responsibility? In particular, the ferocity and lack of restraint concerning "collateral damage" in the bombings on Tokyo, Hiroshima, and

---

. The phrase was on a sign painted on glass plate mounted on a walnut base on President Truman's desk in the White House. It was a gift made in the Federal Reformatory in El Reno, Oklahoma, from the U.S. Marshal for the Western District of Missouri, Fred M. Canfil. It should be noted that Truman received the desk plate in October 1945, nearly two months after the atomic bombings of Japan.

Nagasaki was accelerated by dehumanization, hate, revenge, and deficient empathy for the Japanese. The nature of the attack on Pearl Harbor as a "sneak attack" and the different race and culture of the Japanese from the white European background of the vast majority of America made it much easier to dehumanize and hate the Japanese and to seek revenge. While "44 percent of American soldiers in World War II said they would 'really like to kill a Japanese soldier,' only 6 percent expressed that degree of enthusiasm for killing Germans."[223] Niall Ferguson, professor of history at Harvard University, shows the prevalence of dehumanization and hate of Japanese soldiers by Allied forces:

> This brings us to one of the most troubling aspects of the Second World War: the fact that Allied troops often regarded the Japanese in the same way that Germans regarded Russians—as Untermenschen [sub-humans]. General Sir Thomas Blamey, who commanded the Australians in New Guinea, told his troops that their foes were 'a cross between the human being and the ape', 'vermin', 'something primitive' that had to be 'exterminated' to preserve 'civilization'. "The Japs...had renounced the right to be regarded as human," recalled Major John Winstanley, who fought with the Royal West Kent Regiment at Kohima. "We thought of them as vermin to be exterminated." To Lieutenant Lintorn Highlett of the Dorsetshires, they were "formidable fighting insects"—an echo of General Slim's description of the Japanese soldiers as "part of an insect horde with all its power and horror." Wartime cartoonists often portrayed the Japanese as monkeys or apes. Such sentiments were even more widespread among Americans....[224]

The consensus of history on the matter of the conduct of American and British forces late in World War II has not been reached but the authors believe a more enlightened view of human nature, that we seek to promote through this book, will ultimately view these atomic bombings and firebombing campaigns as a form of evil behavior. Certainly, less culpable than the aggression of the Axis powers who provoked it, but evil nonetheless.

As we are well aware, atomic weapons have already been used in targeting civilian population centers—the question of justification for their use is not what is most important to understand at this moment in time. What is important to understand for the moment is how, in times of perceived crisis, through a causal chain of diffusion of responsibility, devaluation of *out-groups*, sanctioning by authority, the elimination of empathy, and a step-by-step process leading to the destruction of human life, the most horrific acts of destruction and mass murder are possible at virtually anytime and anyplace by almost anyone. To doubt this means to ignore not only the Holocaust, but the Crusades, the Inquisition, the Armenian genocide of 1915-16, the Rape of Nanking, China by Japanese soldiers in 1937, the Soviet Union under Stalin, the Cultural Revolution under Mao, lynching of African-Americans in the United States in the century after the Civil War, the Khmer Rouge in Cambodia under Pol Pot, the 1994 genocide in Rwanda, Serbian ethnic cleansing in Bosnia and Kosovo in 1990s, the September 11, 2001 attacks in the United States, the present crisis in the Darfur region of Sudan, and many other wars and incidents too numerous to list. As Milgram observed,

> [There is] a dangerously typical situation in complex society: it is psychologically easy to ignore responsibility when one is only an intermediate link in a chain of evil action and is far removed from the final consequences of the action. Even Eichmann was sickened when he toured concentration camps, but to participate in mass murder, he had only to sit at a desk and shuffle papers. At the same time, the man in the camp who actually dropped [Zyklon-B] into the gas chambers was able to justify *his* behavior on the grounds that he was only following orders from above. Thus, there is a fragmentation of the total human act; no one man decides to carry out the evil act and is confronted with its consequences.[225]

We need desperately at this point in human history to understand and learn from the life of Eichmann. Eichmann represents the potential in most of us to lose our way morally when situational factors such as sanctioning by apparent authority, lack of empathy for a devalued group, hate, and psychological distance makes possible what is now unimaginable to us. Eichmann himself was unique due to the immensity of his crimes but the Holocaust was made possible by tens of thousands like him who in smaller but no less significant ways abdicated their ordinary moral nature in regards to a devalued *out-group*. One example of these *lesser Eichmanns* is Einsatzgruppen C member Wilhelm Findeisen, who served as a gas van operator:

> The van was not used immediately when we arrived in Kiev. When we first arrived, they were only carrying out isolated actions. Being a driver, I had nothing to do with these isolated actions. One evening, several officers appeared and ordered certain people to go with them. They went into a private flat where they picked up a professor and his daughter. These people were then taken to a spot close to a piece of open land where a grave was dug.
>
> The people, i.e. the officers, then gave orders for these two people to be shot. One of the officers said to me, "Findeisen, shoot these people in the neck." I refused to do this as did the other men. The girl must have been about eighteen or nineteen. The officer shot the people himself as the others refused. He swore at us and said we were cowards, but apart from that he did not do anything else.
>
> The gas-van was used for the first time in Kiev. My job was simply to drive the van. The van was loaded at headquarters. About forty people were loaded in, men, women and children. I then had to tell the people they were being taken away for work detail. Some steps were put against the van and the people were pushed in. Then the door was bolted and the tube connected...I drove through the town and then out to the anti-tank ditches where the vehicle was opened. This was done by prisoners. The bodies were then thrown in the anti-tank ditches.[226]

To grasp and absorb Findeisen's statement is to begin to understand the Eichmann phenomenon, the *banality of evil*, and how war, genocide, terrorism, and mass murder are made possible by the behavior of ordinary people. Findeisen displayed a sense of moral understanding by refusing to shoot the professor and his daughter and even disobeyed a direct order from an officer to do so. Despite the myth that German police, security, and military officers would be shot for disobeying an order to execute civilians, the reality was that "no one would be punished for such refusal" and the worst that happened was being labeled a "coward" or being transferred.[227] It was possible not to take part in the "final solution" and many chose not to do so in an active role, thus distancing themselves psychologically from the horror they knew was all around them. Thanks to the diabolical genius of Himmler, enough space, in form of psychological distance, was created to permit the participation of tens of thousands of ordinary individuals in mass murder. While Findeisen refused to execute the professor and his daughter, he did routinely drive around a van filled with some forty victims, including children, while they agonizingly suffocated on carbon monoxide gas. And he routinely stood by while other victims dumped the bodies into anti-tank ditches.

A series of letters home from SS-Obersturmführer (First Lieutenant) Karl Kretschmer, serving in the Einsatzgruppen in Russia during the fall of 1942, to his wife and children reveals the personality and psychological state of an ordinary man involved, like Findeisen, in carrying out the daily mass murder as part of the Holocaust.[228]

No. 6 Sunday, 27 September 1942

My dear Soska,

How I'd like to be with you all. What you see here makes you either brutal or sentimental. I am no longer in the area of Stalingrad but further north in the middle of the front.... After my experiences in Russia, my lovely home means more to me than anything else in the world....

As I said, I am in a very gloomy mood. I must pull myself out of it. The sight of the dead (including women and children) is not very cheering. But we are fighting this war for the survival or non-survival of our people.... As the war is in our opinion a Jewish war, the Jew is the first to feel it. Here in Russia, wherever the German soldier is, no Jew remains. You can imagine that at first I needed some time to get to grips with this. Please do not talk to Frau Kern about this....

"Buy" is not the right word, the money is worth nothing, we barter. We happen to be in possession of old clothes, which are very much sought after. We can get everything here. The clothes belonged to people who are no longer alive today. So you don't need to send me any clothing or the like. We have got enough here to last us for a year. Please could you get hold of some salt for me—the white Kaisers-Kaffe type in packets....

I wrote to you that I might be able to find you a Persian rug. It now turns out that it won't be possible. First, I am no longer in the right area and second, the Jewish dealers are no longer alive.... This is my sixth letter. Today, I dispatched parcels no. 2 (butter) and 3 (two tins of sardines in oil, 2 rubber balls, 1 x tea and 2 packets of sweets for the children).... Once the cold weather sets in, you'll be getting a goose now and again when somebody goes on leave.... We live like princes.... Today, Sunday, we had roast goose (1/4 each)....

Take care of the children for me

With longing and love

In my heart,

your Karl

[Date not known]

Even if the end result is that the people here die of hunger, we will still take food for ourselves. But it need not go that far. That would only be if the worst came to the worst. We have got to appear to be tough here or else we will lose the war. There is no room for pity of any kind. You women and children back home could not expect any mercy or pity if the enemy got the upper hand. For that reason, we are mopping up where necessary but otherwise, the Russians are willing, simple, and obedient. There are no Jews here anymore.

Kursk, 15.10.1942

No. 11

Beloved wife, dear children,

At 7:00 we have coffee.... I always have four slices of bread. Then we work until 12.00. There is always good food for lunch.... Then back to work again until 18.00. For supper there is either something hot: roast potatoes with scrambled eggs or other dishes, or something cold: bread and some salami. You can see that our bodily needs are taken care of....

We spend the evenings either playing cards, boozing, or sitting together with the boss.... The first few days, I was tired and could not take very much but after that I managed to see the night through and was actually the last to quit the field.

I have already told you about the shooting—that I could not say no here either. But they've more or less said they've finally found a good chap to run the administrative side of things. The last one was by all accounts a coward. That's the way people are judged here. But you can trust your Daddy. He thinks about you all the time and is not shooting immoderately. So that's our life.

I hope the package for Wurzel will get there in time for his birthday. It would make me very happy.

Lots of kisses and greetings for the children

For their dear mummy a long deep kiss

You are my everything

Your Papa.

O.U., 19 October 1942

Dear Mutti, dear children,

Anyway, you need not worry that we are living badly here. We have to eat and drink well because of the nature of our work, as I have described to you in detail. Otherwise, we would crack up. You Papa will be very careful and strike the right balance. It's not very pleasant stuff. I would far rather sleep....

Are the children still behaving? Is Muckerle working hard at school? Has Volkmar stopped wetting his bed? He'll soon be a big man and should not be doing a thing like that anymore. And how about washing hands and brushing teeth? You know how important it is not to be sloppy. Dagi, too, should now become accustomed to sitting properly at table and not put her elbows on the table....

If it weren't for the stupid thoughts about what we are doing in this country, the Einsatz here would be wonderful, since it has put me in a position where I can support you all very well. Since, as I already wrote to you, I consider the last Einsatz to be justified and indeed approve of the consequences it had, the phrase: 'stupid thoughts' is not strictly accurate. Rather it is a weakness not to be able to stand the sight of dead people; the best way of overcoming it is to do it more often. Then it becomes a habit.... For the more one thinks about the whole business, the more one comes to the conclusion that it's the only thing we can do to safeguard unconditionally the security of our people and our future. I do not therefore want to think and write about it any further. I would only make your heart heavy needlessly. We men here at the front will win through. Our faith in the Fuhrer fulfills us and gives us the strength to carry out our difficult and thankless task....

Kretschmer was a committed member of the Einsatzgruppen who, on a daily basis, committed mass murder of innocent men, women, and children, yet, after reading his letters, one may become somewhat ambivalent about his evilness. Just as we may be ambivalent, so was Kretschmer about his activities in Russia. But for his participation in the "final solution," Kretschmer comes across as a normal family man who displays traits we consider admirable in terms of his care and concern for the well-being of his family. Kretschmer faithfully sends parcels home of food and even sweets and rubber balls for his children. He misses his family and wishes to be home again with them. He struggles with the nature of his unpleasant work and does not want to burden his wife with his gloom. Kretschmer, like Eichmann, is not a psychopath, and probably did not hate Jews but accepted their devalued *out-group* status, like Eichmann as well. Kretschmer's sanity, *unlike* Eichmann, was, however, hanging by a thread. Eichmann did not get his hands dirty with the blood of his victims like Kretschmer and his psychological distance from the actual killing afforded him refuge from the pangs of conscience. Kretschmer attempted to stifle his conscience through drowning the guilt in food, booze, and card playing, by focusing on all the good he was doing for his dear family, and by rationalizations that were full of holes, like his victims. He demeans his conscience as "stupid thoughts" and believes all would be "wonderful" indeed, but for these "stupid thoughts." He accepted Himmler's appeal that to give in to the "stupid thoughts" would be weakness and that it was a sign of strength to carry out these "not very pleasant" tasks for the good of *his* people. He resolves to shut down his empathy by showing no pity and to overcome his conscience by killing "more often" so that it "becomes a habit." To preserve his status as being tough and not being a coward, to not let down his comrades and conform to expected group behavior, to be able to ease the burden of wartime on his family, perhaps to avoid duty on the real front, and to fulfill his obligations to the SS, Kretschmer sold his soul and, deep down, he knew it. While we can be somewhat sympathetic to his plight, we also realize that in addition to the mass murder of innocent men, women, children, and babies, Kretschmer used the clothing of his dead victims to barter for food and goods for himself and his family, gorged himself on good food and alcohol while the spared villagers faced starvation, and sent home the rubber balls of a murdered Jewish child.

We need to consider that Kretschmer, as a member of the SS, was perhaps *not* typical of the German military and police forces in the Nazi-occupied territories of Eastern Europe and that his willingness to kill was therefore exacerbated by his authoritarian nature and commitment to Nazi ideology. Shortly after World War II, social theorist Theodor Adorno proposed that a certain personality type called the "authoritarian personality" were violence-prone and attracted to Nazism and other fascist organizations. Adorno compiled a list of the crucial traits as a test for such authoritarian personality called the "F-scale"—The "F" standing for Fascist. While the notion of authoritarian personality as measured by the F-Scale is generally not accepted as an explanation for who took part in the Holocaust, the notion of an authoritarian personality has taken hold in psychology as a particular personality type that tends to adopt a blind adherence to conventional values, become submissive to authority, and to believe aggression against out-groups is justified.

Authoritarian personality can be thought of as a personality trait that is within the range of traits of psychologically normal people and can range across a spectrum from low to high. Philip Zimbardo summarizes the research of John Steiner on the authoritarianism of the SS:

> Having lived through the horrors of Auschwitz, John Steiner (my dear friend and sociologist colleague) returned for decades to Germany to interview hundreds of former Nazi SS men, from privates to generals. He needed to know what had made these men embrace such unspeakable evil day in and day out. Steiner found that many of these men were high on the F-Scale measure of authoritarianism, which attracted them to the subculture of violence in the SS. He refers to them as "sleepers," people with certain traits that are latent and may never be expressed except when particular situations activate these violent tendencies. He concludes that "the situation tended to be the most immediate determinant of SS behavior," rousing "sleepers" into active killers. However, from his massive interview data Steiner also found that these men had led normal—violence-free—lives both before and after their violent years in the concentration camp setting.[229]

Kretschmer shows us that these SS men could not only live normal lives before and after taking part in the Nazi atrocities, but could also maintain a distinct normal self in the midst of the atrocity through a process Zimbardo calls *compartmentalization*.

> People can do terrible things when they allow the role they play to have rigid boundaries that circumscribe what is appropriate, expected, and reinforced in a given setting. Such rigidity in the role shuts off the traditional morality and values that govern their lives when they are in "normal mode." The ego-defense mechanism of compartmentalization allows us to mentally bind conflicting aspects of our beliefs and experiences into separate chambers that prevent interpretation or cross talk.[230]

While daily taking part in the mass murders, Kretschmer was also the tender and caring husband and father doing his best to provide for his family. As revealed in his own words, he was, "either brutal or sentimental." His mental angst occurs only when he tries to reconcile his murderous activities with his normal values during introspective moments when he takes down the barriers of his compartmentalized mind. Psychiatrist Robert J. Lifton found a similar phenomenon occurred in the minds of the Nazi doctors of Auschwitz who made the selections of concentration camp inmates for labor, gassing, or "experiments."

> Lifton asks how the Nazi doctors could do what they did and at the same time (some of them) show kindness to inmates, treat prisoners who were

pressed into work as doctors with professional courtesy, and go home to be kind husbands and fathers. His answer is that the Auschwitz environment forced them to adapt. They did so by *doubling*. This is a process whereby two opposing selves are created, one of which is responsible for evil. The two selves seem encapsulated, walled off from each other to avoid internal conflict.[231]

Kretschmer and the other SS men of the Einsatzgruppen tended to be high on the F-Scale of authoritarianism[232], which contributed to the relative ease of their willingness to take part in the Holocaust and accept the justifications for their actions provided by Himmler and other Nazi leaders. They also lived in a culture in which "obedience to authority and giving oneself over to a leader had positive value" and where "authoritarian values also pervaded the most basic of institutions, the family."[233] Excessive obedience to authority does not excuse nor substantially explain the Holocaust, but it does provide insight into one factor that allowed for the acceptance of genocide to occur with greater ease. Had certain Nazi organizations of relatively high authoritarianism, like the SS, not thrived, the scope of Holocaust would have been substantially diminished. But there was also substantial effort contributing to the Holocaust by the most ordinary of people, including individuals taking part directly in the acts of murder with their own hands. The best examples of these individuals were the "ordinary men" of Reserve Police Battalion 101.

Reserve Police Battalion 101

Christopher R. Browning, a professor of history at Pacific Lutheran University, conducted extensive research of a battalion of slightly less than 500 members of the German Order Police sent into Poland in June 1942 to carry out the "final solution." This research resulted in his book, *Ordinary Men: Reserve Police Battalion 101 and the Final Solution in Poland*.[234] Poland had the largest Jewish population of Europe (3 million in 1933) and most of them lived dispersed in smaller cities and towns. It would take an extraordinary effort involving massive manpower to eradicate the Jews of Poland, according to Hitler's wishes.[235] The Order Police were Germany's civilian police forces at the municipal and regional levels. Twenty battalions of about 500 men each were sent into Poland to help secure the newly occupied territories and to carry out the "final solution."

Browning, while examining documents related to indictments and judgments from German trials of Nazis who committed crimes against Polish Jews, discovered the well-documented investigation of Reserve Police Battalion 101 conducted by the Office of the State Prosecutor in Hamburg from 1962 to 1972. Browning was able to study the interrogations of 210 men, which permitted him to conduct a "detailed narrative reconstruction and analysis of the internal dynamics of this killing unit."[236] In Browning's words,

"Never before had I seen the monstrous deeds of the Holocaust so starkly juxtaposed with the human faces of the killers."[237]

Reserve Police Battalion 101 began its service in the newly annexed areas of western Poland after the German invasion in September 1939. Beginning in May 1940, the battalion took part in the forced resettlement to central Poland of nearly 37,000 "undesirables"—including Poles, Jews, and Romany—"as part of a demographic scheme of Hitler and Himmler's to 'germanize' these newly annexed regions."[238] From mid-October 1941 to late February 1942, the battalion was involved in the forced deportation to the east of Jews and Romany from Hamburg, Germany. In June 1942, the battalion returned to Poland; however, the composition of the battalion had changed significantly, with more than 80 percent of the men recently inducted into the battalion.

> But for the most part, Reserve Police Battalion 101 was now composed of men without any experience of German occupation methods in eastern Europe, or for that matter—with the exception of the very oldest who were World War I veterans—any kind of military service....

> The battalion was divided into three companies, each of approximately 140 men when at full strength.... Each company was divided into three platoons....

> The battalion was commanded by fifty-three-year-old Major Wilhelm Trapp, a World War I veteran and recipient of the Iron Cross First Class. After the war, he became a career policeman and rose through the ranks.... Trapp was clearly not considered SS material....

> Of the rank and file, the vast majority were from the Hamburg area. About 63 percent were of working-class background, but a few were skilled laborers. The majority of them held typical Hamburg working-class jobs: dock workers and truck drivers were most numerous, but there were also many warehouse and construction workers, machine operators, seamen, and waiters. About 35 percent were lower-middle-class, virtually all of them white-collar workers. Three-quarters were in sales of some sort; the other one-quarter performed various office jobs, in both the government and private sector.... The average age of the men was thirty-nine; over half were between thirty-seven and forty-two, a group considered too old for the army but most heavily conscripted for reserve police duty after September 1939.

> Among the rank and file policemen, about 25 percent (43 from a sample of 174) were [Nazi] Party members in 1942....

> The men of Reserve Police Battalion 101 were from the lower orders of German society.... Most came from Hamburg, by reputation one of the least nazified cities in Germany, and the majority came from a social class that had been anti-Nazi in its political culture. These men would not seem to have

been a very promising group from which to recruit mass murderers on behalf of the Nazi vision of racial utopia free from Jews.[239]

Browning's research clearly shows the men of Reserve Police Battalion 101 were simply a group of ordinary "average Joes," the majority of whom were not high on the F-Scale of authoritarianism, like many drawn to service in the SS, and of whom, we can safely surmise, the vast majority were not psychopaths.

In the early morning hours of July 13, 1942, the men of Reserve Police Battalion 101 assembled in the Polish village of Jozefow to receive instructions from Major Trapp on their first major action in Poland. They probably were expecting to take part in another relocation action. In their prior actions in Hamburg, it is very likely that most were aware of the fate of those being placed on the trains and that there was the occasional need for someone to kill a person unable to travel to the departure stations. Thus far, their psychological distance from the actual killing allowed them to fairly easily justify their actions. But, until this day in Jozefow, a village with 1,800 Jewish inhabitants, there was never the expectation and pressure for any of them to take part in the actual mass murder of innocent women and children.

Major Trapp, "Pale and nervous, with choking voice and tears in his eyes...visibly fought to control himself as he spoke."

> The battalion, he said plaintively, had to perform a frightfully unpleasant task. This assignment was not to his liking, indeed it was highly regrettable, but the orders came from the highest authorities. If it would make their task any easier, the men should remember that in Germany, the bombs were falling on women and children....

> He then turned to the matter at hand. The Jews had instigated the American boycott that had damaged Germany.... There were Jews in the village of Jozefow who were involved with partisans.... The battalion had now been ordered to round up these Jews. The male Jews of working age were to be separated and taken to a work camp. The remaining Jews—the women, children, and elderly—were to be shot on the spot by the battalion. Having explained what awaited his men, Trapp then made an extraordinary offer: if any of the older men among them did not feel up to the task that lay before him, he could step out.[240]

Of the nearly 500 men of the battalion, only about a dozen took up the offer to step out to be then relieved of the duty. Trapp stayed away from the forest where the executions took place and was reported by witnesses later that day to be distraught over giving the orders for the executions. Trapp's driver reported that Trapp confided to him, "If this Jewish business is ever avenged on earth, then have mercy on us Germans."[241]

Trapp carried out his orders much like most of the subjects in the Milgram Obedience Experiment who followed the experimenter's directions to deliver the maximum voltage to the "learner": with great reluctance and distress. His rationalizations to the men were more to convince himself of the necessity of the executions he was setting in motion. He, like the vast majority of the "ordinary men" carrying out the Holocaust, shifts responsibility to those above and below himself: "the orders came from the highest authorities" and the victims are deserving of death. Ervin Staub, a psychology professor at the University of Massachusetts, notes that, "One psychological consequence of harm-doing is further devaluation of victims."

> According to the just-world hypothesis, which has received substantial experimental support, people tend to assume that victims have earned their suffering by their actions or character....[242] Strong belief in a just world is associated with rigid application of social rules and belief in the importance of convention, as opposed to empathy and concern with human welfare.[243]

Like Eichmann, Findeisen, and Kretschmer, Trapp was probably not suffering from anti-social personality disorder and was probably not consumed with a hatred of Jews. Like Eichmann, Findeisen, and Kretschmer, however, Trapp's natural empathy for a devalued *out-group* was no match for the situational pressures involving the exigencies of war, obedience, conformity, self-image, and dispersion of responsibility. Zimbardo tells us that the primary lesson of the Stanford Prison Experiment is that "situations matter."

> Within certain powerful social settings, human nature can be transformed in ways as dramatic as the chemical transformation in Robert Louis Stevenson's captivating fable of Dr. Jekyll and Mr. Hyde....
>
> Good people can be induced, seduced, and initiated into behaving in evil ways. They can also be led to act in irrational, stupid, self-destructive, antisocial, and mindless ways when they are immersed in "total situations" that impact human nature in ways that challenge our sense of the stability and consistency of individual personality, of character, and of morality....
>
> Any deed that any human being has ever committed, however horrible, is possible for any of us—under the right or wrong situational circumstances. That knowledge does not excuse evil; rather, it democratizes it, sharing its blame among ordinary actors rather than declaring it the province only of deviants and despots—of Them but not Us.[268]

Had Trapp been required to actually pull the trigger as he had ordered his men, he likely would have been one of those to step out for reassignment. Because, as commander, he could remove himself from even witnessing the brutal killing process, he created enough psychological distance to allow himself to carry on as a crucial link in the "chain of evil" by giving the orders for his subordinates to do the dirty work. Trapp provides a good example of how a simple variable— proximity to the killing and those doing the killing—determines the moral choices of ordinary people that are largely independent of their character. The irony is that Trapp's disengagement from the killing process made him more effective as the doer of evil deeds. Thus, with Eichmann, even further removed from the killing than Trapp, the magnitude of evil could be much greater. Not only did Eichmann not take part in the killing, he didn't even see the victims (as victims about to be murdered) or the killers (while engaged in murderous operations).

Being the battalion's first involvement in mass murder, their methods were crude and ineffective compared to the cruel efficiency that later developed in carrying out the Holocaust. At first, the policemen were paired off with their victims who, after being transported by truck to the forest, were ordered to lie down in a row. The battalion men placed their fixed bayonets "on the backbone above the shoulder blades" as an aiming guide and, when ordered by their first sergeant, fired in unison.[245] Many policemen reported gruesome injuries due to frequent inaccurate shots that caused the victims' heads to explode, spraying blood, brain tissue, and skull fragments on the shooters. Victims were assembled within an earshot of the shooting, creating additional angst among both victims and policemen as it became known to the victims what their fate would be. There were no graves prepared so the dead "were simply left lying in the woods" and there was no official collection of clothing or valuables, though "some of the policemen had enriched themselves with watches, jewelry, and money taken from the victims."[246]

Despite the horror of the killing, Browning estimates that at least 80 percent of the battalion of "ordinary men" continued to shoot until, in a single day, all the 1,500 Jews of Jozefow not selected for work were killed, the vast majority of them women and children. In addition to the dozen or so who initially stepped out when offered by Trapp, others avoided shooting by various means. Some requested to be excused once the reality of the orders finally set in or after initially engaging in the shooting while others simply hid or busied themselves with other activities.

A thirty-seven-year-old tailor in the battalion, referred to under the pseudonym "Georg Kageler" by Browning*, carried out one shooting and then refused to continue after conversing with his next victims, whom he learned were "Germans from Kassel." Kageler stated, "I took the decision not to participate further in the executions. The entire business was now so repugnant to me that I returned to my platoon leader and told him that I was still sick and asked for my release."[247] Kageler was reassigned to guard duty in the marketplace where the victims were assembled for selection for either work or execution. Kageler's story provides a good example of how psychological distance and level of empathy affected his decision to shoot. At first, he accepted the rationalization of the Jews of Jozefow as the enemy, reducing his empathy sufficiently to allow him to take part in the killing. Upon taking part in a conversation with two victims and learning the mother and daughter were

---

* Browning's access to the judicial interrogations was under the condition that he could not use the real names of those interrogated due to German privacy laws.

German Jews, Kageler became empathic as these two people were not the enemy and were more like him than he initially believed and, the conversation itself decreased the psychological distance from their humanity. Unfortunately, Kageler's empathic response was, like Trapp's, weak, in that he merely reduced his own personal burden by creating psychological distance from the actual killing, but still took part as a component of the killing machine by serving guard duty at the collection and selection site.

Trapp and Kageler show, on an individual basis, why the Holocaust was so effective and efficient in carrying the systematic and orderly genocide of European Jews: using the authority of the state, the exigencies of war, and a vicious propaganda campaign that vilified and dehumanized the Jews, the vast majority of Germans and other citizens of the Greater Reich could find a self-justified zone of comfort to either passively stand by or actively take part in the Holocaust. The Nazi leadership clearly applied strong pressure for its military, police, and security forces to actively contribute to the goals of the "final solution" but wisely—in the sense of establishing the most effective and efficient killing machine—allowed those troubled by their conscience to opt out to a lesser role acceptable to their conscience. The Nazi leadership understood that is was far better to allow objectors to find a zone of comfort and still contribute, however minimally, than to punish them and lose entirely their support and engender sympathy for them from others who opposed or who were on the fence. The person in the Nazi leadership who bore the most responsibility for devising this incredibly destructive system of evil which diabolically exploited the frailties of the capacity for empathy was Himmler, a true evil genius. As Browning observes,

> Heinrich Himmler himself sanctioned the toleration of this kind of weakness in his notorious Posen speech of October 4, 1943, to the SS leadership. While exalting obedience as one of the key virtues of all SS men, he explicitly noted an exception, namely, "one whose nerves are finished, one who is weak. Then one can say: Good, go take your pension."[248]

Browning notes that the widespread demoralization of the men after the Jozefow massacre resulted in changes to alleviate "the psychological burden on the men." The men would now mostly be assigned to "ghetto clearing and deportation, not outright massacre on the spot" with the most of the on-the-spot killing undertaken by "Trawnikis," Soviet POWs trained by the SS.[249] As with individual policemen such as Trapp and Kageler, the battalion itself was allowed to adjust to its own level of acceptable psychological distance and still take part effectively in the "final solution." Rather than push these men too hard and risk decimating the battalion, providing them sufficient psychological distance permitted the battalion to be a key component of the Holocaust. Reserve Police Battalion 101, in just a four-month period, took part in the executions of at least 38,000 Jews and deportations of another 45,000 Jews to the Treblinka concentration camp. Browning concludes that,

This change would prove sufficient to allow the men of Reserve Police Battalion 101 to become accustomed to their participation in the Final Solution. When the time came to kill again, the policemen did not "go crazy." Instead, they became increasingly efficient and calloused executioners.[250]

The thousands of officers like Eichmann and Trapp giving the orders to round up the victims and execute them; the tens of thousands of SS *Sonderkommandos* and Order Police like Findeisen, Kretschmer, and Kageler rounding up the victims, shooting the victims and conducting the gassing operations; and, the hundreds of thousands of victims disposing of bodies: all form an "intermediate link in a chain of evil action" that made the Holocaust possible. Given the confluence of certain situational factors, unspeakable and unimaginable violence can become ordinary or, in the words of Arendt, *banal*. As Milgram concludes, "Arendt's conception of the *banality of evil* comes closer to the truth than one might dare imagine."

Shortly after the then fifteen-year-old Elie Wiesel was deported to Auschwitz from the small town of Sighet in Transylvania, Hungary, in the spring of 1944, a six-year-old Jewish child living in Budapest, Hungary, named Ervin Staub and his family went into residence in a "protected" house set up by the Swedish diplomat Raoul Wallenberg. Wallenberg went to Hungary on a mission to save Jewish lives and, using his diplomatic status, issued "letters of protection" that granted Swedish citizenship to thousands of Hungarian Jews after the war. Staub and his family survived the war and Staub attributes this experience as "one source of my intense and lifelong concern with kindness and cruelty."[251] In his book, *The Roots of Evil: The Origins of Genocide and Other Group Violence*, Staub reveals his childhood in Nazi-occupied Hungary reluctantly because of fear "that audiences and readers might discount the validity of what I had to say." Staub uses the Holocaust, the Armenian and Cambodian genocides, and mass killings in Argentina in the 1970s to provide a "psychological understanding of how genocides and mass killings come about." [253] Staub methodically and convincingly describes a process that starts with a society under "difficult life conditions" that identifies an internal devalued subgroup as a threat. "Gradually increasing mistreatment of this subgroup" progresses "along a continuum of destruction," ending in genocide or mass killing.[254] While the "behavior of bystanders can inhibit or facilitate this evolution," Staub concludes that "tragically, human beings have the capacity to come to experience killing other people as nothing extraordinary."[255]

Evil that arises out of ordinary thinking and is committed by ordinary people is the norm, not the exception.... Great evil arises out of ordinary psychological processes that evolve, usually with a progression along the continuum of destruction.... The most kind or the most brutal actions can appear reasonable and justified to people, depending on their perspective.[256]

Herein we find a paradox of evil: *While the evilness of Hitler, Himmler, and Heydrich was greater than Eichmann's, the Eichmann phenomenon of banality represents the greater evil to society.* The Hitlers, Himmlers, and Heydrichs are present in every society in small numbers but cannot succeed without the assistance of the Eichmanns who exist in large numbers in every society. The nature of the Hitlers, Himmlers, and Heydrichs of the world is pathological and highly resistant to change while the nature of Eichmanns of the world is within the psychologically normal range and can be changed. To prevent needless war, genocide, and terrorism, we must first and foremost address the Eichmann phenomenon.

The essence of evil is epitomized by the character and conduct of Himmler and to look at the face of Himmler is took look into the face of abject evil. Himmler consciously, knowing right from wrong, chose the annihilation of a whole race of people simply to further his own insatiable narcissistic needs. His decision to try and stop the exterminations and cover up evidence of the "final solution" late in 1944 and his attempt to negotiate a complete surrender to Eisenhower in exchange for personal immunity reveal his awareness of the morality of his actions and the utter selfishness of his motives. Most disturbing of all, when his meager ability to empathetic response was triggered by exposure to the actual mass murder of helpless civilians and he realized these same empathetic reactions by the Einsatzgruppen were interfering with the progress of the "final solution," rather than reconsider the morality of the exterminations, he used his intellect to find ways to override the natural empathy to the suffering of other human beings through various means such as creating psychological distance from the murder by using more "humane" methods'. These methods include the recruitments of local paramilitary forces and criminals to carryout executions, the carbon monoxide poisoning in gas vans, and finally industrialized mass murder by Zyklon B gassing in the death camps. The most depraved methods, in terms of utter lack of appreciation for the humanity of the victims, were forcing the victims to dig their own graves, the use of victims in the death camps as *capos*—enforcers of control and discipline, and the use of victims to conduct the gassing operations in the death camps.

Yet, people like Himmler, who generally fit a severe form of antisocial personality disorder commonly referred to as *psychopaths* or *sociopaths*, are a constant in society who make up about 1 percent of the general population[257]. Unlike psychotic people who lack capacity for moral judgment and are delusional, psychopaths understand the difference between behavior that is morally acceptable and unacceptable and can accurately assess their environment. We have referred to individuals with psychopathic tendencies who are socially or politically successful and who are charismatic and narcissistic as *Machiavellians*. Recent research suggests that psychopathic traits

---

* "Humane" methods were intended by Himmler to be from the perspective of his SS men and certainly not from the perspective of the victims.

have a genetic basis and result from anatomical differences in the limbic system.[258] Research at the Institute of Psychiatry at King's College, London, has found differences in brain structure of psychopaths that may provide a biological explanation for psychopathy. There is a brain structure called the uncinate fasciculus (UF) consisting of a brain white matter tract that connects the amygdala, responsible for generation of emotion, and the orbitofrontal cortex (OFC), responsible for impulse control and decision making. Researchers found significant reduction in the integrity of the structure of the UF in psychopaths and the degree of abnormality was significantly related to the degree of psychopathy.[259]

The prevalence in society of psychopaths may be the result of an *evolutionary stable strategy* (EES) that permits a limited number of "cheaters" to thrive in social groupings that are structured generally on the non-exploitive and altruistic behavior of the members. The concept of EES was developed by British evolutionary biologist and geneticist Maynard Smith defined "as a strategy which, if most members of a population adopt it, cannot be bettered by an alternative strategy."[260] The classic game theory example of an EES involves a population of a hypothetical species in which there are only two types of fighting strategy named *hawk* and *dove*. Hawks always fight as hard and unrestrained as they can and doves threaten but never hurt anybody.[261] Using a point system to quantify the outcome of individual encounters between hawks and hawks, doves and doves, and hawks and doves, there arises a stable ratio for hawks to doves in the population in which the average points of hawks equal the average points for doves. This stable ratio translates into the proportion of genes for hawk traits and dove traits in the population. When this stable ratio is reached, natural selection does not favor one gene over the other and an EES is reached.

In the hawk and dove game theory example used by Richard Dawkins in his book *The Selfish Gene,* the average payoff in points to an individual in the EES population, with a ratio of hawks to doves of 7 : 5, is 6 ¼. But a population of all doves would do much better with an average payoff to the individual of fifteen. While an all-dove population does much better than EES population of hawks and doves, the all-dove population requires an agreement that all members will be doves.

But, unfortunately, in conspiracies of doves, a single hawk does so extremely well that nothing could stop the evolution of hawks. The conspiracy is therefore bound to be broken by treachery from within. An EES is stable not because it is particularly good for the individuals participating in it, but simply because it is immune to treachery within. It is possible for humans to enter into pacts or conspiracies that are to every individual's advantage, even if these are not stable in the EES sense. But this is only possible because every individual uses his *conscious* foresight, and is able to see that it is in his own long-term interests to obey the rules of the pact. Even in human pacts, there is a constant danger that individuals will stand to gain so much in the *short-term* by breaking the pact that the temptation to do so will be overwhelming…. So, even in man, a species with the gift of conscious foresight, pacts or conspiracies based on long-term best interests teeter constantly on the brink of collapse due to treachery from within.... The general conclusions that are important are that EESs will tend to evolve, that an EES is not the same as the optimum that could be achieved by a group conspiracy, and that common sense can be misleading.[262]

While Machiavellian psychopaths such as Himmler represent a long-term threat to the society as a whole, perhaps their presence in society is due to the evolution of an EES involving a ratio of psychopaths to non-psychopaths.[263] While we all would be better off without the presence of psychopaths, this would require a "conspiracy of doves," which is extremely difficult, if not impossible, to maintain. It seems throughout history that most well-intentioned groups, whether it is a nation or large corporation, or a society based on religion or ideology, are infected by *hawks*. Over the course of our 6 million year history as hominids, a gene for exploitation of others crept in and has been able to survive because it has created an EES that, although not optimal, cannot be bettered by natural selection. Is it a coincidence that prevalence of psychopaths in populations is about 1 percent and for more than 99 percent of our history as hominids, we have lived as small groups of hunter-gathers numbering from about 20 to 150? Did an EES evolve in which one psychopath per social group became a stable ratio resistant to change by natural selection? The low but stable prevalence of psychopathy has been successfully modeled using evolutionary game theory analysis by Andrew M. Colman of the School of Psychology at the University of Leicester.[264] Whatever the answer is to the reason for psychopaths, it must be accepted that they are a constant in all societies and will continually try either to construct social, political, religious, ideological, or business organizations or take over such organizations already in existence.

The political and social ideology of Marxism-Leninism, although on its face espousing a society of equality, has been the political and social system most fertile for nurturing the authoritarian dominance of Machiavellian despots. Mao Zedong, chairman of the People's Republic of China, a country whose population was at the time one-quarter of the world's population, ruled China for nearly three decades from 1949 to his death in 1976. Under Mao's purges and failed economic policies, as many as 70 million people perished. The purges, internal exile and relocations, and failed economic policies of Joseph Stalin, general secretary of the Communist Party of the Soviet Union for three decades until his death in 1953, led to the deaths of as many as 20 million people. Cambodian communist leader Pol Pot's forced agrarian collectivization program from 1975 to 1979 resulted in about 2 million deaths or about one-fifth the total population of the country. The deaths resulting from these Machiavellian-led communist states plus the nearly 60 million deaths resulting from the Second World War[265] instigated by the Machiavellian Nazi leader Hitler account for the vast majority of the 167 to 188 million deaths by organized violence[266] that made the twentieth century, in the words of Niall Ferguson, the "bloodiest century in modern history."[267] Fascism, like

Marxism-Leninism, provides a highly fertile social structure for exploitation by Machiavellians such as Hitler.

Three men—Hitler, Stalin, and Mao—were responsible for more than 160 million deaths, yet to focus on people like them as the way to prevent future catastrophic destruction and loss of life is probably ineffectual and misguided. The next Hitler, Stalin, or Mao is present in every nation, organized religion, and political party and in every community, social organization, club, or business that contains several hundred members or more. Assuming the Machiavellians such as Hitler, Stalin, and Mao make up only 10 percent of the psychopaths who make up 1 percent of the population means that there are 30,000 such Machiavellians in the United States alone˙. To devise strategies to protect ourselves from these Machiavellians means we first must acknowledge that they exist in every large organizational entity and are constantly seeking to get control or maintain control through exploitation of others and resources. The hopes we may have identifying them before they take power or before they create havoc are unrealistic and naïve. Machiavellians are by their very nature charismatic and highly manipulative and we, the decent and good people, are naturally trusting and ineffective at detecting cheaters. They are the *hawks* and we are the *doves*. So how do we move forward to save ourselves—to save humanity?

˙ If this book is even modestly successful, then it is inevitable that several Machiavellians will read it. If you are such a person, there are three possible ways you are able to live with yourself: (1) You are totally oblivious to the pain and suffering you inflict because your empathy deficit is so extreme; or, (2) you are aware of the pain and suffering you cause but simply ignore it because your empathy deficit, while not extreme, is strong enough to negate almost all compassion; or, (3) your empathy deficit is moderate so you rationalize, like SS-Obersturmfuhrer Karl Kretschmer, your destructive behavior using the just world theory—the people getting hurt deserve it. If there is even the slightest chance you are such a person, we implore to step outside yourself and examine your life for signs that you have exploited and abused others to satisfy your own needs for power and self-importance. If you find that you fit the Machiavellian description, we appeal to your intellect to work your way through your empathy deficit for your own betterment and those under your influence. Your lack of empathy is a disability, but as an intelligent person, you should realize your obligation to use your intellect to compensate for the disability. As the hawk and dove game theory and the prisoner's dilemma game theory (that we will look at in the next chapter) show, life can be a win-win situation. As human beings, we have the gift to rebel against our genes for the betterment of all. What more can you possibly do to show the power of your intellect than to conquer a flawed genetic predisposition for the betterment of yourself and others? Please think carefully about it!

Chapter Ten

The Nature of Societies and Governments

*Mankind will, in time, discover that unbridled majorities
are as tyrannical and cruel as unlimited despots.*

- John Adams

Band, Tribe, Chiefdom, and State

We ended the last chapter with a question critical to our survival: In large societies that we know contain "hawks" plotting to exploit the vast majority of us who are doves, how do we devise systems of governance to prevent them from achieving control? First, we need to review the types of societies that we live in and their organization.

Jared Diamond in *Guns, Germs, and Steel: The Fates of Human Societies,* divides human societies into four classifications: band, tribe, chiefdom, and state. Bands have members that number in the dozens and the "organization is often described as 'egalitarian': there is no formalized social stratification into upper and lower classes, no formalized hereditary leadership, and no formalized monopolies of information and decision making."[268] Bands essentially consist of "an extended family or several related extended families" and are the societies humans lived in as hunter-gatherers probably exclusively "until at least 40,000 years ago, and most still did as recently as 11,000 years ago."[269] As we noted earlier, bands are the social organization of our nearest relatives, the primates, and is the social organization under which, over millions of years, our emotions evolved, particularly our capacity for hate and empathy. With the emergence of small areas with abundant resources about 13,000 years ago and the development of food production about 11,000 years ago starting in the Fertile Crescent, a larger organizational entity—the tribe—developed.

Tribes are similar to bands in that they "still have an informal, 'egalitarian' system of government" in which decision making is communal and there are no "ranked lineages or classes."[270] Tribes, however, typically number in the hundreds, usually live in fixed settlements, and consist "of more than one formally recognized kinship group, termed clans, which exchange marriage partners. However, the number of people in a tribe is still low enough that everyone knows everyone else by name and relationships."[271] Diamond points out that bands and tribes do not need a central authority to redistribute goods since the "economy is based on reciprocal exchanges between individuals or families" and that a police force and laws are also not needed because any two members in a dispute "share many kin who apply pressure on them to keep it from becoming violent."[272] With tribes, we have reached the end of the road for our natural genetic based capacity for empathy. As Diamond observes, when two members of different New Guinean tribal villages meet outside of their villages and are unfamiliar to each other, "the two [engage] in a long discussion of their relatives, in an attempt to establish some relationship and hence some reason why the two should not attempt to kill each other."[273] This conversation is an attempt to find empathy because without such empathy, hate fills the vacuum and violence naturally flows.

With societies larger than tribes—chiefdoms and states—people must interact with others who are not part of their known universe of family and clan. Kin altruism and reciprocal altruism based on empathy are not effective in preventing violent interactions. Centralized institutions and rules are required to impose order and to ensure the distribution of food and goods and an elite class of leaders with a monopoly of power is needed to oversee these large societies. These institutions and rules are not deeply imbedded in our nature through genetics but are cultural adaptations, or, to use the language of Richard Dawkins we saw in Chapter Three, *memes*. While the capacity for empathy is limited generally to that group considered our tribe, the capacity for hate is not and can grow to encompass the growing number of potential threats of increased population density and competitors. Thus, the hate-empathy gap has been growing steadily since the establishment of chiefdoms estimated to have started about 5,500 B.C. in the Fertile Crescent.

Chiefdoms range in size from several thousands to several tens of thousands of people, a size that "created serious potential for internal conflict because, for any person living in a chiefdom, the vast majority of other people in the chiefdom were neither closely related by blood or marriage, nor known by name."[274] The need to control internal conflict resulted in the creation of a centralized authority held in the person of a "chief," whose position was filled by hereditary right.[275] With chiefdoms came the first societies with class distinctions; a commoner class and privileged class for the chief's family. We also see for the first time in human societies the institution of slavery. In addition to the killing of persons from outside the chiefdom, those captured would be put to the use of the chiefdom as slaves. For the first time, we see a central authority shaping the extent of human empathy through its coercive power by defining members of the *in-group*—the chiefdom—and the *out-group*—all others. The chief had the exclusive right to use force to impose order and control and to make all significant decisions.[276]

Chiefdoms began a major shift in economies from the "reciprocal exchanges characteristic of bands and tribes" to a system known as "redistributive economy."[277] Reciprocal exchanges are a system of barter where something of value is given by a person with the expectation of receiving back something of equal value. There is no need for a central authority to monitor the transactions or act as a middleman. With agriculture leading to the growth of societies into chiefdoms and states whose success depended on members supporting the society through specialized functions, a central authority was required to collect essential food and goods and redistribute them.

States that first arose in Mesopotamia around 3700 B.C. consist today of populations of over one million. In states, central control and economic specialization are more extreme and organization is based not on kinship as in bands, tribes, and simple chiefdoms, but political and territorial lines.[278] States tend to be multiethnic and in most modern states, leadership is not based on heredity but on ability.

The central authority of chiefdoms and states provides the ideal environment for Machiavellians to take control and exploit their populations. The ability to control the wealth of a large society in the hands of a small elite ruling class inevitably leads to such exploitation because in every large society, there are always "hawks" present waiting for their opportunity to exploit the "doves." In addition to the appropriation of wealth, the populations are subjected to the hardships of warfare based on needless aggression arising from personal needs of the ruler such as the need to restore personal prestige. As John Jay wrote in the *Federalist Papers*, a series of articles that appeared in 1787-88 in support of ratification of the United States Constitution: "Absolute monarchs will often make war when their nations are to get nothing by it, but purposes and objects merely personal, such as a thirst for military glory, revenge for personal affronts, ambition, or private compacts to aggrandize or support their particular families or partisans." At best, chiefdoms and despotic states are under the control of "benevolent dictators" who ensure a basic standard of living and limited freedoms for their subjects. Frederick the Great, King of Prussia from 1740 to 1786, modernized government and supported the arts and education. At worst, we have the likes of Hitler, Stalin, and Mao. Yet, even under the rule of a benevolent dictator, Prussia during the reign of Frederick the Great was in a near constant state of warfare.

Diamond refers to chiefdoms as "kleptocracies" in which goods retained by the ruling class in excess of their need became a "tribute," a precursor of taxes.[279] Chiefdoms and states, in order to consolidate power in the elite ruling class, also established institutionalized religions or ideologies. Diamond notes that "official religions and patriotic fervor of many states make their troops willing to fight suicidally. The latter willingness is one so strongly programmed into us citizens of modern states, by our schools and churches and governments, that we forget what a radical break it marks with previous human history."[280] As in chapter four, in which we saw that chimpanzees who live in bands will not attack a rival band unless their numerical strength assures victory without serious loss, Diamond notes that sacrificial death on behalf of society in human bands and tribes is "unthinkable.... In all the accounts that my New Guinea friends have given me of their former tribal wars, there has been not a single hint of tribal patriotism, of a suicidal charge, or of any other military conduct carrying an accepted risk of being killed. Instead, raids are initiated by ambush or by superior force, so as to minimize at all costs the risk that one might die for one's village."[281]

Intertribal warfare has been occurring as far back as the archeological record indicates and likely has been a constant in all of human history. Professor Lawrence H. Keeley of the University of Illinois has found that about 90 to 95 percent of societies engage in war. Keeley has also found that despite the destructiveness of modern warfare between states, tribal warfare is on average 20 times more deadly than modern warfare with casualty rates as high as 60 percent as compared to 1 percent of combatants in modern warfare.[282] Psychologist Steven Pinker of Harvard University believes "our ancestors were far more violent than we are today" and that "we are probably living in the most peaceful moment of our species' time on earth."[283] For example, Pinker cites the work of criminologist Manual Eisner who found that "homicide rates in Europe had declined from 100 killings per 100,000 people per year in the Middle Ages to less than 1 killing per 100,000 people in modern Europe."[284]

These homicide rates can be misleading if we don't consider the effects of advanced medical technology in keeping present day rates much lower than even in the recent past. The Killology Research Group estimates that the murder rate of today would be at least ten times higher if we had 1930's medical technology and distribution, means of transportation and communication capabilities.[285] How high would the homicide rate in Europe be today if the available medical care was the same as in the Middle Ages when a scratch could lead to a deadly infection?

Despite Pinker's optimism on the declining violent nature of humanity, actual numbers of death from organized violence, as opposed to percentages, from the last century are appalling: The approximate 175 million deaths during the twentieth century due to organized aggression equals almost the entire world population at the time of Jesus Christ. Also disturbing is that given the more enlightened state of mankind concerning aggression as noted by Pinker, the fact that people are still capable of degenerating into the wholesale mass murder of groups of other people who present no direct threat such as during the Holocaust shows the capability for incredible violence still resides in the human psyche. With the increasing availability of weapons of mass destruction, the potential for catastrophic destruction eclipsing the last century is a clear and present danger. A single leader's bad day can lead to the destruction of millions of lives. Also, as noted in chapter two, there are serious threats to humanity that do not involve human aggression such as global warming, pandemic disease, poverty, food shortages, and droughts that cannot be solved by nations that are in the least indifferent and at worst actively seeking to undermine world stability.

Pinker believes that the seventeenth-century English philosopher Thomas Hobbes (1588-1679) "got it right" that life before civilization "in a state of nature was nasty, brutish, and short."[286] For most of the world's people today, life is drudgery, fearful, and shorter than it should be. There is room for great improvement in our ethical nature and sense of obligation to one another. Now is not the time to relax.

The Wisdom of John Adams and the Founding Fathers

Like Pinker, the Founding Fathers of the United States also took heed of the political philosophy of Hobbes in crafting its political philosophy and structure of government as manifested in the Declaration of Independence and Constitution. In *Leviathan*, Hobbes asks us to consider what life would be like without government in "the condition of mere nature." Because of each man's self-interest and desire to control resources at the expense of the other, men would constantly be in a state of war and fear and will "endeavor to destroy or subdue one another." In order to have peace, men must give up their right "to all things" and mutually covenant with others to submit to the authority of a sovereign that must have absolute authority. The sovereign "Commonwealth" has the power to enforce the covenant and the natural laws and to protect the people from danger from within and from without. Hobbes tells us there are three types of sovereign authority: monarchy where the power is vested in an individual representative of the people; aristocracy where power is vested in a select group; and, democracy where power is vested in a body of people in which all may take part. Despite Hobbes belief in the absolute authority of the sovereign, he also believed that the people retained certain liberties, including the liberty to disobey when their lives were in danger, the liberty not to incriminate oneself, and in situations where the sovereign has prescribed no rule, the liberty to act according to one's discretion.

While the Founding Fathers were opposed to monarchy and aristocracy, they did adopt the concept of a democracy in which the people mutually covenant to form a sovereign authority of which all would be subservient. The idea of a mutual covenant can be found in the first three words of the Constitution: "We the People." Also, the concept that a person not be forced to incriminate himself is found in the Fifth Amendment to the Constitution ("nor shall be compelled in any criminal case to be a witness against himself") and the concept of residual liberty residing in the people is found in the Tenth Amendment ("The powers not delegated to the United States by the Constitution, nor prohibited by it to the states, are reserved to the States respectively, or to the people.").

Hobbes implies that it is because of the inherent selfish nature of people that in all cases sovereign authority is required to keep the peace. This is only a partially accurate assessment of human nature. People will behave selfishly most often towards those who are not identified as being in the person's *in-group* and will most often cooperate with those being identified with the person's *in-group*. In the social groups of band and tribe, as Diamond notes, the members are able to generally resolve differences and police themselves without the aid of a central authority. Sovereign authority as described by Hobbes is not required for these groups because, as we believe, the kinship of the members allows for the effects of our natural empathy. Bands and tribes still suffered lives that were "solitary, poor, nasty, brutish, and short" as compared to mature civilization. But this was due not to an inability to live in peace internally, but to a lack of technology capable of producing advancements such as medicine and stable food production, and intertribal warfare. Hobbes and Diamond are, however, in agreement that large societies—chiefdoms and states—require a central authority to maintain peace. The natural empathy that extends to kin is incapable of controlling our mistrust and willingness to exploit those not considered to be part of our tribe. Nationalism is a form of artificially imposed tribalism that must continuously be taught as part of cultural learning and defections by members, such as treason, must be punished severely. A strong central authority is required to impose this learning and punishment.

John Locke (1632-1704) was a British philosopher who perhaps had the greatest impact on the Founding Fathers. In *The First Treatise of Government*, Locke refutes the concept that the only legitimate government is an absolute monarchy ruled by kings under "divine right." In *The Second Treatise of Government*, Locke espouses two critical social-political concepts that influenced the Founding Fathers: natural rights theory and the social contract. According to Locke, all people are created by God "being all equal and independent" and all people have natural rights of "life, health, liberty, or possessions" that existed before the introduction of civil government. All people are, under natural rights, obliged to respect the rights of others. Locke believed that civil governments are necessary to ensure that, when transgressions occur, the punishment should be proportional to the crime. The victim, in a state of nature without government, will tend to overreact to a wrong, leading to social instability. Impartial government magistrates are needed to ensure fair punishments. According to Locke, the only legitimate government is one instituted by the explicit consent of the governed; whose function is to preserve the rights to life, liberty, health, and property. Locke espoused religious toleration and the separation of church and state—concepts adopted by the Founding Fathers found in the Constitution's First Amendment ("Congress shall make no law respecting an establishment of religion, or prohibiting the free exercise thereof...."").

We hear the echo of Locke in the inspirational words of Thomas Jefferson found in the Declaration of Independence, arguably the most politically inspirational words of modern history: "We hold these truths to be self-evident, that all men are created equal, that they are endowed by their Creator with certain unalienable Rights, that among these are Life, Liberty, and the pursuit of Happiness. That to secure these rights, Governments are instituted among Men, deriving their just powers from the consent of the governed."

Another highly influential political philosopher on the Founding Fathers was Charles de Montesquieu (1689-1755) who advocated a republican form of government—in which the people hold sovereign power and elect representatives to exercise the power—as opposed to a pure democracy in which all citizens directly take part in governance. To ensure the liberty of citizens, he advocated for separation of powers through an executive branch, a legislative branch divided into two houses, and an independent judiciary. He also believed that education was critical to the stability of the republic. Montesquieu believed in toleration of different religions; that civil laws should not be based on religious principles nor be used to enforce religious norms of conduct. According to Montesquieu, God did not need the assistance of man in enforcing His laws and that when men attempt to do so, religion becomes an instrument of fanaticism and oppression.

There were numerous other influences that served to frame the political philosophy of the Founding Fathers such as Jean-Jacques Rousseau (1712-1778) or documents such as the Magna Carta and the English Petition of Rights˙, but it was the Enlightenment philosophers Hobbes, Locke, and Montesquieu who provided the forceful reasoning for a limited government derived from the authority of the people that inspired the experiment of American democracy that, to this day, represents, despite its shortcomings, the best model for the organization of societies larger than tribes. Of the Founding Fathers, the individual who we believe contributed the most to incorporating the best ideas of the Enlightenment philosophers into the framework of government was John Adams. We would even go so far as to argue that Adams was the individual who made the single largest contribution to the success of the new republic that called itself "The United States of America."

John Adams was born in Braintree, (now Quincy) Massachusetts, in 1735, the son of John Adams, a farmer and shoemaker, and Susanna Boylston

---

˙ Rousseau wrote *The Social Contract* in which he argued that "Man is born free, yet everywhere he is in chains." His writings were more influential on the 1789 French Revolution than on the American Revolution. The English *Magna Carta* of 1215 provided for rules of law that were fundamental and the highest authority, even higher than the rule of monarchs. It provided fundamental rights to freeman such as a trial by jury and due process of law. Trial by jury is a right found in the Sixth Amendment of the U.S. Constitution and the right not to be deprived of life, liberty, or property without due process of law is found in the Fifth Amendment. The English Petition of Rights of 1628 provided that: taxes could not be levied without the consent of parliament; subjects could not be imprisoned without a showing of cause; quartering of soldiers in homes of citizens was prohibited; imposition of martial law in times of peace was prohibited.

Adams. After graduating Harvard College in 1755, Adams taught school in Worcester, Massachusetts, for a few years and in 1756, began studying law with a Worcester attorney. Adams was admitted to the bar in 1759 at the age of twenty-four. As a young man, Adams was "self-absorbed and ambitious," yet also insecure and anxious about his ability to make his mark on the world.[287] He threw all his energy into the law and was "determined to understand human nature."[288] In his diary from this period, Adams wrote: "Let me search for the clue which led great Shakespeare into the labyrinth of human nature. Let me examine how men think."[289]

Adams began his rise in political stature with his opposition to the Stamp Act of 1765, which was the first direct tax on Americans by the British. Opposition to the Stamp Act was the beginning of the American colonies' quest for liberty and Adams was the voice of that quest through his well-reasoned and salient advocacy and writings in defense of liberties that "are inherent and essential, agreed on as maxims and established as preliminaries even before Parliament existed."[290]

On the evening of March 5, 1770, an angry and boisterous crowd of several hundred gathered at the Custom House in Boston. The city was under occupation by British troops since 1768 in an effort to maintain order in the face of growing opposition to Britain's oppressive policies such as "taxation without representation," trials without a jury, and general writs of assistance, which were search warrants that allowed customs officials to search any premises at any time without having to specify the articles sought or their specific location˙. "Incidents of violence broke out between townsmen and soldiers" and "the atmosphere in the city turned incendiary."[291] On this particular evening, "the crowd pelted the despised redcoats with snowballs, chunks of ice, oyster shells, and stones. In the melee, the soldiers suddenly opened fire, killing five men" in an incident known as the Boston Massacre.[292] The captain and eight soldiers were charged with manslaughter and the passions of the community were at a fever pitch against the British governance for the killings that Samuel Adams† called a "bloody butchery."

Because of popular outrage against the soldiers, any lawyer taking up their defense risked condemnation and a ruined reputation. John Adams was asked

---

˙ The Fourth Amendment to the U.S. Constitution was designed to outlaw general writs of assistance by requiring search warrants to be issued only "upon probable cause…particularly describing the place to be searched, and the person of things to be seized."

† Samuel Adams, a second cousin of John Adams, was a Massachusetts political figure who was an early supporter of opposition to British policies in the American colonies and a key figure in fomenting political resistance to the British, culminating in the American Revolution. He served as a representative to the Second Continental Congress where he signed the Declaration of Independence. Samuel Adams played an important role in the Boston Tea Party of December 1773, an act of political defiance to the British Tea Act in which 342 chests of tea were dumped in Boston Harbor. "Tea Party" politics has made a resurgence in the present American political scene seeking to capture the popular sense of defiance to present political order and zeal for revolutionary change.

to defend the soldiers and accepted in order to defend the principle that everyone was entitled to representation by counsel and a fair trial. Although some historians believe the desire for a fair defense of the soldiers may have been a shrewd political move by Samuel Adams to prove that Boston was not controlled by a lawless mob but the victim of British tyranny, John Adams's decision entailed considerable risk for himself and his family, and was consonant with his lifelong track record of acting with the utmost integrity.

The first trial held was against the British captain, in which Adams secured a not guilty verdict. The second trial was against the eight soldiers, in which six were acquitted and two found guilty of manslaughter. In the second trial, Adams told the jury, "Facts are stubborn things and whatever may be our wishes, our inclinations, or *dictums of our passions* [italics added], they cannot alter the state of facts and evidence."[293] These trials showed Adams's commitment to the rule of law and his profound understanding of the frailties of human nature. Adams sought to understand human nature and his greatest contribution, in our view, was his understanding of how both the citizens and the government can be corrupted by the power of enflamed human passion. For the rest of his political life, Adams would always seek to ensure that the structure of government would have safeguards to protect against the momentary arousal of human passion. In our more scientific and cold analytic approach, we choose to call this passion a *"limbic brain emotional response to a threat to survival or reproductive interests,"* but we are in essence referring to the same thing. The mob that attacked the British soldiers in the Boston Massacre was acting on uncontrolled limbic brain emotion—passion—and the jury sitting in judgment of the soldiers was likely to convict them unjustly out of the same uncontrolled limbic response. Adams was determined not to let it happen again. A couple of years after the trial, Adams would write in his journal:

> Ambition is one of the more ungovernable passions of the human heart. The love of power is insatiable and uncontrollable.... There is a danger from all men. The only maxim of a free government ought to be to trust no man living with power to endanger the public liberty.[294]

In the spring of 1776, while serving as a delegate to the Continental Congress in Philadelphia, Adams was asked for his views on government by a fellow congressman, North Carolina's William Hooper, who was going home to help draft a new constitution for his colony. This letter to Hooper, entitled *Thoughts on Government*, crystallized Adams' views on the structure and role of government and would serve as the foundation of his later writings and for the very form of government that eventually would be adopted by the American colonists. Drawing on the political philosophy of Montesquieu, Adams advocated for a republican form of government with two distinct legislative bodies to prevent the danger of a single legislative body being subject to the "transports of passion."[295] A further check on the power of the legislative branch would be an executive branch with the power to veto legislation. Again drawing on Montesquieu, Adams believed that an independent judiciary with judges appointed for life was essential for the stability of government as well as "Laws for the liberal education of youth, especially for the lower classes of people."[296]

On June 10, 1776, Adams was appointed to the "Committee of Five," along with Thomas Jefferson, Roger Sherman, Robert Livingston, and Benjamin Franklin, to draft a declaration of independence. Despite his own established and respected literary talent, Adams favored Jefferson to author the declaration. Amongst his numerous talents that contributed to the cause of the revolution, Adams was a shrewd judge of character and had an acute political sense. Jefferson, as a Virginian—the largest American colony—would garner the most popular support for independence and was a strong writer in his own right. It was Adams who, during the Second Continental Congress in May 1775, nominated another delegate to Congress from Virginia, George Washington, to command the Continental Army. Adams's biographer, David McCullough, observes, "Had [Adams's] contribution as a member of Congress been only that of casting the two Virginians in their respective, fateful roles, his service to the American cause would have been very great."[297]

The actual vote to declare independence was made on July 2, 1776, with twelve colonies voting in affirmation and one, New York, abstaining. "It was John Adams," McCullough notes, "more than anyone, who had made it happen."[298] Yet, his journey to fulfill his dream of the establishment of an independent republic dedicated to the "greatest quantity of human happiness"* was only just beginning and many years of turmoil and sacrifice lay ahead.

After being named by Congress as a commissioner to work with Benjamin Franklin and Arthur Lee to negotiate an alliance with France, Adams and his ten-year-old son, John Quincy, set sail for France across the North Atlantic aboard the 24-gun frigate *Boston* on February 17, 1778. The journey across the North Atlantic in winter was fraught with danger due to storms, rough seas, and icing, as well as the risk of capture by the British. During the six-and-a-half week journey, there was an armed engagement with the British cruiser, *Martha*, which was captured, and, during which, Adams took an active part in defense of the ship. Adams and his son arrived in Bordeaux on April 1, 1778, only to learn that an alliance with France was already reached on February 6, 1778, before Adams had even departed for France. Despite the mission largely being accomplished, Adams and his son did not depart France until June 17, 1779, arriving in Braintree on August 2, 1779.

In slightly more than three months, Adams would return to France after being chosen by Congress to act as *minister plenipotentiary* for the purpose of negotiation with Great Britain. During this brief interlude at home, Adams would draft what has become the longest operative constitution in the world: the Constitution of the Commonwealth of Massachusetts. The Massachusetts constitution would serve as a model for the federal constitution adopted eight

---

* The phrase is a quote from Adams's *Thoughts on Government*.

years later whose preamble was inspired by these words: "We, therefore, the people of Massachusetts...."

The influence of Locke is heavy upon the preamble to the Massachusetts constitution, drawing on his theories of natural rights and social contract: The purpose of government is "to furnish the individuals who compose it with the power of enjoying in safety and tranquility their natural rights.... The body politic is formed by a voluntary association of individuals: It is a social compact, by which the whole people covenants with each citizen, and each citizen with the whole people, that all shall be governed by certain laws for the common good." The concept of social contract was put into action: the ratification of the constitution required a popular vote of two-thirds.

The Bill of Rights, a series of ten amendments to the U.S. Constitution designed to limit the powers of the federal government over the rights of the people, was not adopted until December 1791, more than three years after the adoption of the constitution. Ensuring the freedoms of the people took front and center in the Massachusetts Constitution: the first part of the Massachusetts Constitution ("Part the First') is "A Declaration of the Rights of the Inhabitants of the Commonwealth of Massachusetts." And, first of these rights appearing in Article I, drawing upon Locke, the Virginia Declaration of Rights`, and the Declaration of Independence, is that "All men are born free and equal, and have certain natural, essential, and unalienable rights."[†] Based on Article I, the Supreme Judicial Court of Massachusetts would abolish slavery in Massachusetts in 1783, the first court in the nation to do so.

The Declaration of Rights continues with twenty-nine more articles, providing an exhaustive enumeration of rights designed to ensure the citizens of Massachusetts would be free of the tyranny imposed by the British, including the freedom to worship according "to the dictates of his own conscience," reasonable compensation for public taking of private property, the right against self-incrimination and the right to confront witnesses in criminal cases, the right to counsel and to a jury trial, freedom of the press and of assembly, and the "right to be secure from all unreasonable searches and seizures." In the last two articles, Adams put into effect two key provisions from his *Thoughts on Government*, which were drawn from the writings of Montesquieu. Article XXIX provides for the "impartial interpretation of the laws.... by judges as free, impartial and independent as the lot of humanity

---

[·] Adopted on June 12, 1776 and drafted by George Mason, the Virginia Declaration of Rights was the inspiration for the language in the Declaration of Independence that "We hold these truths to be self-evident, that all men are created equal" and served as the first constitutional embodiment of the natural rights espoused by the Founding Fathers. This declaration contained many of the rights and protections later found in the U.S. Constitution, including: government power derived from the consent of the people; separation of powers; due process; trial by jury; the right against self-incrimination; the prohibition of cruel and unusual punishments and excessive bail; the prohibition on general warrants (writs of assistance); and, freedom of the press.

[†] Article I was amended in 1976 by Article CVI so that "All *people* are born free and equal...."

will admit." To ensure their independence, the article provides for lifetime appointments to the bench "for the security of the rights of the people." The foundational principle of separation of powers is made absolutely certain in Article XXX which provides that:

> In the government of this commonwealth, the legislative department shall never exercise the executive and judicial powers, or either of them: the executive shall never exercise the legislative and judicial powers, or either of them: the judicial shall never exercise the legislative and executive powers, or either of them: to the end it may be a government of laws and not of men.

The second part of the Massachusetts constitution, "The Frame of Government," divides the power of the government into two legislative branches, a Senate and House of Representatives, "each of which shall have a negative on the other," a governor with veto power over the acts of the legislature, and a judiciary. In a unique provision "which was like no other declaration to be found in any constitution ever written until then, or since,"[299] Adams, drawing upon his own *Thoughts on Government* and Montesquieu, makes education a basic responsibility of government.

> Wisdom and knowledge, as well as virtue, diffused generally among the body of the people being necessary for the preservation of their rights and liberties...it shall be the duty of legislators and magistrates in all future periods of this commonwealth to cherish the interests of literature and the sciences.

The Massachusetts constitution is a profound statement of the principles of government necessary to overcome the dangers of human nature in the organization of large societies. In it, Adams drew upon the greatest thinkers of the Enlightenment, as well as a deep and insightful understanding of history, to construct a living document that, to this day, provides the foundation for, arguably, the best form of government known to man. All that we've tried to do in this book in providing an evolutionary, genetic, cultural, and psychological basis for human nature was well known and appreciated by Adams. Even more remarkable was Adams's and the other Founding Fathers' ability and courage to put into action their understanding of human nature for the betterment of mankind.

Despite a world containing seven billion people, we continue to struggle, fight, and sow the seeds of our own destruction because of a lack of true leaders of the caliber of Adams. Instead of a society that nurtures self-interested politicians, we should strive to develop leaders who are Philosopher-Scientist-Statesmen like Adams. It was Plato who disliked democracy because it was always in a state of flux, being swayed by opinion rather than reason and knowledge. Plato also believed most people were unfit to rule because they lacked wisdom and self-restraint and were likely to respond emotionally rather than for what is rationally good for society. Plato favored an aristocracy ruled by "philosopher-kings" trained to be guided by reason rather than passion, to have escaped the "Cave" and seen the "Good." Adams, who was accused by some of being aristocratic, no doubt agreed with Plato's ruling class elitism but was wisely wary of the ability of self-serving individuals to penetrate and take over any system of governance without sufficient checks and balances. Adams was also more optimistic than Plato about the underlying intelligence and wisdom of the common man despite man's ability to be swayed by momentary passions. The government chosen by Adams and the other Founding Fathers wisely found a balance between pure democracy and Platonic aristocracy. This was a representative democracy with foundational separation of powers. Adams's homage to Plato was, however, his instance on "wisdom and knowledge" being "diffused generally among the body of the people" as part of the Massachusetts constitution. We believe it is now imperative that society promotes an educational and political system that allows persons with the temperament of "philosopher-kings" to serve as public officials; men and women who, to use our terms, resist limbic, stereotypical and binary thinking, and who engage in deliberate cognitive empathy and rational decision making.

Adams set sail for France once again on November 15, 1779, but this time with his nine-year-old son, Charles, in addition to John Quincy. This journey across the Atlantic would prove to be more perilous than the first. Due to a serious leak that nearly sunk the ship, the *Sensible* proceeded to the nearest friendly port at El Ferrol, Spain, arriving on December 8, 1779. Rather than wait for repairs to be made, Adams chose to make the 1,000-mile journal over land and across the Pyrenees Mountains to Paris riding on mules. The journey took nearly two months, with Adams arriving at Paris on February 9, 1780. Adams probably would have arrived sooner had he chose to wait for the ship to be repaired. His decision to travel by land reflected not only his determination to carry out his mission but also a certain obstinacy and impatience. These character traits, while not winning him many friends in the diplomatic circles of the French court, helped enable Adams to accomplish key milestones in support of the war against Great Britain.

Growing impatient in Paris, Adams decided on his own as a private citizen, without the authority of Congress, to seek a loan to support the war effort from the Dutch Republic, traveling to Amsterdam in July of 1780 with his two sons. By the beginning of 1781, Adams was appointed minister plenipotentiary to the Dutch Republic but had made no progress in securing a loan due to the strong commercial ties between the Dutch and British and the lack of success so far in the American war effort against the British. Moreover, the shrewd and powerful French Foreign Minister, the Comte de Vergennes, displeased with Adams's mission as peacemaker and meddling in European power politics, was actively seeking to have Congress remove him from his position as the sole American peacemaker in Europe. In June of 1781, Congress acquiesced to the demands of the French by making Adams one of five commissioners to negotiate with the British and by requiring the approval of the French of any actions taken. Late that summer, Adams would suffer the greatest mental and physical distress of his life. Exhausted mentally and physically, alone, his commission to negotiate weakened by Congress, and without success in securing a loan from the Dutch, Adams fell ill with fever, possibly malaria or typhus, that nearly killed him. Once again, his determination and stubbornness pulled him through the illness and dejection.

The fortunes of Adams and America would improve tremendously with the surrender of British General Cornwallis and his army to General Washington and French General Rochambeau at Yorktown, Virginia, on October 19, 1781. The tide had turned and victory for America now was inevitable. In the spring of 1782, the Dutch recognized American independence and admitted Adams as the United States ambassador who would open the first American embassy in the world. In June, Adams would secure a loan of $2 million from three Amsterdam banking houses and in October, he would sign a treaty of commerce with the Dutch Republic. Late in October, Adams would be back in Paris and, along with Franklin and John Jay, began formal negotiations with the British. Nearly one year later, on September 3, 1783, Adams, Franklin, and Jay would sign the final peace treaty with Great Britain. As well as gaining formal independence from the British, the treaty also ceded all territory west to Mississippi River as well as navigation rights on the Mississippi River and the right to take fish along the coast of Newfoundland and other British territories in America.

In his final role as the face of America in Europe, Adams would serve as the first ambassador of the breakaway United States of America to its former sovereign, Great Britain. On June 1, 1785, Adams would formally present himself to King George III as minister plenipotentiary for the United States, the same king he and his nation disparaged as a "tyrant" who was "unfit to be the ruler of a free people" in the Declaration of Independence nine years earlier. In addition to the historic importance of the moment for America, this was the high point of Adams's political life that may not have been exceeded except for perhaps his election as president of the United States.

Before departing London and Europe for the last time in March of 1788, Adams would weigh in on the debate at home concerning the adoption of a new constitution. In early 1787, Adams wrote a paper called *A Defence of the Constitutions of Government of the United States of America* in support of the constitution with an exposition largely restating his principles for government found in *Thoughts on Government* and what he put into practice in the Massachusetts constitution. David McCullough, in his biography, *John Adams*, observes:

> Where it departed most notably from what he had written before was in its pronouncements on human nature.... Human beings were capable of great good, but also great evil. Thus, it had always been and thus it would ever be. He quoted Rousseau's description of "that hideous sight, the human heart," and recounted that even Dr. Priestly had said that such were weaknesses and folly of men, "their love of domination, selfishness, and depravity," that none

could be elevated above others without risk of danger. How he wished it were not so, Adams wrote. Thucydides had said the source of all evils was "a thirst of power, from rapacious and ambitious passions," and Adams agreed. "Religion, superstition, oaths, education, laws, all give way before passions, interest, and power."[300]

We of course agree with Adams and throughout this book have attempted to show through the social and biological sciences what he and the Founding Fathers already knew about human nature. And like Adams, we will attempt to provide insight into building societies that account for the frailties of human nature. Unlike Adams, however, we must consider the complexities of the globalized twenty-first century that includes seven billion people, a worldwide economy, the instant transmission of ideas across the globe, and weapons of mass destruction capable of destroying the planet.

Adams would go on to serve as the nation's first vice president for two terms under Washington and would serve as the nation's second president for one term from 1797 to 1801. Although a capable administrator, his greatest achievements towards the founding of a new nation and creating a model for sound "government of laws and not of men" were behind him, both as viewed from the lens of history and in his own opinion.

The most notable accomplishment of his presidency was carrying out his steadfast conviction that neutrality with France, despite its involvement in a war with much of Europe and an undeclared war on American shipping, was the best course for America. Adams was able to successfully guide the nation through three and one-half years of divisive clamor for and against the war with France until a peace treaty was reached in October of 1800. While holding out for peace, Adams also pushed Congress to create a Department of the Navy, enabling America to defend its interests around the world. One of Adams's last acts of his presidency also proved to be one of his most important and enduring, one that helped to ensure the rule of law under the constitution: the appointment of John Marshall as Supreme Court Chief Justice, who would serve for thirty-four years on the Court as one of the greatest, if not greatest, chief justices in history.

In the spirit of Adams and the Founding Fathers, we will now attempt to use the collective wisdom of the ages and the best the biological and social sciences has to offer on human nature to construct models for human behavior and interaction for individuals, organizations, communities, and nations. We hope these models will be used as guides to individuals, organizations, communities, and nations to create a better world.

Chapter Eleven
An Initial Solution to the Question of Man's Inhumanity to Man

No Man is an island, entire of itself...any man's death diminishes me, because I am involved in mankind, and therefore never send to know for whom the bell tolls; it tolls for thee.

-John Donne (1572-1631)
Devotions Upon Emergent Occasions, Meditation XVII

When human lives are endangered, when human dignity is in jeopardy, national borders and sensitivities become irrelevant. Wherever men and women are persecuted because of their race, religion, or political views, that place must—at that moment—become the center of the universe....
As long as one dissident is in prison, our freedom will not be true.
As long as one child is hungry, our life will be filled with anguish and shame."

-Elie Wiesel
Nobel Peace Prize acceptance speech, December 10, 1986

The Evolution of Cooperation: The Prisoner's Dilemma

Professor **Robert Axelrod** of the University of Michigan's Ford School of Public Policy sought to answer this question: "Under what conditions will cooperation emerge in a world of egoists without central authority?"[301]

Should a friend keep providing favors to another friend who never reciprocates? Should a business provide prompt service to another business that is about to be bankrupt? How intensely should the United States try to punish the Soviet Union for a particular hostile act, and what pattern of behavior can the United States use to best elicit cooperative behavior from the Soviet Union?[302]

By "egoists," he means individuals (or individual groups or nations) who have their self-interest as their primary motivation. The phrase "without central authority" means the decision to cooperate or not is based strictly on the individual's choice without the influence of any higher authority. Axelrod intimates that we collectively have adopted the view of Thomas Hobbes that "cooperation could not develop without a central authority, and consequently a strong government was necessary."[303]

Using a game called the iterated Prisoner's Dilemma, in which two players seek to gain the most points through a series of decisions whether to cooperate with or defect against each other, Axelrod created a Computer Prisoner's Dilemma Tournament. He invited experts in game theory to submit a computer program with decision rules on when the player (playing against the computer programmed with its own rules) should cooperate or defect with the goal of obtaining the most points. All the players had to use for information about their opponent is the prior decision history against that particular opponent. "The players can communicate with each other only through the sequence of their own behavior."[304] "Entries came from game theorists in economics, psychology, sociology, political science, and mathematics."[305]

The Prisoner's Dilemma is based on a hypothetical situation in which two confederates in the commission of a serious crime are arrested by the police and separately questioned by the police. Each suspect, without knowing what the other will do, can either cooperate with the other and keep quiet or can defect and implicate the other seeking the best deal for himself. "No matter what the other does, defection yields a higher payoff than cooperation. The dilemma is that if both defect, both do worse than if both had cooperated."[306] The outcomes of the interactions are quantified through a point system that determines the "payoff." For purposes of explaining the point system, we can be Player A in a match with Player B (who is the computer in Axelrod's tournament). If Player A and Player B both cooperate, they do fairly well and both receive 3 points, the *reward for mutual cooperation*. In practical terms, the two suspects don't implicate each other and the cops are stuck with a weak case that results in a minimal punishment. If we defect and Player B cooperates, we get the maximum 5 points for the *temptation to defect* and Player B gets 0 points called the *sucker's payoff*. Again, in practical terms, because we implicated Player B and helped the cops, we got the best deal and walked away (5 points), while player B, the sucker, held fast and cooperated with us and got the maximum punishment (0 points). If we defect (implicate Player B) and Player B defects (implicating us), we both get 1 point, the *punishment for mutual defection*. Since we both implicated each other, the cops have a strong case in which each player gets a little bit of a break for defecting but still got a long prison sentence. This is still better than being the sucker who gets 0 points for cooperating with a confederate who defects and implicates you getting the best deal for him and screwing you!

If this interaction with Player B, or any other person, *is a one-time interaction,* then it always pays better to defect against the other person. If the other player is going to cooperate, you are better off defecting and getting 5 points as opposed to cooperating and getting 3 points. If the other player is going to defect, then you are also better off defecting by getting at least 1 point instead of the sucker's payoff of 0 points. If the other player follows the same strategy, then all interactions involve mutual defections and the obtaining of a low score of 1 point for each interaction "which is worse than the 3 points of the reward that you both could have gotten had you both cooperated. Individual rationality leads to a worse outcome for both than is possible. Hence the dilemma."[307] While defection makes sense for a single interaction, for a series of interactions against the same opponent, mutual defection leads to a *lose-lose* situation (a 1-point average per interaction) while mutual cooperation leads to a *win-win* situation (a 3-point average per interaction). Even if players alternate getting 5 points for defecting against a cooperating player and then getting zero points for cooperating against a defecting player, the best they can average over the course of a series of interactions is 2.5 points, which is still less than the 3 points for mutual cooperation.

Almost all games and contests played against an opponent, whether individual or team competitions, are *zero-sum* games. For every winner, there is a loser, and, for every loser, there is a winner. The wins and the losses cancel out mathematically, hence the description as being "zero-sum." At the end of the Major League Baseball season, adding up all the wins and losses will leave zero. Some games, like the Prisoner's Dilemma are *non-zero-sum* games, in which you can have two winners (win-win) and two losers (lose-lose). Unfortunately, we tend to live our lives—individually and collectively, particularly in Western cultures—like we are playing a zero-sum game, believing that the only way we can get ahead is through someone else's loss. So when playing the Prisoner's Dilemma, we tend to apply the logic of zero-sum games, believing that the only way to win is to make the other player lose and so we always defect and the other player, thinking like us, does the same. What could have been a win-win for both sides ends up being a lose-lose. If only we could have realized that the Prisoner's Dilemma is a non-zero-sum game and that, instead of assuming that the other side will always defect, we could have had a win-win situation by giving the other side a chance to cooperate and then responded in kind.

Life is a non-zero-sum game that we so often play as a zero-sum game, turning opportunities for win-win into lose-lose. War is the ultimate zero sum game we have played since to dawn of civilizations over seven thousand years ago. Yet, even in war, under the right circumstances, opposing sides can learn to cooperate. The most famous example of spontaneously developing cooperation occurred during the trench warfare of World War I. Soldiers facing each other in trenches along the Western Front developed a system called "live-and-let-live." During the times between major engagements when the soldiers where hunkered down in the trenches, they deliberately avoided attacking the other side so long as the other side did the same.

> The live-and-let-live system was endemic in trench warfare. It flourished despite the best efforts of senior officers to stop it, despite the passions aroused by combat, despite the military logic of kill or be killed, and despite the ease with which the high command was able to repress any local efforts to arrange a direct truce.[308]

While World War I was, overall, a zero-sum game, along quiet sectors of the Western Front arose pockets of non-zero-sum game interactions with both sides generally choosing to avoid shooting to kill unless in retaliation for the other side's decision to shoot to kill. The key to allowing for the development of mutual cooperation was the special nature of trench warfare in which "the same small units faced each other in immobile sectors for extended periods of time."[309] The system of live-and-let-live deteriorated when the British High Command ordered hundreds of small raids on enemy trenches. Results from these raids could be monitored, leaving no way to pretend a raid was undertaken; if successful, prisoners were taken and, if unsuccessful, there would be casualties.

> The cooperative exchanges of mutual restraint actually changed the nature of the interaction. They tended to make the two sides care about each other's welfare.... The converse was also true. When the pattern of mutual cooperation deteriorated due to mandatory raiding, a powerful ethic of revenge was evoked. This ethic was not just a question of calmly following a strategy based on reciprocity. It was a question of doing what seemed moral and proper to fulfill one's obligation to a fallen comrade. And revenge evoked revenge. Thus, both cooperation and defection were self-reinforcing.... The live-and-let-live system that emerged in the bitter trench warfare of World War I demonstrates that friendship is hardly necessary for cooperation based on reciprocity to get started. Under suitable circumstances, cooperation can develop even between antagonists.[310]

Returning to Axelrod's Computer Prisoner's Dilemma Tournament, the question proposed was this: Which strategy, in a series of interactions (a total of 200 moves) against the same opponent (a random computer program), produced the highest score? Of the fourteen submitted entries from experts in the five disciplines of psychology, economics, political science, mathematics, and sociology, a program called TIT FOR TAT, submitted by Professor Anatol Rapoport of the University of Toronto, won the tournament. This program turned out to be the simplest of all the submitted programs: cooperate on the first move and then always repeat what the other player did on the previous move. In a game of 200 moves, if each player always defected, then each would player would finish with 200 points (1 point each for each move). If each player cooperated on every move, then each player would finish with 600 points (3 points for each move)˙. TIT FOR TAT, the winner, averaged 504 points per game.[311] Axelrod classified all of the top eight entries as "nice," meaning that all the top entries were never the first to defect.

> What accounts for TIT FOR TAT's robust success is its combination of being nice, retaliatory, forgiving, and clear. Its niceness prevents it from getting into unnecessary trouble. Its retaliation discourages the other side from persisting whenever defection is tried. Its forgiveness helps restore mutual cooperation. And its clarity makes it intelligible to the other player, thereby eliciting long-term cooperation.

Axelrod persuasively argues that even in biological systems, ranging from bacteria to humans, cooperation can evolve into evolutionary stable strategies (discussed in the last chapter) using Dawkins proposition of the "selfish gene" as the unit of natural selection in evolution. In environments in which bacteria consistently interact with the same organisms, the bacteria can "learn" which strategies lead to greater success and can play the game. While an always defect strategy is always an evolutionary stable strategy, the question is: How can an evolutionary trend of cooperative behavior get started and become stable? The two forms of altruism discussed earlier found consistent with evolution, *kin altruism* and *reciprocal altruism*, are both capable of creating an evolutionary stable strategy for cooperation. A sacrifice for other individuals who share a substantial amount of the same genes leading to the successful propagation of those genes can give rise to an evolutionary stable strategy of cooperating with related individuals. Reciprocal altruism can also lead to cooperation in a population of always defecting individuals if the cooperative strategy occurs, initially randomly as a mutation, as a cluster that is a nontrivial proportion of the interactions each has. Once there is a sufficient probability that interaction between two individuals will continue, then cooperation becomes stable.

The very history of life is one of cooperation between individuals starting with the first replicators (believed by most in the field of biology to be a primeval form of RNA) combining to form DNA. Segments of DNA (genes and chromosomes), combined to form the first cells, the prokaryotes, which contained no nucleus, which in turn combined to form the eukaryotes, cells with a nucleus of genetic material. Single eukaryotic cells began to cooperate to form colonies and within colonies, cells began to take on specialized roles, leading to the complexity of multicellular life forms, including us. Many biologists, including E.O. Wilson, now believe that members of a species organized into a distinct society, such as a colony of ants, form a

---

˙ A score of 0 for one player and 1000 for the other is possible if one player constantly cooperated with a player who always defected.

"superorganism" with each individual functioning like a cell does in the body of an individual.

We saw in chapter four that chimpanzees frequently cooperated through such behavior as grooming and sharing of food. In the animal kingdom, nature abounds with cooperative behavior towards non-related members of a species: female vampire bats will share blood by regurgitating blood into the mouths of unrelated female bats with whom they roost; ravens feasting on carrion will make loud calls to attract other ravens and even return to their roost to recruit more ravens; wolves will hunt together in packs; honeypot worker ants whose only job is to hang upside down as a source of nutrition for the queen; numerous species of grazing mammals that live in herds for protection from predators. While the common view of evolution is that of survival of the fittest through fierce competition—of "nature, red in tooth and claw" —nature more often than not seeks out ways that avoid direct competition as a means for survival.

Axelrod provides "four simple suggestions for how to do well in a durable iterated Prisoner's Dilemma" that "might serve as good advice to national leaders as well."[312]

"1. Don't Be Envious"

The most important aspects of life are *non-zero-games*, in which the other player doing well enhances your ability to do well (a *win-win*), whether you are an individual or nation. Think about the most important relationships in your life: family, friends, coworkers, and neighbors—all of them doing well is not a threat to you and their success contributes to your success. Likewise, their failure can contribute to your failure. If a nation has a stable government, security, a healthy economy, essential freedoms, and a decent standard of living, it is less likely to be an aggressor and less likely to be a burden on other nations.

If you measure your own success by comparison to these other players and they are doing better than you, which is common if you seek cooperation, you are likely to become envious. Envy tends to make you want to take the other player down, which means you will be tempted to defect. Defection will lead the other player to defect and will lead to a self-destructive cycle for you and the other (a *lose-lose*). The TIT FOR TAT strategy (always cooperate on the first move and copy the other player on subsequent moves), which is the most successful strategy in a world of egoists, by its own rules can never let you do better than the other player—the best you can do is achieve the same score or slightly less. According to Axelrod:

> TIT FOR TAT won the tournament, not by beating the other player, but by eliciting behavior from the other player which allowed both to do well. TIT FOR TAT was so consistent at eliciting mutually rewarding outcomes that it attained a higher overall score than any other strategy. So in a non-zero-sum world you do not have to do better than the other player to do well for yourself.

Even in the free market world of capitalism where the best strategy for business would seem to be the traditional Darwinian concept of survival of the fittest through competition, cooperation began to take hold, much as in the trenches of World War I, through formation of monopolies and price fixing. Cooperation was so successful for businesses in the United States in the late nineteenth-century that the government had to step in to level the playing field for consumers through antitrust legislation such as the Sherman Antitrust Act of 1890. It took the coercive power of the United States government to force business to become competitive! The example of anticompetitive business practices highlights an important point about cooperation: cooperation itself is neither ethical nor unethical but merely a means to an end. Anticompetitive business practices were good for business but bad for the consumer. The premise of the Prisoner's Dilemma itself was based on how two criminals, presumptively bad people, can beat the system and get away with the commission of a serious crime! So we must also ensure that cooperation is harnessed for good purposes. To do this, we must always ask, "How does the cooperation of the players affect those outside the game?" If the negative impact of the cooperation on those outside the game outweighs the positive effects to the players, the players should look to alternatives for improving on their goals. Looking outside one's group of players really means looking outside one's *in-group,* which means improving one's capacity for empathy. True international cooperation, if it can be obtained, is the ultimate *win-win* because there is no group outside the players to consider—the players constitute the whole world! If all nations are making choices that benefit all other nations, then all players benefit, leaving no one outside the game who could be hurt.

Just as cooperation itself is neither ethical nor unethical, so, too, is competition itself neither ethical nor unethical. In an evolutionary sense, competition does lead to improvement in the struggle for survival. In our everyday lives, competition can lead to better performance through such competitive activities as sports or preparing for entrance to college. In the business example above, we found the competitive nature of business improves the economy and supports the consumer. The test for useful and proper competition is this: In the process of improving the performance of the competitors, does the competition destroy or seriously debilitate the competitor who failed to win? If the competition has the tendency to cause undue suffering or hardship on the loser, the cost is too high. We should seek competition that allows the loser to fight another day. Competition in business may cause one business to fail, but the owners can regroup and try again if they so desire. The loss was not fatal. War is a competition which fails the test because its purpose is the destruction of the enemy.

The Prisoner's Dilemma contains a powerful lesson for us to live our lives individually and collectively, not by seeking to outdo each other, but by seeking to mutually improve ourselves and others. It reinforces a principle foundational to the Judeo-Christian heritage found in the Ten Commandments: "Thou shall not covet thy neighbor's house."

"2. Don't Be the First to Defect"

Axelrod calls rules in which the player's first move is always to cooperate "nice" and found they consistently did better than rules that were not nice in the Prisoner's Dilemma Tournament. The best way to elicit cooperation is to be the first to offer cooperation. By starting out an interaction with a new player with defection, the message is clearly one of noncooperation, engendering defection by the other player. "Nice guys" can finish first in the *non-zero-sum* game of life.

President Barack Obama, emboldened by democratic majorities in both houses of Congress during the first two years of his term, engaged in political defection against the Republicans by forcing through Congress his affordable healthcare bill ("Obamacare") without even minimal bipartisan support. The minimization of Republican input became most severe after the swearing in of Minnesota Democratic Senator Al Franken on July 7, 2009, giving the Democrats a filibuster-proof majority in the Senate. Regarding passing of Obamacare, President Obama engaged in *zero-sum* politics in which his win was the Republican's loss. In terms of Axelrod's Prisoner's Dilemma scoring, President Obama sought the maximum payoff of 5 points, with the Republicans getting zero points. Had this bill been the only legislation sought by President Obama for his entire presidency, such a strategy would have been effective from his self-interested standpoint. It appears President Obama did not pay enough attention to the fact that his presidency's effectiveness, despite who controlled each house of Congress, would depend largely on bipartisan efforts. Another option for passing of Obamacare would have been to seek true cooperation from the Republicans using a *win-win, non-zero sum* game strategy, resulting in 3 points for himself and 3 points for the Republicans. Although it would have involved many compromises and a win for the Republicans, it would have set the stage early in his presidency for cooperation and bipartisan efforts. This defection by President Obama was a strategic error that caused a severe response of defections on the part of Republicans in Congress. The Republicans were now intent on evening the score through their own *zero-sum*, *win-lose* strategies.

The filibuster-proof majority in the Senate was short-lived, with the swearing in of Republican Senator Scott Brown, who replaced Senator Edward Kennedy, on February 4, 2010 and the Democratic majority in the House of Representatives was lost in the November 2010 elections. For politicians, staying in office and staying in power are the equivalent of survival and so threats to political office and power implicate limbic brain binary and "us versus them" thinking, leading to a political form of hate that is obsessed with destroying the opponent. Evidence of limbic hate-fueled responses were apparent. During President Obama's speech to a joint session of Congress in September 2009, Republican Representative Joe Wilson of South Carolina yelled out "You lie!" In October 2010, Senate Minority Leader Mitch McConnell stated that the "most important thing" Republicans were seeking "is for President Obama to be a one-term president." Once in control of the House in January 2011, the Republicans immediately filed a bill to repeal "Obamacare," called the "Repealing the Job-Killing Health Care Law Act." President Obama and the Democrats' minimization of the Republicans during the beginning of his term led to a series of defections, resulting in political gridlock and complete lack of bipartisan efforts. There was a brief respite from the gridlock in the lame duck session after the November 2010 elections, but this was mainly due to the fact that failure to enact a law to extend the Bush-era tax cuts would result in all taxpayers seeing tax increases. The prospect of the American public's anger at all politicians, regardless of party, who failed to extend the tax cuts was enough to allow for limited cooperation. After this brief respite, the partisan gridlock resumed, causing a near paralysis of Congress that plagued the rest of Obama's term in office and resulted in the lowest Congressional approval ratings ever recorded. It is tragic that in this time of extreme difficulty and danger for America and the world, many of the leaders of the most powerful nation on Earth are locked into a series of *zero-sum* defections based on primitive limbic *Us versus Them* thinking that has resulted in a serious weakening of the government's ability to protect its citizens.

"3. Reciprocate Both Cooperation and Defection"

Reciprocity can work both ways. Being too nice can lead to being exploited. So, by letting the other player know you will not be exploited by responding to a defection with defection, you have a decent chance of changing his or her behavior. Hopefully, a rational player will realize the benefits of mutual cooperation, as opposed to mutual defection. The key to defection designed to elicit cooperation is its proportionality. In the Prisoner's Dilemma game, it is one for one. In real life, a defection of equal proportion to the other's defection may not be desirable. In nations under threat of insurgency or terrorism, the response to provocation usually exacts a much higher penalty for the defection but usually serves to embolden the enemy and intensify the conflict. The 2006 Israeli-Hezbollah War began by a Hezbollah "defection" by firing missiles into Israel border towns and the killing of three Israeli soldiers and capture of two. A thirty-four-day war ensued in which Israel retaliated through a massive bombing campaign that severely damaged the infrastructure of Lebanon and displaced hundreds of thousands of Lebanese. Although Hezbollah lost more fighters (about 500) than Israel lost soldiers (121), their ability as a guerilla group to withstand the punishing attacks of the most sophisticated and powerful military force in the Middle East was largely seen as a political victory for Hezbollah and a setback for Israel. These defections were clearly a *lose-lose* situation; however, one side's loss can be greater than the other's.

When two players are locked into a series of defections, as Israel is with its Arab neighbors, a way to break the cycle may be for the stronger of the players to retaliate slightly less in magnitude than the weaker player. Perhaps, a response equal to about 80 percent of the force of the provocation will be effective in that the response is still substantial but noticeably reduced. Not responding to provocations only encourages more defections; and overreaction, if not completely successful, emboldens the other player.

"4. Don't Be Too Clever"

The danger of complex rules is that by appearing to be random, they will fail to convey a message of your intentions to the other player. The only effective way of communication on the Prisoner's Dilemma is through the history of your moves. TIT FOR TAT conveys a clear and concise message that you are willing to cooperate *but will not tolerate defection*. The more complex the rule, the more likely the other player will not understand your message and assume no intention to cooperate, resulting in a policy of defection. By trying to outsmart the other player, you will probably end up outsmarting yourself.

Axelrod offers some ideas to help induce cooperation between players. The stability of cooperation based on reciprocity is based on the players having continuous and long-standing interactions in which they keep track of each other's past behavior.

"1. Enlarge the Shadow of the Future"

The willingness to cooperate with the other player is enhanced when "the future is sufficiently important relative to the present."[313] As we described earlier, in a one-time interaction, a rule of defection makes the most sense to each player, despite the potential reward for mutual cooperation. To make the future important, to "enlarge [its] shadow" requires making the "interactions more durable" and to "make the interactions more frequent."[314] Durable interactions are prolonged interactions that allow for patterns of cooperation to develop and to take hold. By increasing the frequency of the interactions, the next move appears more imminent and therefore takes on more importance. It also allows the players to take large issues in which there is a large temptation to defect for a large payoff, and break them down into small pieces where risking cooperation does not result in a potential catastrophic loss if the other player defects. The smaller gain from defecting on a small piece also appears small when compared to the potential gain from cooperation over the course of several moves.

"2. Change the Payoffs"

Picking up on the notion that making the long-term benefit of cooperation appear better than the short-term gain of defection, a change in the payoff for cooperation versus defection can "make the long-term incentive for mutual cooperation greater than the short-term incentive for defection"[315] The danger of increasing the punishment for defection, however, is that, unless it breaks the will of the other player, it may actually increase their motivation and desire to exact revenge. A better way to change the payoff to induce cooperation may be to increase the reward for cooperation while maintaining one-for-one defection or perhaps even reducing slightly the punishment for defection if you are the player who is in the more powerful position.

"3. Teach People to Care about Each Other"

This advice for promoting cooperation is extremely difficult without underlying empathy for the others for whom we should care about. Before we are capable of seriously caring about those outside of our natural *in-group*, we must find ways to enlarge the concept of membership in our *in-group* so that our natural empathy will flow to these outsiders. Teaching people to care about each other therefore means first finding ways to identify with those outside our natural *in-group* (much like the two New Guinean villagers from different tribes who meet and seek ways to find a relationship so as to avoid trying to kill each other) and then taking the time to understand the other's plight so that natural empathy will start to take hold. Only then will we have a decent chance of truly caring about the others who initially were not part of our natural *in-group*.

"4. Teach Reciprocity"

Axelrod is a realist who believes a rule of reciprocity found in TIT FOR TAT, while not the "height of morality" because of its insistence on an "eye for an eye," is a better rule for living than the morally superior rule of unconditional cooperation (which is Prisoner's Dilemma's version of the Golden Rule).[316]

> The problem with this view is that turning the other cheek provides an incentive for the other player to exploit you. Unconditional cooperation cannot only hurt you, but it can hurt other innocent bystanders with whom the successful exploiters will interact later. Unconditional cooperation tends to spoil the other player; it leaves a burden on the rest of the community to reform the spoiled player, suggesting that reciprocity is a better foundation for morality than is unconditional cooperation.[316]

While reciprocity is the best rule for encouraging cooperation, the danger lies in the tendency also to allow players to get stuck in a cycle of mutual defection, resulting in a conflict such as between Israel and its Arab neighbors. As discussed above, however, the use of a slightly less proportional response by the stronger player may result in restoring mutual cooperation.

"5. Improve Recognition Abilities"

In order for cooperation to take hold through reciprocity, each player must be able to recognize the other player from past interactions and the history of those interactions. Axelrod notes than even bacteria can recognize the interactions with another player through an exclusive relationship with that other player who is the host to the bacterium. In human affairs, effective control of nuclear weapons can be hampered by lack of verification: not knowing "what move the other player has actually made."[318] The difficulty the world is having with controlling Iran's production of fissionable weapons-grade uranium for potential use in nuclear weapons is due in part to lack of confidence in its claims. Reciprocity cannot develop, and therefore cooperation, where there is doubt that Iran is doing as it says it does. "Therefore, the scope of sustainable cooperation can be expanded by any improvements in the players' ability to recognize each other from the past, and to be confident about the prior actions that have actually been taken."[319]

Principles for Determining When to Cooperate and When to Compete

Whether as individuals, organizations, or nations, we are constantly making decisions as to either cooperate or compete with others. We are guided by our self-interest, family interest, or by the *in-group* we happen to identify with at the moment. As the prisoner's dilemma has shown us, in general, it pays for us and the other player to cooperate; most interactions can and should be *win-win*. However, there are times when competition, despite its *win-lose* nature, is, in the long run, better for all, as we saw in the American business model. What follows are principles to help you decide when to cooperate and when to compete based on the assumption that you and the other players are generally self-interested. We have chosen to use the word "compete" as opposed to "defect," as used in the prisoner's dilemma because it is more positive and more accurately reflects the nature of opposing others, which can be described as competition for limited resources, whether it be mating opportunities, fertile territory, sports championships, or business markets.

Principles for Cooperation and Competition

For purposes of these principles, a **"person"** includes:
- a natural person;
- any organized group of people, including business entities, special interest groups, collective bargaining associations, trade associations, sports teams, and political parties; and,
- Nations and their political subdivisions, including provinces, states, counties, municipalities, and government departments and agencies.

"Appreciable risk" means the chance of harm is any chance that is more than minor or insignificant. In terms of percent, appreciable risk may be expressed as always involving the likelihood of harm being at 50 percent or more. The more serious the harm, the lower the likelihood of harm is needed to qualify as appreciable. For harms of the greatest magnitude, a likelihood of occurrence of only 10 percent is enough to qualify as appreciable.

Principle (1): Except as provided hereinafter, a person shall always seek to cooperate in any interaction with another person.

Principle (2): Cooperation with another person shall not be undertaken when:

(a) The benefit to the person's cooperating is substantially outweighed by serious harm to persons outside of the cooperation; or,

(b) The outcome of the cooperation results in the appreciable risk that a person not a party in the cooperation will, through no fault of their own, suffer:

- Death or catastrophic loss; or,
- Irreparable harm of a serious and substantial nature.

Principle (3): Competition may be undertaken with another provided the other consents to the competition and the outcome of the competition does not result in the appreciable risk that either the parties to the competition or those outside the competition, through no fault of their own, will suffer:

- Death or catastrophic loss; or,
- Irreparable harm of a serious and substantial nature.

Consent under this principle may be implied by the voluntary participation in a system in which competition is an integral part of such system and obvious to an outside objective observer. For example, starting a business in a free market economy would constitute consent to engage in competition.

An example of acceptable competition based on competition is participation in organized sports in which reasonable precautions are taken to prevent serious injuries.*

Principle (4): Competition may be undertaken against another person without their consent when such other person has engaged in unjustified competition against the party seeking competition, provided:

- The impact of the competition is reasonably gauged to be proportional in potential harm to such other person to that suffered by the person seeking competition; and,
- Reasonable and diligent efforts are made to eliminate or minimize potential harm to those outside the competition.

The United States' invasion of Afghanistan after the 9/11 attacks, which were directed by individuals aligned with Al Qaeda having refuge and support by elements of the Taliban, was justified competition with Al Qaeda and the Taliban

---

* Due to medical concerns of children being susceptible to concussions and the serious medical conditions that result from repeated concussions, questions as to the safety of youth (American full contact) football are being raised, which may result in changes such as raising the age of participation, mandated medical evaluations, and rules changes to minimize forceful contact.

based on the proportional response and efforts not to harm noncombatants. Now after more than a decade of military operations in Afghanistan, the justification is weakening as the nexus of direct harm to the United States from the individuals being killed and captured weakens and the number of civilian casualties increases. The invasion of Iraq led by the United States appears under the Principles *not* to have been justified. The issue of responsible parties for 9/11 inside Iraq was questionable as was its control of weapons of mass destruction that posed a direct threat to the United States. The intelligence community inside the United States also appears to have failed to properly vet intelligence about Iraq's intentions and weapons programs due in part to the administration's unwritten, undeclared, but clearly communicated desire to punish Iraq for intransigence largely unrelated to the form of Islamic extremism behind the 9/11 attacks. Unfortunately, the administration came under the spell of limbic stereotypical thinking fueled by bias and an existential crisis. Under the model in Chapter Seven of bias to atrocity, the bias against Iraq based on the Gulf War of 1991 and its continuing opposition to United States and Israeli interests quickly progressed in the minds of certain key officials in the administration to actual hate. While the bias was justified (although dangerous if not tempered by neocortical analysis), the hate was not. Strong bias, binary thinking, hate, and a true crisis led many officials to place too much weight in questionable intelligence in a desire to eliminate the threat and, for those who did question privately, obedience and fear of appearing disloyal muted serious questioning.

Principle (5): For a person to be considered part of either a cooperative or competitive enterprise, they must knowingly, purposefully, and directly participate and stand to directly either benefit or suffer harm from such participation. Nonparticipation in either cooperative or competitive enterprises should be liberally construed. For example, being a citizen and non-combative of a country at war means such citizen is not in competition with the combatants of the opposing nation or sub-state actor.

Principle (6): A person engaging in cooperation or competition shall comply with international law and the laws of the sovereign with jurisdiction except when:
   (a) The competition itself is against such law and is justified under Principles (1) through (5); or,
   (b) The cooperation or competition contemplated cannot be lawfully engaged in and competition against the law is justified under Principles (1) through (5).

During the Civil Rights Movement in the 1950s in the South of the United States, civil disobedience to segregationist laws by African-Americans was a form of justified competition with the laws and policies of the government.

Table of Selfishness and Altruism: A Road Map to Rebellion against the Genes

Although we have genetic modules for both selfishness and altruism, the expression of these traits is largely controlled by situational factors discussed earlier in this book such as *in-group* or *out-group* status, seriousness of threat to self-interest or identified *in-group*, cultural norms such as obedience, and psychological distance from actual violence. It is also possible to engage in altruistic behavior through sheer force of will where situational factors would normally not lead the individual in that direction. In other words, we can, through the use of our neocortical brain, to use a phrase by Dawkins, rebel against our genes. Seeking opportunities to further our own interests and those of others through altruistic behavior is simply another way of seeking *win-win* situations through cooperation under the paradigm of the prisoner's dilemma or, to use the term of evolutionary biologists, to engage in reciprocal altruism. It is possible for individuals, groups, and nations to rate their actions on an algorithmic scale of selfishness and altruism so that these people, groups, and nations can consciously strive at all times for *win-win* opportunities that will advance their own interest and the interests of others and, ultimately, those of society at large. The hierarchy of desirable behavior towards the self and others is ranked in order or preference as follows:

RANKING	BEHAVIOR TOWARDS SELF	BEHAVIOR TOWARDS OTHERS	CLASSIFICATION
1.	Beneficial	Beneficial	Reciprocal Altruist (win-win)
2.	Harmful	Beneficial	Disinterested Altruist (lose-win)
3.	Harmful	Harmful	Destructive (lose-lose)
4.	Beneficial	Harmful	Antisocial (win-lose)

You may question why reciprocal altruism (*win-win*) is ranked as a more desirable social behavior than disinterested altruism (*lose -win*) since the disinterested altruist is the ultimate in self-sacrifice. The reason being that their self-sacrifice generally means they will not be around as long as or as effective as the reciprocal altruist. By helping themselves while helping others, the reciprocal altruist will generally be around longer to help others than the disinterested altruist and so is more beneficial to society. Likewise, the destructive (*lose-lose*) person is deemed less harmful to society than the antisocial (*win-lose*) person because the destructive person will not be around as long as the antisocial person, thereby limiting their harm to society. A suicide bomber is not as dangerous, in the long-term, as a terror group leader

171

such as Osama bin Laden. Antisocial people, especially the Machiavellians, are the most dangerous to society because of their potential for a lifetime of harmful behavior towards society.

Individual or collective acts of individuals, groups, or nations can be rated for *relative* harm or benefit and *absolute* harm or benefit using the following scoring system.

Measuring Relative Harm or Benefit

This system rates the relative harm or benefit through a scoring system that quantifies the harm or benefit as the product of the number of people affected times the amount of harm or benefit. A numerical value or "score" is assigned based on the number of people affected from 1, representing a single person to 780, representing 102,334,155 or more people. The larger the score, the greater the number of people classified under that score. So, while a score of 6 represents 3 to 4 people, a score of 55 represents 89 to 143 people. This represents the phenomena that when making decisions about large numbers of people, the relative value of each person is decreased in the sense of both the person making the decision and an observer. A person who commits a double murder is viewed much more harshly than if the person commits single murder. Our opinion of a killer of thirty-seven people doesn't change much if it turns out he or she killed thirty-eight or thirty-nine. The killer's opinion likewise is not affected much, either. The reason the table contains large numbers that are not nice round numbers is that the basis for each higher number of people in each higher score is the Fibonacci series of numbers in which each number is the sum of the previous two numbers. This results in a sequence of numbers that not only get bigger but the difference between numbers grows as well. The harm/benefit score for each population also grows larger but at a much slower pace to also account for the phenomena that as groups grow larger and larger, the relative value of each individual diminishes. So while 3 people receive a score of 6, which is two times (200 percent) the number of people, a group of 300 people receive a score of 78, which is one-quarter (25 percent) the number of people. The following table includes in the first column the population groupings based on 39 groupings from 1 to 102,334,155. In the second column is simply the ranking of the groups from 1 to 39. The third column contains the score based on the population group which represents the relative weight given each population group. The fourth column represents the relative harm for each population group based on the death of all members of the group calculated by multiplying the population group score by a relative harm factor of -9 (explained further below). The fifth column represents the relative benefit for each population group based on saving the lives of all members of the group calculated by multiplying the population group score by a relative benefit factor of +9 (explained further below).

Table (11-1) for Scoring Population Size for Determinations of Relative Harm

POPULATION	RANK	SCORE	DEATH VALUE (SCORE x -9)	SAVE LIFE VALUE (SCORE x +9)
1	1	1	-9	9
2	2	3	-27	27
3-4	3	6	-54	54
5-7	4	10	-90	90
8-12	5	15	-135	135
13-20	6	21	-189	189
21-33	7	28	-252	252
34-54	8	36	-324	324
55-88	9	45	-405	405
89-143	10	55	-495	495
144-232	11	66	-594	594
233-376	12	78	-702	702
377-609	13	91	-819	819
610-986	14	105	-945	945
987-1,596	15	120	-1,080	1,080
1,597-2,583	16	136	-1,224	1,224
2,584-4,180	17	153	-1,377	1,377
4,181-6,764	18	171	-1,539	1,539
6,765-10,945	19	190	-1,710	1,710
10,946-17,710	20	210	-1,890	1,890
17,711- 28,656	21	231	-2,079	2,079
28,657- 46,367	22	253	-2,277	2,277
46,368-75,024	23	276	-2,484	2,484
75,025-121,392	24	300	-2,700	2,700
121,393-196,417	25	325	-2,925	2,925
196,418-317,810	26	351	-3,159	3,159
317,811-514,228	27	378	-3,402	3,402
514,229-832,039	28	406	-3,654	3,654
832,040- 1,346,268	29	435	-3,915	3,915

1,346,269-2,178,308	30	465	-4,185	4,185
2,178,309-3,524,577	31	496	-4,464	4,464
2,178,309-3,524,577	31	496	-4,464	4,464
3,524,578-5,702,886	32	528	-4,752	4,752
5,702,887-9,227,464	33	561	-5,049	5,049
9,227,465-14,930,351	34	595	-5,355	5,355
14,930,352-24,157,816	35	630	-5,670	5,670
24,157,817-39,088,168	36	666	-5,994	5,994
39,088,169-63,245,985	37	703	-6,327	6,327
63,245,986-102,334,154	38	741	-6,669	6,669
102,334,155+	39	780	-7,020	7,020

In the next table (11-2), the relative harm or benefit is quantified on a scale of -9 to +9 with -9 representing the most harm, zero representing no harm or benefit, and +9 representing maximum benefit.

Table (11-2) for Scoring Harm or Benefit

HARM/BENEFIT	SCORE
- Death - Permanent catastrophic physical or psychological injury - Indefinite/long-term imprisonment in extreme cruel conditions	-9
- Rape - Permanent/long-term serious physical or psychological damage - Torture - Indefinite imprisonment in extremely poor conditions - Moderate/short-term imprisonment in extreme cruel conditions	-8
- Assaults causing serious injury - Moderate-term serious psychological damage - Indefinite imprisonment in humane conditions - Moderate/short-term imprisonment in extremely poor conditions - Complete destruction of property or financial interests	-7

- Assaults causing moderate injuries - Short-term serious psychological damage - Moderate imprisonment in humane conditions - Significant damage to property or financial interests	-6
- Assault causing minor injury or psychological damage - short-term imprisonment in humane conditions - Moderate damage to property or financial interests	-5
- Death threats or threats to cause serious physical injury - Short-term psychological abuse	-4
- Small damage to property or financial interests	-3
- Threats to cause moderate physical injury - Short detentions in poor conditions	-2
- Threats against property or financial interests - Short detentions in humane conditions	-1
- No harm or benefit	0
- Short-term psychological improvement - Short-term moderate improvement in health or living conditions	1
- Small property or financial benefit	2
- Short-term substantial improvement in health or living conditions - Small improvement in freedoms - Moderate-term moderate improvement in health or living conditions	3
- Moderate-term psychological improvement - Moderate property or financial improvement	4
- Moderate-term substantial improvement in health or living conditions - Preventing a serious injury	5
- Permanent/long-term psychological improvement - Permanent/long-term moderate improvement in health or living conditions	6
- Substantial property or financial benefit - Moderate improvement in freedoms	7
- Substantial improvement in freedoms - Preventing a catastrophic physical injury or illness	8
- Permanent/long-term substantial improvement in health or living conditions - Saving a life	9

To calculate the Relative Harm or Benefit (R), we multiple the population score (p) times the harm/benefit score (r). The equation is thus: $R = p \times r$. Relative Harm or Benefit can be expanded into three categories: Deaths, Injuries/Social Conditions, and Property. First, for a particular incident or series of incidents involving death, a product is obtained for the number people score (p) times -9 (the harm/benefit score for death). Next, the number score for a particular class of injured/helped people is multiplied by the score for the harm or benefit (-8 to +9, depending on the nature of the harm or benefit). Finally, the number score for particular class of people whose property is damaged/improved is multiplied by the score for the harm or benefit to the property (-7 to +7, depending on the nature of the harm or benefit). The calculation for the relative harm or benefit using the three categories is thus:

$$R = (P_{deaths} \times -9) + (P_{injuries} \times r_{injuries}) + (P_{property} \times r_{property})$$

For example, the calculation of Relative Harm for a suicide bomber who kills 20 people, seriously injures 50 people, and causes significant property damage to 10 people is:

$$R = (21 \times -9) + (36 \times -7) + (15 \times -6)$$
$$R = -189 + -252 + -90$$
$$R = -531$$

The calculation of the Relative Benefit of a donor, who provides $500,000 to a community resulting in medical care that cures 20 people of serious illness, provides long-term, moderate improvement in the health conditions of 50 people, and a substantial property improvement for 10 people is:

$$R = (21 \times 9) + (36 \times 6) + (15 \times 7)$$
$$R = 189 + 216 + 105$$
$$R = 510$$

The calculation of Relative Harm or Benefit is not a value judgment as to the goodness or badness of the motives of the actor(s) whose actions are quantified. It is simply a statement measuring the results in terms of effect on those impacted by the conduct without passing judgment as to the propriety of the conduct. Even when harmful acts are fully justified, having a system to calculate the harm or benefit—that can be used consistently and with less subjectivity—is necessary to ensure that the expected benefit clearly outweighs the harm and that harm is minimized despite the justification for use of violent or destructive force. The conduct of the suicide bomber in the example above will be viewed by the group who promoted it as the desirable outcome of an altruistic act, while the society whose people were victim will view the conduct as evil. While the Relative Harm has a negative value in this case—in terms of its impact on the victims—this number is not a judgment as to the justification or appropriateness of the conduct. It is simply a quantification of effect. For example, the dropping of the atomic bomb on Hiroshima has, in terms of deaths and injuries alone, a Relative Harm value, based on a conservative estimate of 90,000 deaths and 70,000 injuries, of -4,908. We are not sidestepping judgments as to absolute good and evil—those rules follow in later in the chapter.

Measuring Absolute Harm or Benefit

Absolute Harm or Benefit (A) is a value that represents the effect of harmful or beneficial conduct, with each person being of equal value. There is no diminishing of value as the population of those affected grows. It is absolute in the sense of the number people involved; the scoring of harm or benefit based on Table 2 still involves a subjective element that is used to calculate Absolute Harm or Benefit. Absolute Harm or Benefit is simply the product of the total number of people affected ("n") times the harm/benefit score ("r") in Table 2. The equation is thus: $A = n \times r$. Like Relative Harm or Benefit, Absolute Harm or Benefit can be expanded into three categories: Deaths, Injuries/Social Conditions, and Property. The calculation for the Absolute Harm or Benefit using the three categories is thus:

$$A = (n_{deaths} \times -9) + (n_{injuries} \times r_{injuries}) + (n_{property} \times r_{property})$$

The larger the number of people affected, the greater the effect of Absolute Harm or Benefit over Relative Harm or Benefit. The Relative Harm value in terms of death and injury from the atomic bomb dropped on Hiroshima was determined to be -4,908. The Absolute Harm value, in which each victim's value is equal, is -1,370,000 (calculation: $A = [90,000 \times -9] + [70,000 \times -8]$).

Absolute Harm or Benefit is a linear relationship; if you plotted the relationship on a graph, you would have a straight line in which the amount of harm of benefit increases in direct proportion to the number of people affected[*]. Relative Harm or Benefit plotted on a graph would look like a curved line that increases sharply in slope but then flattens out, representing the relationship of relative harm or benefit which increase slightly while the number of people increases dramatically[†].

---

[*]   A linear relationship that can be expressed algebraically, using the harm factor for death, as $y = -9x$, where y is the harm and x the number of people.

[†]   As opposed to a linear relationship, this relationship is considered exponential.

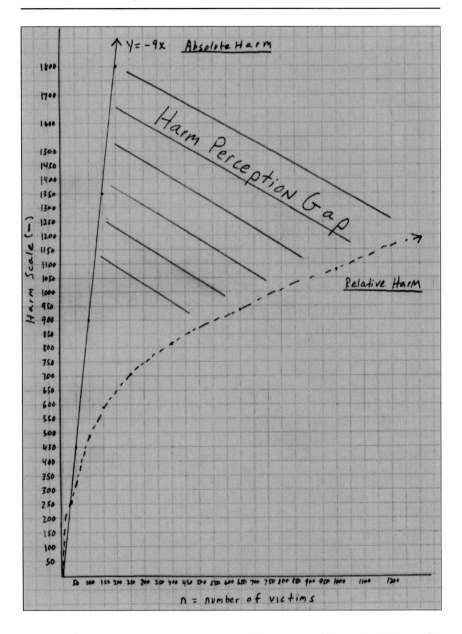

Graph of Absolute Harm versus Relative Harm: Above 50 victims, the perception of harm falls below the actual harm. The gap grows extremely large as the number of victims increases. Our inability to accurately grasp the magnitude of harm for large numbers of victims is a product of our hunter-gatherer past in which, for the vast majority of human history, people lived in bands that rarely exceeded a few dozen individuals.

In terms of perception, our perception of the magnitude of harm, reflected in Relative Harm, increases beyond the Absolute Harm for up to about 50 people involved. For about 50 people, the perception of magnitude of Relative Harm is about the same as the magnitude of Absolute Harm. Above about 50 people, the perception of magnitude of Relative Harm falls farther and farther behind the ever-growing magnitude of Absolute Harm as the number of people involved increases. The outrage we experience considering the crimes of Adolph Hitler, leading to a world war with tens of millions of deaths, although more than the outrage for the serial killer, Ted Bundy, estimated to have murdered 35 people, does not reflect the absolute enormity of Hitler's crimes as compared to Bundy. Our emotions are fairly good at gauging the harm of bad behavior that affects up to about 50 victims, but beyond that, we simply lack the emotional capacity to comprehend fully the nature of harm for larger numbers of victims. We can understand intellectually the larger numbers, but cannot understand them emotionally. Biochemist and Nobel laureate Albert Szent-Gyorgyi observed,

> I am deeply moved if I see one man suffering and would risk my life for him. Then I talk impersonally about the possible pulverization of our big cities, with a hundred million dead. I am unable to multiply one man's suffering by a hundred million.

Our emotional brain developed during the millions of years of living in small societies that rarely grew beyond 50 people. Our emotional capacity is a reflection of this evolutionary history. Thus, the dilemma of modern societies in the twenty-first century: Our neocortical capacity to build weapons of mass destruction and to plan and carry out enormous acts of aggression, but our emotional capacity limited to the world of small hunter-gatherers bands. We can comprehend intellectually a number such as 90,000 killed in the atomic bomb attack on Hiroshima, but we are incapable emotionally of appreciating anything even approaching one-thousandth its destructive impact. Even if we tried to interview 100 survivors of Hiroshima, just to gain a minute glimpse of the emotional impact, we would become numb emotionally after interviewing a few dozen. So, when considering our decisions and evaluating others for the magnitude of the harm or benefit, it is important to consider both the Relative and Absolute measurements. The Relative magnitude will allow us to consider our limited perception and that of others, and the Absolute magnitude will force us to consider a more realistic impact of our harmful and helpful behavior.

Combining the original table in this section that ranked desirable behavior by harm or benefit to self and others with the Relative and Absolute Harm or Benefit score for specific conduct or collective conduct provides a road map for evaluating both the desirability and undesirability of conduct and its magnitude. Use of this table can promote deliberate and intelligent effort to seek *win-win* situations rather than rely upon situational variables to guide us like a leaf blowing in the wind. Given the choice of the possibility of maximum benefit at the expense of another or moderate benefit for us and the other, we usually opt for the former. As the prisoner's dilemma shows us, this may make sense in a single interaction with another, but, when we must continually deal with the same people and groups, this behavior results in a *lose-lose*. Globalization means ever-increasing interconnectedness so we must seek opportunities for *win-win* opportunities and discard our *lose-lose* habits.

Road Map to *Win-Win* Behavior and Reduction of *Lose-Lose* Behavior

RANKING	BEHAVIOR TOWARDS SELF	SELF SCORE (R = A)[4]	BEHAVIOR TOWARDS OTHERS	OTHERS' RELATIVE SCORE (R)	OTHERS' ABSOLUTE SCORE (A)	CLASSIFICATION
1.	Beneficial (+)		Beneficial (+)			Reciprocal Altruist (win-win)
2.	Harmful (-)		Beneficial (+)			Disinterested Altruist (lose-win)
3.	Harmful (-)		Harmful (-)			Destructive (lose-lose)
4.	Beneficial (+)		Harmful (-)			Anti-social (win-lose)

Using the table, we should always monitor our conduct so that it fits into ranking number one with maximum scores for ourselves and others. We should encourage the disinterested altruists in ranking number two to take better care of themselves so that their long-term effectiveness in helping others is maximized. We should at the least avoid people in ranking three and four and if possible, discourage or prevent their harmful behavior. As governments and organizations, and as members of societies and organizations, we should always be on the lookout for the Machiavellians in ranking four and seek their removal from power through appropriate means and support systems of governance that minimize their ability to take power or abuse power. Below is the *Road Map to Win-Win* table with examples of each classification:

EXAMPLE	BEHAVIOR TOWARDS SELF	SELF SCORE (R = A)[*]	BEHAVIOR TOWARDS OTHERS	OTHERS' RELATIVE SCORE (R)	OTHERS' ABSOLUTE SCORE (A)	CLASSIFICATION
Raoul Wallenberg[†] Saved 70,000	Beneficial (+)	+9	Beneficial (+)	+2,484	+630,000	Reciprocal Altruist (win-win)
Ross A. McGinnis[‡] Saved 4	Harmful (-)	-9	Beneficial (+)	+54	+36	Disinterested Altruist (lose-win)
Timothy McVeigh 168 Killed 500 Injured	Harmful (-)	-9	Harmful (-)	-1140	-4512	Destructive (lose-lose)
Mao Zedong 70 million deaths	Beneficial (+)	+9	Harmful (-)	-6,669	-630,000,000	Anti-social (win-lose)

Had Richard Reid, the Shoe Bomber, succeeded in his plan to take down American Airlines flight 63 on December 22, 2001, and killed the passengers and crew, we could calculate the harm as follows:

---

[*] The Relative Harm or Benefit and the Absolute Harm or Benefit are the same for a single person.

[†] Wallenberg was a Swedish diplomat who went to Budapest, Hungary, in July 1944, with the mission to save Jews from the Nazis. Through the invention of a special Swedish passport issued to Jews, safe houses, bribes and threats, up to 100,000 Jews were saved from deportation to death camps by Eichmann and the Nazis.

[‡] McGinnis was a U.S. Army soldier serving in Iraq. He used his body to shield a grenade, saving the lives of four soldiers on December 4, 2006. He was posthumously awarded the Medal of Honor.

R_{deaths} = 66 x -9 = **-594**
A_{deaths} = 197 passengers x -9 = **-1773**
$R_{families}$ = 105 x -6 = -630
$A_{families}$ = 800 approximate affected people x -6 = **-4800**
$R_{economic}$ = 435 x -3 = **-1305**
$A_{economic}$ = 1,000,000 estimate economically affected x -3 = -3,000,000

Total R = -594 + -630 + -1305 = **-2529**
Total A = -1773 + -4800 + -3,000,000 = **-3,006,573**

RANKING	BEHAVIOR TOWARDS SELF	SELF SCORE (R = A)*	BEHAVIOR TOWARDS OTHERS	OTHERS' RELATIVE SCORE (R)	OTHERS' ABSOLUTE SCORE (A)	CLASSIFICATION
3.	Harmful (-)	-9	Harmful (-)	-2529	-3,006,573	Destructive (lose-lose)

While the choice of criteria to measure is flexible and somewhat subjective as well the extent of those affected by the harm, as long as a consistent approach is used, the table provides a method for evaluating behavior and gauging a response if deemed justified. The investment by Al Qaeda in outfitting and training Reid was, from their perspective, well worth the effort based on the score for Absolute Harm.

The Paradox of Defining Good and Evil

In order to prevent evil, we must know evil. In a world of seven billion people, 195 sovereign nations, more than twenty major religions, and several thousand cultures, a universal definition seems improbable. Yet, due to the shrinking of the planet through globalization, we are bumping into one another with alarming frequency. This jostling of people, groups, cultures, and nations increasingly involves disagreement over values, often leading to tension and aggression. Without a set of universal values to define good and evil, the continued shrinking of the world will result in ever-increasing tension and aggression. If we believe we have universally defined good and evil, it will inevitably be *interpreted* in a manner to justify behavior perceived as *good* by some and will be *interpreted* as *evil* by others, also resulting in tension and aggression. This is the paradox of defining good and evil: By neglecting to define evil, we allow the self-interest of a person or group to define it, often to the detriment of others; by defining evil, we provide the justification for behavior by a person or group that is likewise often detrimental to others.

A pure and absolute definition of good and evil cannot work for the entire world community, although it can work within a particular group with strong shared values such as a religious-based community. The closest we can come to

---

* Persons who seek to live, despite the fact their altruistic acts may put them in greater danger, are scored as +9.

absolute principles of good and evil, without invoking a deity or other supernatural cause, involves aligning our principles with our shared genetic heritage developed over our 5 million-year hunter-gatherer past. Examples of genetic-based prohibitions that appear to be universal are the incest prohibition and killing of *in-group* members. Any workable definition will also require flexibility to allow localized definitions of good and evil that will be respected unless in conflict with the few but near-absolute genetic based definitions. We see wisdom in the observation of George Orwell that, "Mankind is not likely to salvage civilization unless he can evolve a system of good and evil which is independent of heaven and hell." We see his comment as insightful not because notions of good and evil are independent of religion and not because secular and religious understanding of good and evil cannot coexist. The wisdom is contained in the idea that religious-based doctrines are absolute and inflexible, according the adherents of a particular religion and therefore immediately create conflict when applied to those outside the particular belief system. Yet, to survive as a species, we must be able, internationally, to agree on some very basic rules of behavior as being foundational. It turns out that when we look at the behaviors most people across most cultures seem to agree upon as being desirable and undesirable, we also find a strong basis for them in evolutionary biology. As we stated in chapter two, we find some evolutionary models useful and believe, without reaching any ultimate conclusions as to the source of our moral sense, we can use these models to understand ourselves and make the world a better place. Perhaps, use of the words "good" and "evil" make this goal insurmountable because of their strong religious connotation. But these are the words that most clearly strike at the heart of the matter and are still even used today by social scientists.

Fortunately, the vast majority of us do in actuality share these basic genetic dispositions as to what is good and what is evil. However, because of the limitations of our hunter-gatherer past when these genetic based dispositions formed, we have trouble applying them to anyone not deemed to be part of our *in-group*. Because of the smallness of the world and the massive destructive power of tools created by our powerful neocortical brain, we know intellectually that the *in-group* must be all of humanity if we are to survive. Yet, our more primitive emotional brain, which dominates our decision making, clings to family and tribal distinctions, resulting in very limited inclusiveness into the *in-group* and automatically reduced empathy for anyone deemed as belonging to the *out-group*. Persons identified as belonging to the *out-group* are easily subject to demonization and dehumanization when members of the *in-group* are experiencing a perceived existential threat. Moreover, determinations of *in-group* and *out-group* can shift and are subject to manipulation by figures of authority. The definition of good and evil can work if we can teach ourselves, in an exercise of the power of our neocortical brain, that all peoples are part of our family and tribe and therefore part of the *in-group* for purposes of determining moral behavior.

Because of the limitations of our genetic-based determinations of *in-group* status, we have and will continue to have great difficulty in agreeing on the status of the unborn. We have not been prepared by our genetic heritage to have clear genetic based guidance on the status of the unborn and will continue to struggle on a personal and societal level with their status.

Eleven Universal Model Foundations for Determinations of Good and Evil

1) All people of the world are of one tribe in the sense of a family or strongly cohesive local community.

2) All large human organizations of any type whatsoever (generally with greater than 150 members) are inherently corruptible and, due to the statistical population distribution of Machiavellians, are presumptively corrupted by Machiavellian influence unless they demonstrate sufficient organizational structures and processes that identify, prevent, and eliminate the exploitation of the general membership by those in governance of the organization.

3) *Universal evil behavior* is any intentional or reckless act or omission by a person that results in unjustified death or injury to another or damage or destruction of another's property or interests.

4) *Universal evil behavior* includes
   a) Sexual contact between parents and children or between siblings; or
   b) Sexual contact with preadolescent children; or
   c) Sexual contact with another compelled through force or threat of force; or
   d) Sexual contact with a married person not one's own spouse; or
   e) Stealing the property of another or malicious damage or destruction of the property of another; or
   f) Significant restraints on freedom, kidnapping, and slavery; or
   g) Wanton or needless destruction or injury to animal and plant life.

5) Any death, injury, or damage or destruction to property by the intentional or reckless act or omission is presumptively unjustified with the burden upon the person who caused such death, injury, damage, or destruction to prove justification.
   a) Justification for causing death or serious bodily injury is limited to cases where the person causing death or serious bodily injury is acting on the well-founded fear of imminent death or serious bodily injury to themselves, through no fault of their own, or other innocent person.
   b) Justification for causing injury is limited to cases where the person causing injury is acting on the well-founded fear of imminent injury to themselves through no fault of their own or other innocent person.
   c) Justification for causing damage or destruction to property of another is limited to cases where the person causing damage or destruction is acting on the well-founded belief that such damage or destruction was necessary to prevent a clearly greater harm.

183

d) Justification for significant restraint on freedoms and involuntary confinement is limited to proportional punishment for crimes adjudicated by a lawfully-constituted and impartial body of the sovereign state.

6) *Relative evil behavior* can be any behavior that is harmful to the interests of another that is prohibited by duly-enacted laws of a sovereign and that do not conflict with sections one through five inclusive.

7) *Good behavior* should be practiced whenever possible and encouraged in others.

8) *Good behavior* includes

   a) Sharing of resources with those in need;
   b) Cooperation towards mutually beneficial goals;
   c) Respecting the diversity and differences of others;
   d) Aiding others in peril and defending others subject to unjustified attack.

9) Whenever *universal evil behavior* occurs, people are obligated to identify it and work together to correct it.

10) No nation shall deprive any person under its jurisdiction, nor allow any person within its jurisdiction to deprive any person of life, health, safety, liberty, or property based upon the determination of an individual that such deprivation is sanctioned, approved, or demanded by a supernatural being.

   a) All imposition of punishments by nations shall be in accordance with duly-enacted laws administered by duly-elected or appointed officials.
   b) Such duly-enacted laws may, however, represent a collective view of moral standards imposed by their faith.
   c) Violations of private contracts or agreements may provide for monetary awards provided they are proportional to the violation.
   d) Private organizations, including schools and religious organizations, may, if not prohibited by local law, impose physical punishments on members who voluntarily are members provided the punishment does not result in death, severing of any limb or portion of the body, broken bones, severe pain, impairment or loss of function of any bodily function, bleeding, bruising, soft tissue damage, or lasting psychological damage

11) A "person" is defined to include a natural person, group, or nation.

   a) A natural person exists when born.
   b) The unborn who have reached the stage of unambiguous viability are *special status natural persons* whose lives have the protective status of persons unless superseded by the death or grave harm to the mother or other equivalent grave harm.

The Role of the United Nations

In the late eighteenth century, German Philosopher Immanuel Kant's *Perpetual Peace, A Philosophical Sketch* thoughtfully portrayed a peaceful world community whereby states are independent entities that respect the rights of its own citizens and welcome the international community to share in a global sense of community. Kant captured the essence of world peace and cooperation by expressing the idea that we, as a global community, must first ensure that citizens of a state or country are treated with dignity and respect by its own leaders. We must then apply the same fundamentals of human decency to our international community and perhaps, most importantly, to ensure that other nations do the same.

To uphold the virtue that every human has the basic right to life and that sovereign nation states must coexist peacefully, man has struggled to create a set of laws that will prevent people and nations from abridging these basic rights. We have been woefully inadequate in preventing injustice on an individual level and even more so on a global scale in preventing large scale atrocities, including ethnic cleansing, genocide, and war.

The League of Nations was created at the end of WW I, "The War to End All Wars," with the express purpose of preventing another world war. At its inception, it was thought to be a powerful elixir that would sooth the constant drumbeat of nations rallying to war. Although The League of Nations at its height had fifty-eight members and experienced some success in preventing skirmishes among nations, it was completely ineffectual in carrying out its primary mission: preventing future world wars. Shortly after the creation of the League of Nations, the winds of war began to stir across the globe. World War II raged across Europe and the South Pacific and displayed to the world the most heinous, vile examples of man's capacity for evil that history has ever known. At the conclusion of this Second World War, the world had once again sought to unite peoples and nations in the spirit of cooperation and to put an end to future wars: in October of 1945, the United Nations was born.

The introduction to the United Nations Charter reads:

WE THE PEOPLES OF THE UNITED NATIONS DETERMINED

To save the succeeding generations from the scourge of war, which twice in our lifetime has brought untold sorrow to mankind, and to reaffirm faith in fundamental human rights, in the dignity and worth of the human person, in the equal rights of men and women and of nations large and small, and to establish conditions under which justice and respect for the obligations arising from treaties and other sources of international law can be maintained, and to promote social progress and better standards of life in larger freedom,

AND FOR THESE ENDS

To practice tolerance and live together in peace with one another as good neighbours, and to unite our strength to maintain international peace and security, and to ensure, by the acceptance of principles and the institution of methods, that armed force shall not be used, save in the common interest, and to employ international machinery for the promotion of the economic and social advancement of all peoples....

With nearly two hundred nations coming together under this post-World War II agreement to uphold the spirit of peace and cooperation in a covenant that clearly delineates the duties and responsibilities of each sovereign nation, we surely will have lasting peace. Then came the first Indochina war, the Greek civil war, the Korean War, the Arab-Israeli War, Tunisian War, Algerian War, Vietnam War, Angola war, Cambodian Civil War, Invasion of Czechoslovakia, Lebanese Civil War, Soviet War in Afghanistan, Iran-Iraq War, Invasion of Granada, the Gulf War, Rwandan Civil War, Bosnian War, Kosovo War, Invasion of Iraq and Iraq War, War in Somalia, the still ongoing wars in Iraq and Afghanistan and skirmishes and tensions in many other countries around the world. Amazingly enough, this list represents only a small percentage of the wars, battles, invasions, ethnic cleansings, conflicts, and genocides that have taken place since the creation of the United Nations.

Though the United Nations charter may be imperfect, the authors believe strongly that it is our best hope to prevent future wars and other global atrocities. The United Nations Charter must reflect the realities of what causes conflict and ultimately human destruction. We must not allow a select few nations or a cohort of nations to monopolize power and control of a body that holds world peace in its hands. The United Nations Security Council must have the authority to quickly intervene in any internal national conflict or any aggression across borders, to prevent the slaughter of innocent civilians and conventional or nuclear war.

We have clearly shown the path that all men take leading individuals and nations from "bias to atrocity"; at the same time, the world has never seen such access to information on a global scale. We must keep access to this information open to all so that the world can monitor nations and governments in order to prevent tragedies. We have provided some suggested additions to the United Nations charter. By committing our global actions to the International Court of Justice and the International Criminal Court, we can seek global justice and closely monitor how justice is served.

MINIMUM REQUIREMENTS FOR NATIONAL GOVERNMENTS TO BE IMPOSED BY THE UNITED NATIONS

In order to maximize the ability of the world to promote cooperation, peace, stability, health, and safety the United Nations through its Security Council must commit to adopting and enforcing three basic doctrines that

- Limit the ability of Machiavellians to rule nations
- Encourage nations to adopt governments that limit needless conflict and aggression through minimum standards

186

- Require swift and effective international intervention when nations fail to deal with other nations under the *Eleven Universal Model Foundations for Determinations of Good and Evil* or when a nation internally engages in, or permits, genocide and other similar egregious harm

THREE INTERNATIONAL DOCTRINES OF COOPERATION, PEACE, STABILITY, HEALTH AND SAFETY

I. **Rules of Construction**

 A. Except as hereinafter provided, actions under these *Doctrines* may be taken by the affirmative vote of any twelve members of the Security Council. If less than twelve members—constituting a quorum—are voting, actions under these *Doctrines* may be taken by the affirmative vote of at least 75 percent of the voting members.
 B. These *Doctrines* do limit any other actions available to the Security Council under the Charter of the United Nations.

II. **Doctrines**

Doctrine (1): Machiavellian Heads of State shall be identified and their influence over international matters limited to the greatest extent possible through appropriate sanctions. Nations under autocratic rule of a Machiavellian leader shall be identified and isolated by the entire international community and maximum pressure exerted to bring about a nonviolent change to acceptable government. Such nations shall have no seat in the Security Council or any other committee or subcommittee, shall not have the right to vote in the General Assembly, and shall be barred from speaking in the General Assembly, except to respond to inquiries from the Assembly.

For purposes of this *Doctrine*, a "Machiavellian" is a person who has demonstrated by clear and convincing evidence, the following *Attributes*:

 I. Clinical psychopathy, antisocial personality disorder, narcissistic personality disorder, borderline personality disorder, or psychosis, as determined under the most current version of the Diagnostic and Statistical Manual of Mental Disorders (DSM);
 II. An established pattern throughout their public life of deception and exploitation; and,
 III. An established pattern of suppressing basic human rights of citizens in furtherance of political or personal goals or needs.

The Security Council shall appoint a Psychology Committee composed of thirty psychiatrists and psychologists who represent at least twenty nations.

Eligible members must have received their training in psychiatry or psychology at an accredited and internationally recognized academic institution of higher learning and be licensed to practice and in good standing in their home country. By vote of any ten members of the Security Council, a Machiavellian Review Subcommittee shall be appointed to evaluate a designated Head of State suspected of being classifiable as a Machiavellian. The Machiavellian Review Subcomittee shall consist of five members of the Psychology Committee selected randomly provided that no nation is represented by more than one member and the nation of the Head of State under review shall not be eligible to participate. The Subcomittee may conduct an investigation that includes the examination of records and other evidence and testimony of witnesses. The Subcomittee may also request the assistance of recognized experts in political science, diplomacy, or intelligence in findings of fact or evaluation of evidence. Upon request of the Subcomittee, the Security Council, upon the concurrence of any ten members, may demand records or other evidence, or production of witnesses of any member nation. The Security Council may impose appropriate sanctions on any nation refusing to provide requested records, evidence, or witnesses. An adverse interpretation may be made by the Subcomittee concerning any information wrongly withheld by a nation whose Head of State is subject of inquiry.

The Subcomittee shall determine if the designated Head of State is classifiable as a Machiavellian under *Attributes* I, II, and III. Such determination must be by unanimous vote of the Subcomittee members.

Proceedings of the Subcomittee shall be held in private but the Subcomittee, upon conclusion of its inquiry shall, within fifteen days, release publicly a report of its findings of fact and conclusions. For purposes of the report, individual identities and specific information may be withheld if necessary for legitimate safety or security concerns. The Subcomittee shall complete its inquiry within sixty days from its creation unless an extension for good cause is granted by vote of any ten members of the Security Council. In no event shall an inquiry exceed 120 days.

An affirmative vote of any twelve members of the Security Council is required for certification of the classification of a Head of State as Machiavellian. An affirmative vote of any twelve members is required for decertification from the classification of a Head of State as Machiavellian. If less than twelve members that constitute a quorum are voting, actions under this paragraph may be taken by the affirmative vote of at least 75 percent of the voting members.

Doctrine (2): Nations will be treated as full members of the international community, with full rights of representation in the United Nations that demonstrate adherence to the *Minimum Standards of Governance*. These standards are:

- All power of the government is explicitly delineated in a foundational document or constitution created and continuing by consent of the citizens, so that the government is one "of laws and not of men." For purposes of approving foundational documents, constitutions, and for electing representatives, all adult citizens, except those who have lost voting rights through lawful proceedings of duly constituted courts or administrative bodies, shall be entitled to vote under the principle of *one person-one vote*. Once a foundational document or constitution is established, amendments or voiding may only occur only through a supermajority vote of not less than 60 percent nor more than 80 percent of the voting citizens or their duly elected legislative body.

- The powers of the government shall be separated into at least three distinct branches: an executive, legislative, and judicial. There shall be a meaningful separation of powers so that no single branch can be viewed as having absolute or near absolute control of the government.
  o The executive branch may not enact laws but may, when authorized by the legislative branch, adopt and enforce regulations over specified areas of commerce and trade.
  o The executive branch may exercise veto power over any legislation, but if such veto power exists, the legislative branch shall have the power to override the veto through a supermajority vote of not less than 60 percent nor more than 80 percent.
  o The executive branch may exercise command and control of the military forces, including the right to engage in military action against other nations or non-state actors in other nations during emergencies, when immediate action is necessary to protect substantial threat to national security; provided, however, that declarations of war or long-term military interventions shall only be authorized by the legislative branch.
  o The legislative branch shall consist of at least 100 members who shall represent districts that are divided by an approximate equal number of citizens per district. Members shall be elected by direct vote of citizens who reside in the legislators' respective districts of representation. Additional legislative bodies may exist provided that all laws require approval of a body meeting the requirements of the previous sentence.
  o The legislative branch shall have the authority to remove for serious misconduct any elected or appointed government official, including a head of state, legislative member, or judicial member by a supermajority vote of not less than 60 percent nor more than 80 percent.
  o The judicial branch shall consist of judges who are elected or appointed to terms of not less than four years. They shall not be removed from office except for serious misconduct by the legislative branch.

- ○ The judicial branch shall be the final arbiter of the meaning of the laws and the constitutionality of laws. It shall have the power to void laws inconsistent with the constitution.
- The foundational document or constitution shall include a bill of rights that guarantees citizens' lives, property, and essential liberties are protected and cannot be deprived except by due process of law in proceedings of duly constituted courts or administrative bodies.
- In any nation with a federated system of government, in which there are internal subdivisions of government that exercise sovereignty for areas not delegated to the national government, such internal subdivisions shall conform to the *Minimum Standards of Governance*.

Any nation not meeting the *Minimum Standards of Governance* shall not be entitled to a seat in the Security Council and shall lose its vote in the General Assembly when the Security Council determines it has engaged in unjustified aggression against other nations, or in serious and substantial harm to the welfare of its citizens. Such right to vote shall not be restored until the aggression or harm to its citizens is corrected to the satisfaction of the Security Council. The Security Council may also adopt sanctions against such nations engaged in unjustified aggression against other nations or in serious harm to the welfare of their citizens.

Doctrine (3): All nations shall adhere to the *Eleven Universal Model Foundations for Determinations of Good and Evil* in their dealings with other nations. They shall not engage in, or passively allow or promote, genocide or ethnic cleansing, within their jurisdiction. All nations shall not wage war upon its own citizens and shall not, within their jurisdiction, fail to address a humanitarian crisis through reasonable efforts based on available resources. For purposes of this *Doctrine*, "wage war upon its citizens" means the employment of military or paramilitary forces against civilians using lethal force or the indiscriminate use of lethal force by such forces that is likely to harm civilians. The minimum number of civilians harmed or placed in jeopardy required to qualify as waging war is 1000 in any sixty-day period. Civilians include all noncombatants or persons not actively engaged in combat activity.

Any nation not adhering to the *Eleven Universal Model Foundations* in international relations, or engaged in, or passively allowing or promoting, genocide or ethnic cleansing, or waging war upon its citizens, or failing to address a humanitarian crisis within its jurisdiction shall not be entitled to a seat in the Security Council and shall lose its vote in the General Assembly. Such right to vote shall not be restored until the violations are corrected to the satisfaction of the Security Council. The Security Council may also adopt sanctions against such nations failing to follow the *Eleven Universal Model Foundations* in their international relations or for involvement in genocide or ethnic cleansing, waging war upon citizens, or failing to address a humanitarian crisis. In cases of genocide or ethnic cleansing, waging war upon citizens, or failing to address a humanitarian crisis, swift and unequivocal action by the entire international community is required including, when necessary, military intervention.

For purposes of this Doctrine, a failure to adhere to the *Eleven Universal Model Foundations* in international relations occurs when a nation engages in any act or omission that constitutes a serious and substantial violation of clauses (3), (4), (5), (9), or (10) against any other nation that results in, or has the clear potential to result in, serious harm to such other nation's national security or defense, economic health, access to or control of natural resources, or, the health and safety of its citizens.

We should note the fragile nature of our empathy and the ease in which hate can pervade meaning-based systems of belief or political identity. Our natural desire to help other human beings is not based on an intellectual process but based on the identification of the other as being like ourselves or close kin. In other words, we become motivated to help when the other person becomes the emotional equivalent of our self or our close family. The neural circuitry of empathy means that we do not help others because we know it is the right thing to do in an abstract sense; we do it because we have equated that person in need as being us in an emotional sense. The Golden Rule is based on our most basic emotional drives and endures because of this foundation. Hate can easily be nurtured against any out-group and when combined with dehumanization of the out-group and an existential threat posed by the out-group, extreme and merciless aggression is the expected outcome. Our international community must unite under the authority of the United Nations to promote governments that adhere to principles that prevent Machiavellian corruption, assure basic human rights, and peaceful coexistence with neighbors.

Some exceptional human beings have made empathy a conscious deliberative process, but for the vast majority of us, it is still a fragile emotional process subject to distortion and manipulation and limited to narrowly defined *in-groups*. Our future as a species may depend on most of us developing neocortical empathy, in addition to our limited capacity for emotional empathy and our willingness to confront and eliminate hatred in ourselves, and in our neighbors, community, nation, and the world.

Epilogue

S ince the earliest humans walked upright as "bipedal apes," we have seen humankind commit acts of ruthless aggression and terror against humankind, wiping away millions of people from the face of the earth.

History has shown us that our species has, within every population or large organization, those among us who, at the expense of others, seek to control, manipulate, and conquer for their own aggrandizement, despite the logic that life can be a non-zero sum game. Over the ages, this quest for domination has led to the extermination of tens of millions of innocent lives; if our course does not alter dramatically, hundreds of millions more will be lost.

History has also shown us that the vast majority of "normal people" will stand idly by, indifferent to the suffering and death that surrounds them, and that others will be manipulated to assist in the carnage simply due to situational factors such as a perceived existential crisis, presence of Machiavellian leadership, or dehumanization of an identified out-group believed to be collectively responsible for the threat.

We have shown that there are two special emotional states that natural selection has given us to ensure our survival and reproduction by ruthlessly eliminating other human beings deemed a threat to survival or reproduction, or, by making great sacrifices for those human beings we deem to be our family and tribe. Hate and empathy are the polar opposites that determine who lives and who dies and can easily be manipulated by situations and charismatic leaders.

Humanity now faces its end because the capacity for hate, which co-opts the most powerful and evolved cognitive functions of the brain, is limitless in reach and well-suited for the complex globalized society of the twenty-first century; whereas empathy is purely emotional and still limited in scope based on our hunter-gatherer past. To compensate for the deficiency of our natural empathy, we have stressed the need for people to engage in "neocortical empathy," whereby a deliberate conscious effort is made to recognize the humanity of all peoples.

Richard Colvin Reid attempted to detonate a bomb that was carefully crafted and artfully concealed in his shoe. As we trace the path of his existence on this earth and follow his footsteps to death's door, we reach the only conclusion possible: Reid is human; he has all the human traits that evolution has brought every one of us. Reid's path from working class citizen to international terrorist is well worn. Others have come before him, and others will follow, but the cycle can and must be stopped.

In this book, we have taken the bold step of providing a universal definition of Good and Evil based on evolutionary models. We have provided guidance on when people, groups, and nations should cooperate and compete so that all will benefit based on sound scientific principles of evolutionary biology and game theory. We have further provided a working template for the United Nations that will ensure an august international body, empowered to act using universal principles, capable of policing world affairs.

We have identified the need to apply scientific insight into human nature from psychology, evolutionary biology, and neuroscience into political systems so that we may curb human aggression. The lessons learned and applied here will break the cycle of aggression on a global scale, reduce the number of deaths attributed to those individuals seeking power and domination and, most importantly, they will eliminate future genocide and wars.

We have acknowledged the reluctance of many to accept models based on evolution and natural selection for guiding the conduct of human affairs, but have stressed that they are simply models and not ultimate judgments as to the source of the human spirit. Is there any living person among us who can absolutely tell us by what means a supernatural being or force has chosen to implement the design of creation?

Each one of us has the capacity to tolerate or commit acts of immense destruction or to engage in acts of great kindness. An understanding of our nature can truly limit the former and increase the latter and put us on the path to a non-zero sum, win-win global society. Each of us does indeed have the power to move the world for better or worse: For it is true under the law of universal gravitation that *When a pebble falls, the Earth rises to meet it.*

Notes

1   Wilson, E. 2004. *On Human Nature*. Harvard University Press, Cambridge, MA. p. ix

2   http://www.usnews.com/news/national/articles/2008/12/12/even-the-world-of-ants-has-its-suicide-bombers. Accessed November 26, 2011.

3   Ibid.

4   We called the standard for denying access to critical infrastructure "elevated suspicion," which was challenged as unconstitutional in a lawsuit filed against the authors in the U.S. District Court for Massachusetts by a lawyer for the American Civil Liberties Union (Downing v. MassPort, et al., Civil Action No. 2004-12513-RBC). In a bench ruling, Magistrate Judge Robert B. Collings ruled the use of elevated suspicion to deny access was not unconstitutional on its face.

5   Brown, L. May 2009. Could Food Shortages Bring Down Civilization? *Scientific American* Volume 300, Number 5: 50-57

6   Ibid, 57.

7   Wilson, E. 1998. *Consilience: The Unity of Knowledge*. Vintage Books, New York, NY. p. 291.

8   Hawking, S. 1988. *A Brief History of Time: From the Big Bang to Black Holes*. Bantam Books, New York, NY. p. 60.

9   The complete works of Charles Darwin can be accessed online at http://darwin-online.org.uk/

10 Darwin, F. 1887. *The Life and Letters of Charles Darwin*. D. Appleton, London.

11 Wilson. 1998. p. 171.

12 Ibid, 13.

13 Laughlin, R. 2005. *A Different Universe: Reinventing Physics from the Bottom Down*. Basic Books, New York, NY. p. 208

14 Ibid, p. xiv.

[15]   Ibid, p. 31.
[16]   Ibid, p. 158.
[17]   Diamond, J. 1999. *Guns, Germs, and Steel: The Fates of Human Societies.* W.W. Norton & Company, New York, NY. p. 25.
[18]   Ibid, p. 153.
[19]   Ibid, p.408, 421.
[20]   Ferguson, N. 2006. *The War of the Word: Twentieth-Century Conflict and the Descent of the West.* The Penguin Press, New York, NY. p. xxxiv
[21]   Ibid, p. xli
[22]   Zimbardo, P. 2008. *The Lucifer Effect: Understanding How Good People Turn Evil.* Random House Trade Paperbacks, New York, NY. p. 281.
[23]   Ibid, p. 195.
[24]   Ibid, p. 33.
[25]   Ibid, p. 31.
[26]   Ibid, p. 172.
[27]   Ibid, p. 211.
[28]   http://www.buffalostate.edu/orgs/bcp/brainbasics/triune.html. Accessed on November 3, 2009.
[29]   Ibid.
[30]   Ibid.
[31]   Ibid.
[32]   *See* Dozier, R. 2002. *Why We Hate: Understanding, Curbing, and Eliminating Hate in Ourselves and Our World.* Contemporary Books, Chicago.
[33]   Ibid, 4, 15.
[34]   Ibid, 19, 66.
[35]   Ibid, 4, 13.
[36]   Ibid, 49
[37]   *See* Arendt, H. 1963. *Eichmann in Jerusalem: A Report on the Banality of Evil.* Penguin Books, Toronto, Canada.
[38]   Dozier, 281.
[39]   Guth, A. 1997. *The Inflationary Universe.* Perseus Books, Reading, MA. p.15
[40]   Hawking, S. 1988. *A Brief History of Time: From the Big Bang to Black Holes.* Bantam Books, New York, NY. pp. 105-106.
[41]   Gribbin, J. 2006. *The Origins of the Future: Ten Questions for the Next Ten Years.* Yale University Press, New Haven, CT. p. 60.
[42]   Guth, p. 108.
[43]   Genesis 1:3
[44]   Greene, B. 1999. *The Elegant Universe: Superstrings, Hidden Dimensions, and the Quest for the Ultimate Theory.* W.W. Norton and Company, Inc., New York. p. 349.
[45]   Genesis 1:2
[46]   Genesis 1:9
[47]   Davies, P. 2003. *The Origin of Life.* Penguin Books, London, U.K. p.1

48 Ibid, p. 141.
49 The Lost City story is based on: Bradley, A. (2009, December). Expanding the Limits of Life. *Scientific American, 301(6)*, 62-67.
50 Davies, p. 13.
51 Ibid, p.12.
52 Ibid, pp. 17-18.
53 Dawkins, R. 2006. *The Selfish Gene*. Oxford University Press, Oxford, U.K. p. viii.
54 Ibid, pp. 1-2.
55 Ibid, p. 60.
56 Ibid, p. 88.
57 Ibid, p. 19.
58 Dawkins, R. 2005. *The Ancestor's Tale: A Pilgrimage to the Dawn of Evolution*. Houghton Mifflin Company, New York. p. 555.
59 Gould, S. (1994, October). The Evolution of Life on Earth. *Scientific American*, 85-91.
60 Wilson, E. 1999. *Consilience: The Unity of Knowledge*. Vintage Books, New York. p. 210.
61 Ibid, p. 171.
62 Dawkins (2006), pp. 200-201.
63 Wilson, E. 2004. *On Human Nature*. Harvard University Press, Cambridge, MA. p. 196.
64 Wilson, E. 2004. *On Human Nature*. Harvard University Press, Cambridge, MA. p. 104.
65 Leakey, R. 1993. *Origins Reconsidered: In Search of What Makes Us Human*. Anchor Books, New York. p. xv.
66 Diamond, J. 1999. *Guns, Germs, and Steel: The Fates of Human Societies*. W.W. Norton & Company, New York. pp. 267-268.
67 Pollard, K. (2009, May). What Makes Us Human? *Scientific American, 300(5)*, 44-49.
68 Ibid.
69 See http://www.templeton.org/evolution. Accessed on 10/09/2009.
70 De Waal, F. (2009, November). Fair Play: Monkeys Share Our Sense of Injustice. *New Scientist* issue 2734 accessed online at http://www.newscientist.com/article/mg20427341.100-fair-play-monkeys-share-our-sense-of-injustice.html
71 Goodall, J. 2010. *Through a Window: My Thirty Years with the Chimpanzees of Gombe*. Mariner Books, Boston. p. 22.
72 Ibid, p. p. 50
73 Ibid, pp. 58-61.
74 Ibid, p. 64.
75 Ibid, p. 65.
76 Ibid, p. 100.
77 Ehrlich, P. 2002. *Human Natures: Genes, Cultures, and the Human Prospect*. Penguin Books, New York. pp. 179-180.

[78] Wright, R. 1995. *The Moral Animal - Why We Are the Way We Are: The New Science of Evolutionary Psychology*. Vintage Books, New York. p.90.

[79] Erlich, p. 180.

[80] Wilson, pp. 125-126. *See also* Wright, p. 90.

[81] Wright, p. 91.

[82] Goodall, p. 25.

[83] Ballantyne, C. (2009, May). *Scientific American, 300(5)*, 27.

[84] Horgan, J. (2009, May). Taming the Urge to War. *Scientific American, 300(5)*, 16-17.

[85] Goodall, p. 116.

[86] Ibid, pp. 117-118.

[87] Ibid, p. 122.

[88] Ibid, pp. 239-240.

[89] Ibid.

[90] The account is summarized in Ehrlich, P. 2002. *Human Natures: Genes, Cultures, and the Human Prospect*. Penguin Books, New York. pp. 204-206.

[91] Ibid, p. 204.

[92] Ibid, p. 206.

[93] Horgan, p. 17.

[94] Wilson (2004), p. 82.

[95] Ibid, p. 125.

[96] Numbers 31:7, King James Version.

[97] Chang, I. 1997. *The Rape of Nanking: The Forgotten Holocaust of World War II*. Penguin Books, New York. p. 4.

[98] Zerjal, T. et al. 2003. The genetic legacy of the Mongols. *American Journal of Human Genetics, 23*, 717-721.

[99] Chang, J. et al. 2011. The face that launched a thousand ships: the mating-warring association in men. *Personality and Social Psychology Bulletin, 37(7)*, 976-984.

[100] Vaughan, P. 2003. *The Monogamy Myth: A Personal Handbook for Recovering from Affairs*. Newmarket Press, New York. p.7.

[101] http://www.divorcestatistics.org/ accessed August 15, 2010.

[102] Wright, pp. 96-99.

[103] Leakey, p. 103.

[104] Ibid, pp. 89-90

[105] Ibid, p. 82.

[106] Dawkins, R. 2005. *The Ancestor's Tale: A Pilgrimage to the Dawn of Evolution*. Houghton Mifflin Company, New York. p. 75

[107] Schick, K, and Toth, D. 1993. *Making Silent Stones Speak*. Simon and Schuster, New York. pp. 133-134

[108] Leakey, p.142.

[109] Ibid, pp. 46-47

[110] Ibid, pp. 3-6.

[111] Ibid, p. 55.

[112] Ehrlich, p. 88.

[113] Ibid, p. 92.

[114] Leakey, p.67.

[115] Ibid, p. 182.

[116] Dawkins (2005), p. 53.

[117] Ehrlich, p. 170.

[118] Dawkins (2005), p. 35

[119] Ehrlich, p. 236

[120] Ibid, p.238

[121] Ibid, p.6

[122] Ibid, p. 166

[123] Leakey, p. xviii.

[124] Wilson (2004) states that "there is no evidence that a widespread unitary aggressive instinct exists." See p. 103

[125] Leakey notes that the males, who come from the same genetic stock, "have good biological reasons for working toward common ends." See p. 140.

[126] Wilson (2004), p. 34.

[127] Ibid, p.119.

[128] Ibid, p. 101.

[129] Ehrlich, p. 258.

[130] Lawler, A. (2009, December). Out of Eden. *Discover,* 64-68.

[131] Ehrlich, p. 279.

[132] See http://www.psych.ucsb.edu/research/cep/primer.html. Accessed on 10/09/2009.

[133] Ekman, P. 2003. *Emotions Revealed: Recognizing Faces and Feelings to Improve Communication and Emotional Life.* Henry Holt and Company, New York. p. 216.

[134] Ibid, pp. 21-24.

[135] Gazzaniga, M. 2008. *Human: The Science Behind What Makes Us Unique.* Harper Collins, New York. pp. 20-21.

[136] Ekman, p. 113.

[137] Ibid.

[139] Dozier, R. 2002. *Why We Hate: Understanding, Curbing, and Eliminating Hate in Ourselves and Our World.* Contemporary Books, Chicago. p. 2.

[139] MacLean, P. 1970. *The Triune Brain, Emotion and Scientific Bias.* In *The Neurosciences: Second Study Program.* F.O. Schmitt, ed. Rockefeller University Press. pp. 336-49.

[140] LeDoux, J. 1996. *The Emotional Brain: The Mysterious Underpinnings of Emotional Life.* Simon & Schuster Paperbacks, New York. pp. 157-168.

[141] Ohman, A and Soares, J. 1994. *"Unconscious Anxiety": Phobic Responses to Masked Stimuli.* Journal of Abnormal Psychology. Vol. 103, No. 2, 231-240.

[142] Gazzaniga, pp. 67-68.

[143] LeDoux, pp. 157-168.

[144] Gazzaniga, p. 168.

145 Ibid, p. 73.

146 Ibid, p. 74.

147 Ibid, p. 18.

148 Ibid, pp. 21-22.

149 Dozier, pp. 10-11.

150 Greene, J. 2010. *Joshua Greene's Homepage*. http://www.wjh.harvard.edu/percent7Ejgreene/

151 Ibid.

152 Greene, J. 2003. *From Neural 'Is" to Moral 'Ought': What are the Moral Implications of Neuroscientific Moral Psychology?* Nature Reviews. Vol. 4, 847-850.

153 Ibid.

154 Ibid.

155 Greene, J. 2010. Article "Less than It Should" appearing in *Does Moral Action Depend on Reasoning?* John Templeton Foundation, West Conshohocken, PA. p. 30. Accessed August 8, 2010 at www.templeton.org/reason.

156 Ibid.

157 Immordino-Yang, M. 2011. *Me, My "Self" and You: Neuropsychological Relations between Social Emotion, Self-Awareness, and Morality.* Emotion Review. Vol. 3, No. 3, 313-315.

158 Wright, R. 1994. *The Moral Animal: Why We Are the Way We Are: The New Science of Evolutionary Psychology.* Vintage Books, New York. p. 191.

159 Ibid, p. 13.

160 Ibid, p. 223.

161 Batson, C.D. 1987. Prosocial Motivation: Is it Ever Truly Altruistic? In L. Berkowitz (Ed.), *Advances in Experimental Social Psychology* (Vol. 20, pp. 65-122). Academic Press, New York. Batson, C.D. 1991. *The Altruism Question: Toward a Social-psychological Answer.* Erlbaum, Hillsdale, NJ.

162 Batson, C.D. 2004. Benefits and Liabilities of Empathy-Induced Altruism. In A. Miller (Ed.), *The Social Psychology of Good and Evil* (Chapter 14, pp. 359-385). The Guilford Press, New York.

163 Ibid, pp. 360-361.

164 Science Daily. 2010. *First Direct Recording made of Mirror Neurons in Human Brain.* Accessed online on 4-13-2010 at http://www.sciencedaily.com/releases/2010/04/100412162112.htm

165 Gallese, V., et al. 2011. *Mirror Neuron Forum.* Perspectives on Psychological Science. 6(4): 369-504.

166 Ibid.

167 Waytz, A. and Epley, N. 2011. *Social Connection Enables Dehumanization.* Journal of Experimental Social Psychology, doi: 10.1016/j.jesp.2011.07.012.

168 De Waal, F. 2010. The Evolution of Empathy. In D. Keltner, et al (Eds.) *The Compassionate Instinct* (p. 23). W.W. Norton & Company, New York.

169 Ibid, pp. 23-24.

[170] Singer, T. and Lamm, C. 2009. *The Social Neuroscience of Empathy*. The Year in Cognitive Neuroscience 2009: Ann. N.Y. Acad. Sci. 1156: 81-96

[171] Ibid, p. 88.

[172] Trout, J. 2009. *Why Empathy Matters: The Science and Psychology of Better Judgment*. Penguin Books, New York. The observation of the author is a summary of the following research: Krebs, D. 1975. "Empathy and Altruism". *Journal of Personality and Social Psychology*. 32: 1134-46.

[173] Singer, T., et al. 2006. *Empathic Neural Responses Are Modulated by the Perceived Fairness of Others*. Nature. 439(7075): 466-469.

[174] Baron-Cohen, S. 2011. *The Science of Evil: On Empathy and the Origins of Cruelty*. Basic Books, New York. p. 183.

[175] Ibid, p. 6.

[176] Ibid, p. 15.

[177] Ibid, pp. 27-28.

[178] Ibid, p. 29.

[179] Ibid, p. 38.

[180] Zeki, S. and Romaya, J.P. 2008. *Neural Correlates of Hate*. PLoS ONE: 3(10): e3556.

[181] Ibid.

[182] Baron-Cohen, pp. 6-7.

[183] Chapman, H., et al. 2009. *In Bad Taste: Evidence for the Oral Origins of Moral Disgust*. Science. 323 (5918): 1222

[184] Zeki, S. and Romaya, J.P. 2008. *Neural Correlates of Hate*. PLoS ONE: 3(10): e3556.

[185] Fiske, S. 2004. What's in a Category? In Miller, A., (ed.), *The Social Psychology of Good and Evil*. The Guilford Press, New York. p. 128. Citing: Fiske, S. (1998). Stereotyping, prejudice, and discrimination. In Gilbert, D. et al (Eds.), *Handbook of Social Psychology* (4th ed., Vol. 2, pp. 357-411). McGraw-Hill, New York. Fiske, S. (2000). Stereotyping, prejudice, and discrimination at the seam between the centuries: Evolution, culture, mind and brain. *European Journal of Social Psychology*, 30, 299-322. Macrae, C. and Bodenhausen, G. (2000). Thinking categorically about others. In Fiske, S. et al (Eds.), *Annual Review of Psychology* (Vol. 51, pp. 93-120). Annual Reviews, Palo Alto, CA.

[186] Ibid. Citing: Hart, A. et al. (2000). Differential response in the human amygdala to racial outgroup versus ingroup face stimuli. *Neuroreport*, 11, 2351-2355. Phelps, E. et al. (2000). Performance on indirect measures of race evaluation predicts amygdala activation. *Journal of Cognitive Neuroscience*, 12, 729-738.

[187] Kawakami, K. et al. (2009). Mispredicting affective and behavioral responses to racism. *Science*, 323, 276-278.

[188] Dozier, R. 2002. *Why We Hate: Understanding, Curbing, and Eliminating Hate in Ourselves and Our World*. Contemporary Books, Chicago. p. 10.

[189] Ibid, p. 11.

190 http://www.memritv.org/clip_transcript/en/1925.htm accessed on 11-28-2008.

191 Zeki S., Romaya J.P. (2008) *Neural Correlates of Hate*. PLoS ONE 3(10): e3556. doi:10.1371/journal.pone.0003556.

192 Ibid.

193 Ibid.

194 http://www.cbsnews.com/stories/2003/05/23/60minutes/main 555344.shtml. Accessed on 5-30-2011.

195 Ibid.

196 Duntley, J., Buss, D. 2004. The Evolution of Hate. In Miller, A. (ed.), *The Social Psychology of Good and Evil*. The Guilford Press, New York. pp. 102-103.

197 Ibid, p. 103.

198 http://www.memritv.org/clip_transcript/en/2058.htm. Accessed on 5-30-2011.

199 Browning C. 1993. *Ordinary Men: Reserve Police Battalion 101 and the Final Solution in Poland*. Harper Collins, New York. p. xvi.

200 Johnson E. and Reuband, K. 2006. *What We Knew: Terror, Mass Murder, and Everyday Life in Nazi Germany*. Basic Books, Cambridge, MA. p. 232.

201 Klee, E., et al, Ed. 1991. *"The Good Old Days": The Holocaust as Seen by Its Perpetrators and Bystanders*. Konecky & Konecky, Old Saybrook, Connecticut. p. xxi.

202 Ibid. p. xiv.

203 Milgram, S. 2004. *Obedience to Authority*. Perennial Classics, New York. pp. 8-9.

204 Arendt, H. 1963. *Eichmann in Jerusalem: A Report on the Banality of Evil*. Penguin Books, Toronto, Canada.

205 Longerich, P. 2012. *Heinrich Himmler*. Oxford University Press, Oxford. p. 236.

206 Ibid. p.215.

207 Ibid. p.281.

208 Ibid.

209 Ibid. p.231.

210 Ibid. p.233.

211 Kressler, N. 2002. *Mass Hate: The Global Rise of Genocide and Terror*. The Perseus Books Group, Cambridge, Massachusetts. p. 109.

212 Dewar G. 2008. *The Road to Psychopathy? Why Bullying in Children Affects Us All*. Accessed on 1-24-10 at http://www.parentingscience.com/bullying-in-children.html

213 Frankl, V. 2006. *Man's Search for Meaning*. Beacon Press, Boston. pp. 11-12.

214 Wiesel, E. 2006. *Night*. Hill and Wang, New York. pp. 31-32.

215 Portions of the McVeigh audio recordings were broadcast on the Rachel Maddow Show on April 19, 2010 on MSNBC TV and accessed on July 8, 2010 at http://www.msnbc.msn.com/id/36135258/ns/msnbc_tv/

[216] Arendt, H. 1963. *Eichmann in Jerusalem: A Report on the Banality of Evil.* Penguin Books, Toronto, Canada.

[217] The Nizkor Project accessed January 11, 2010 at http://www.nizkor.org/ftp.cgi/camps/aktion.reinhard/treblinka/eichmann.004

[218] Arendt, H. 1963. *Eichmann in Jerusalem: A Report on the Banality of Evil.* Penguin Books, Toronto, Canada.

[219] Ibid.

[220] *See generally* Grossman, D. 1995. *On Killing: The Psychological Cost of Learning to Kill in War and Society.* Little, Brown and Company, New York.

[221] Kressler, N. 2002. *Mass Hate: The Global Rise of Genocide and Terror.* The Perseus Books Group, Cambridge, Massachusetts. p. 107.

[222] Grossman, D. 1995. *On Killing: The Psychological Cost of Learning to Kill in War and Society.* Little, Brown and Company, New York. pp. 101-102.

[223] Ibid, p. 162 citing Stouffer, S.A., et al. 1949. *The American Soldier.* 5 vols. Princeton University Press, Princeton, New Jersey.

[224] Ferguson, N. 2006. *The War of the World: Twentieth Century Conflict and the Descent of the West.* Penguin Press, New York. p.546.

[225] Milgram, S. 2004. *Obedience to Authority.* Perennial Classics, New York. p. 11.

[226] Klee, E., et al, Ed. 1991. *"The Good Old Days": The Holocaust as Seen by Its Perpetrators and Bystanders.* Konecky & Konecky, Old Saybrook, Connecticut. pp. 71-72.

[227] Ibid, p. xiii. *See also* Browning C. 1993. *Ordinary Men: Reserve Police Battalion 101 and the Final Solution in Poland.* Harper Collins, New York. p.170. ("Quite simply, in the past forty-five years no defense attorney or defendant in any of the hundreds of postwar trials has been able to document a single case in which refusal to obey an order to kill unarmed civilians resulted in the allegedly inevitable dire punishment [of being sent to a concentration camp or immediate execution.]")

[228] Ibid, pp. 163-171.

[229] Zimbardo, P. 2008. *The Lucifer Effect: Understanding How Good People Turn Evil.* Random House Trade Paperbacks, New York. p. 287. *Citing* Steiner, J. 1980. "The SS Yesterday and Today: A Sociopsychological View," in *Survivors, Victims, and Perpetrators: Essays on the Nazi Holocaust* (ed. J.E. Dinsdale). Hemisphere Publishing Corporation, Washington D.C. p. 433.

[230] Ibid, p. 214.

[231] Staub, E. 1989. *The Roots of Evil: The Origins of Genocide and Other Group Violence.* Cambridge University Press, New York. p. 143. *Citing* Lifton, R. (1986). *The Nazi Doctors: Medical Killing and the Psychology of Genocide.* Basic Books, New York.

[232] Ibid, pp. 132-34.

[233] Ibid, p. 109.

234 Browning C. 1993. *Ordinary Men: Reserve Police Battalion 101 and the Final Solution in Poland.* Harper Collins, New York.

235 Ibid, p. xvi.

236 Ibid, pp. xvi-xvii.

237 Ibid, p. xvi.

238 Ibid, pp. 38-39.

239 Ibid, pp. 44-48.

240 Ibid, p. 2.

241 Ibid, p. 58.

242 Staub, E. 1989. *The Roots of Evil: The Origins of Genocide and Other Group Violence.* Cambridge University Press, New York. p. 79. *Citing* Lerner, M. and Simmons C. 1996. Observer's Reaction to the "Innocent Victim": Compassion or Rejection? *Journal of Personality and Social Psychology, 4,* 203-10. Lerner M. 1980. *The Belief in a Just World: A Fundamental Delusion.* Plenum Press, New York. Smith, R. et al. 1976. Role and Justice Considerations in the Attribution of Responsibility to a Rape Victim. *Journal of Research in Personality, 10,* 346-57.

243 Ibid. *Citing* Staub, E. 1978. *Positive Social Behavior and Morality.* Vol. 1, Social and Personal Influences. Academic Press, New York.

244 Zimbardo, P. 2008. *The Lucifer Effect: Understanding How Good People Turn Evil.* Random House Trade Paperbacks, New York. pp. 210-11.

245 Browning C. 1993. *Ordinary Men: Reserve Police Battalion 101 and the Final Solution in Poland.* Harper Collins, New York. p. 61.

246 Ibid, p. 69.

247 Ibid, p. 67.

248 Ibid, pp. 74-75.

249 Ibid, pp. 76-77.

250 Ibid, p. 77.

251 Milgram, S. 2004. *Obedience to Authority.* Perennial Classics, New York. p. 6.

252 Staub, E. 1989. *The Roots of Evil: The Origins of Genocide and Other Group Violence.* Cambridge University Press, New York. p. xii.

253 Ibid, p. xiv.

254 Ibid, p.4, 13.

255 Ibid, p. 13.

256 Ibid, pp. 126-127.

257 Hare, R. 1993. *Without Conscience: The Disturbing World of the Psychopaths Among Us.* Simon and Shuster, New York. p.74.

258 *See generally* Oakley, B. 2008. *Evil Genes: Why Rome Fell, Hitler Rose, Enron Failed, and My Sister Stole My Mother's Boyfriend.* Prometheus Books, Amherst, NY.

259 King's College London (2009, August 5). Brain Difference In Psychopaths Identified. *ScienceDaily.* Retrieved August 6, 2009, from http://www.sciencedaily.com /releases/2009/08/090804090946.htm

260 Dawkins, R. 2006. *The Selfish Gene.* Oxford University Press, Oxford, U.K. p. 69.

261 Ibid.

262 Ibid, pp. 72-75

263 Colman, A.M., & Wilson, J.C. (1997). Antisocial personality disorder: An evolutionary game theory analysis. *Legal & Criminological Psychology.* 2: 23-34.

264 Ibid.

265 Ferguson, N. 2006. *The War of the World: Twentieth Century Conflict and the Descent of the West.* Penguin Press, New York. p. 649.

266 Ibid.

267 Ibid, p. xxxiv.

268 Diamond, J. 1999. *Guns, Germs, and Steel: The Fates of Human Societies.* W.W. Norton & Company, New York. pp. 268-269.

269 Ibid, pp. 267-268.

270 Ibid, p. 272.

271 Ibid, p. 271.

272 Ibid, pp. 271-272.

273 Ibid.

274 Ibid, p. 273.

275 Ibid.

276 Ibid.

277 Ibid, p.275.

278 Ibid, p.278-280.

279 Ibid, p.275-276.

280 Ibid, p.281.

281 Ibid, p.282.

282 Keeley, L. 1996. *War Before Civilization: the Myth of the Peaceful Savage.* Oxford University Press.

283 Pinker, S. *Why Is There Peace?* Chapter appearing in *The Compassionate Instinct*, Keltner, D. et al, ed. 2010. W.W. Norton & Company, New York. p. 260-261.

284 Ibid, p. 262.

285 http://killology.org/art_weap_sum_medical.htm. Accessed November 23, 2011.

286 Pinker, p. 264.

287 McCullough, D. 2001. *John Adams.* Touchstone, New York. pp.46-49.

288 Ibid, p. 48.

289 Ibid. pp. 48-49.

290 Ibid, p. 60. The quote is from Adams' essay *A Dissertation on the Canon and the Feudal Law* published as an unsigned essay in the *Gazette* during the height of the controversy over the Stamp Act.

291 Ibid, p. 65.

292 Ibid.

293 Ibid, p. 68.

294 Ibid, p. 70.
295 Ibid, p, 103.
296 Ibid.
297 Ibid, p. 120.
298 Ibid, p. 129.
299 Ibid, p. 222.
300 Ibid, p. 377.
301 Axelrod, R. 1984. *The Evolution of Cooperation*. Basic Books, New York. p. 3.
302 Ibid, p. vii.
303 Ibid, p. 4.
304 Ibid, p. 12.
305 Ibid, p. viii.
306 Ibid, p. 8.
307 Ibid, p. 9.
308 Ibid, p. 74.
309 Ibid, p. 77.
310 Ibid, pp. 85, 87.
311 Ibid, p. 33.
312 Ibid, p. 110-123, 190.
313 Ibid, p. 126.
314 Ibid, p. 129.
315 Ibid, p. 134.
316 Ibid, p. 137.
317 Ibid, p. 136.
318 Ibid, p. 140.
319 Ibid.

Index